*Joyce and
the Anglo-Irish*

COSTERUS NEW SERIES 119

Series Editors:
C.C. Barfoot, Hans Bertens, Theo D'haen
and Erik Kooper

Joyce and the Anglo-Irish

A Study of Joyce and the Literary Revival

Len Platt

 Amsterdam-Atlanta, GA 1998

ISBN 90-420-0624-2

Cover design: Hendrik van Delft
Cover illustration: Drawing by Hendrik van Leeuwen

© Editions Rodopi B.V.
   Amsterdam - Atlanta, GA 1998

Printed in The Netherlands

Acknowledgements

I am indebted to the many individuals who attended the London Joyce Seminar, particularly in the early years. My especial thanks to Robert Hampson, and to the late Charles Peake who led the Seminar until 1988 and was my research supervisor in the early 1980s. His dedicated scholarship was deeply impressive and had a lasting effect on my approach to Joyce.

I also owe a substantial debt to Michael Peake, who read various drafts of *Joyce and the Anglo Irish* and made many useful suggestions. Even more importantly, Mike listened patiently to half-baked ideas and helped to develop these into something more digestible.

Andrew Gibson is a founding member of the London Joyce Seminar. He is also much implicated in this book. We developed our views on Joyce together — to the extent that I'm no longer certain where my ideas end and his begin. Thanks to Andrew's generosity, this is no great problem. He has been hugely supportive, and I blame him for this book to the extent that without his encouragement and enthusiasm, it would certainly have failed to surface. Not satisfied with all that, he also applied his 'French polish' to a very late draft of *Joyce and the Anglo-Irish*, and saved me considerable embarrassment by so doing.

There are many others who listened and advised. For encouragement, hints and provocation, I would particularly like to thank Malcolm Barry, Jo O'Halloran, Clive Hart, Bill McCormack, Fritz Senn, Robert Spoo and Tony Stone.

And finally, to my family — Sally, Lucy and Charlie — my deepest gratitude. Their part in this is a complex business. Suffice it to say, they have been here from the outset and of that I am very glad.

Contents

Bibliographical References	5
Introduction	7
1 Opening Encounters	18
2 Usurper	48
3 Corresponding with the Greeks	99
4 Revivalism in Popular Culture: 'Sirens' and 'Cyclops'	128
5 'Circe' and the Irish Literary Theatre	157
6 'Our Modern Babylon': Modernity and the National Culture in 'Eumaeus' and 'Ithaca'	180
7 Engendering Nation: Nationalism and Sexuality in 'Nausicaa', 'Oxen of the Sun' and 'Penelope'	203
Appendix: *The Deliverer* and 'Circe'	234
Bibliography	237
Index	245

Bibliographical References

References to the following works are included in the text parenthetically. All *Ulysses* quotations are from *The Corrected Text*, edited by Hans Walter Gabler et al. (New York: Random House, 1986), and are followed by episode and line numbers. References to other works are included in the text in the abbreviated forms noted below and keyed to the editions indicated. I have followed the citational style used in the *James Joyce Quarterly*.

CW	*The Critical Writings of James Joyce*, ed. Ellsworth Mason and Richard Ellmann (London: Faber & Faber, 1959)
D	James Joyce, *Dubliners,* an annotated edn with introduction, notes and afterwords by John Wyse Jackson and Bernard McGinley (London: Sinclair-Stevenson, 1993)
FW	James Joyce, *Finnegans Wake*, 3rd edn (London: Faber & Faber, 1964)
JJ	Richard Ellmann, *James Joyce*, revised edn (New York: Oxford University Press, 1982)
Letters I, II, III	*Letters of James Joyce*, Vol. I, ed. Stuart Gilbert (London: Faber and Faber, 1957). Vols II and III, edited by Richard Ellmann (London: Faber & Faber, 1966)

P	James Joyce, *A Portrait of the Artist as a Young Man*, the definitive text corrected from the Dublin holograph by Chester G. Anderson and edited by Richard Ellmann (London: Jonathan Cape, 1968)
SH	James Joyce, *Stephen Hero*, ed. Theodore Spencer et al. (London: Jonathan Cape, 1956)
Yeats, *Auto*	W. B. Yeats, *Autobiographies* (London: Macmillan, 1955)
Yeats, *CPO*	W. B. Yeats, *The Collected Poems*, 2nd edn (London: Macmillan, 1950 edn)
Yeats, *CPL*	W. B. Yeats, *The Collected Plays*, 2nd edn (London: Macmillan, 1952 edn)
Yeats, *E & I*	W. B. Yeats, *Essays and Introductions* (London: Macmillan, 1961)
Yeats, *Ex*	W. B. Yeats, *Explorations* (London: Macmillan, 1961)
Yeats, *Mem*	W. B. Yeats *Memoirs*: Autobiography — First Draft Journal, transcribed and edited by Denis Donoghue (London: Macmillan, 1972)
Yeats, *Myth*	W. B. Yeats, *Mythologies* (London: Macmillan, 1989)
Yeats, *UP1*	*Uncollected Prose by W. B. Yeats*, ed. John P. Frayne, Vol. I (London: Macmillan, 1970)

Introduction

Post-war criticism constructed Joyce as the voice of common-sense humanity. When it came to politics generally, and nationalism in particular, Joyce was presented as holding the liberal centre. Youthful, and distinctly theoretical, flirtations with socialism and even anarchism put Joyce broadly on the correct side. This tradition acknowledged that Joyce's great vocation was art and argued that art was, by and large, indifferent to politics. The issue of nationalism, however, produced an exception to this elevation of art and artists. Even artists were required to take position on the ideology which, apparently, had split the world. Joyce, almost alone amongst the major modernists, was untainted by any associations with the extreme right. He has been presented as a liberal humanitarian, unequivocal in his stand against anti-Semitism and against what has been perceived as the violent and bloody bigotry of Irish nationalism. Revivalism has played a part, albeit a small one, in this tradition of Joyce studies. The perceived indifference to both language and literary revivals apparently marks the distance between Joyce and Irish nationalism, although, in fact, nationalism and revivalism are not necessarily the same thing. This distance is often taken as evidence of an enmity between provincial and metropolitan, primitive and modern, and Ireland and Europe. Influential American and English critical traditions, often supported by naïve historical readings, have formulated, then, this liberal humanist Joyce who turns his back on nativistic Ireland and the excesses of Irish nationalism to embrace and reproduce the relativity, innovation and multiplicity of modern European culture. The significance of Joyce's fictions as canonical modern texts has thus been shifted from the Irish cultural domain. This is one reason why the fact of Joyce's resistance to revivalism has been little more than a long-standing footnote to critical work on Joyce. In this classic tradition of Joyce studies, Joyce's interaction with such movements as the Gaelic League and the Irish Literary Revival has been approached largely as a 'content' issue — of local, contextual significance certainly, but not at all critical to what is really important about *Ulysses*, and that is its 'modernity', or its 'textuality'.[1]

One of the central arguments of this study is that Joyce's response to revivalism, far from being marginal, is actually fundamental to the *quality* of *Ulysses*, to the kind of text that *Ulysses* is. Indeed, this is the first and foremost challenge of *Joyce and the Anglo-Irish*. It explores a context which has received little serious attention from Joyceans, yet which has an essential impact on *Ulysses*. Joyce's response to the movement that claimed to represent the national consciousness is engineered with extraordinary vigour and persistence here. *Ulysses* is not merely fortuitously different to revivalism. It is, at almost every point, in precise and explicit antithesis. Against the Literary Revival's celebration of an aristocratic culture of heroism is Joyce's celebration of the culture of Dublin's streets, his mock-heroic; against the neo-Platonic aesthetic of Yeats and Russell, Joyce's concoction of Aristotle and Aquinas; against their mysticism, his realism; against the Revival's vegetarianism, his own Leopold Bloom who eats 'with relish the inner organs of beast and fowls' (4.1-2); against its evocations of a timeless idyllic rurality are Joyce's

---

[1] There is an interesting example of exactly this kind of content/form division in a very early account of Irish revivalism, Ernest Boyd's *Irish Literary Renaissance*, revised edn (London: Grant Richards, 1922). Boyd suggests that 'no Irish writer is more Irish than Joyce; none shows more unmistakably the imprint of his race and traditions' (405). By 'race and traditions', Boyd has Catholicism in mind. In Joyce's work he sees 'such an analysis of repressed and stunted instincts as only an Irishman could have made to explain the curious conditions of Irish puritanism'.

In his representation of the Literary Revival, Boyd wants to insist on a syncretic concept of nationality, but it is quite apparent that the Anglo-Irish heroes of his analysis, O'Grady, Yeats, Russell and Synge, for example, are 'Irish' primarily by virtue of their ennoblement of the Irish character, whereas Joyce is 'Irish' because he has been oppressed by the priests. Boyd makes great claims for Joyce as a national writer. The problem is that Joyce represents the 'wrong' Ireland, one in which 'the glamour of love is absent'; where there exists 'a crude horror and fascination of the body as seen by the great Catholic heretics' (410); which focuses on 'all that is mean and furtive in Dublin society' (408).

The further problem in Boyd's attempt to claim Joyce for Ireland is that Boyd can find few Irish precursors for Joyce — only one, in fact: George Moore. But the European influences on Joyce range from Rabelais to Zola and include Flaubert, Jules Romain and the German expressionists, Walter Hasenclauer and George Kaiser. It is in an attempt to sort out this problem that Boyd makes the claim, repeated by so many later Joyceans, that the 'technical' qualities of *Ulysses* are 'European', but the 'matter', is, in Boyd's coy term, 'local' (411).

excessively time-specific urban fictions. The reverse side to Joyce's classical detachment is the impatient temper of romanticism which he ascribed to the Revival. While the Revival often stressed the unconscious, 'spiritual' element in art-manufacture, Joyce's fictions contain the most intricate designs and patterns (he saw a parallel in this respect between *Ulysses* and the complex decorative art of *The Book of Kells*, an art 'at which the ancient Irish excelled' — *CW*, 161).[2] A central argument here is that this antithesis is not, as was previously thought, the accidental product of aesthetic difference, but is rather a designed assault on the foundations of revivalism.

The main purpose of this introduction is to establish some bearings on why *Ulysses* engages revivalism in this way. In order to do so it is necessary to describe some of the central characteristics both of revivalism generally and the Irish Literary Revival in particular. It is not the intention here to give a potted history of revivalism in Irish culture, but rather to outline some of the key features of revivalism, as it is constructed in this study. Firstly, however, my usage of the words 'revivalism' and 'Revival' requires a brief explanation. The capitalised word 'Revival' will always refer to one particular movement, the Literary Revival, in this study. The reason for this privileging will become clear in due course. The term 'revivalism' (and 'revivalist'), taking a lower case initial letter, is used here to define a process of identifying with a historical and, usually, 'native' culture. 'Revivalism', then, refers not to a particular group or movement, but to a cultural practice. This practice will be characterized and theorized in what follows, but the essential point is that revivalism invariably involves the attempt to transform a pre-modern, often archaic, tradition into something living.

Revivalism is invariably nationalistic and is by no means exclusive to Ireland. On the contrary, it is difficult to think of a modern society which is not, almost continuously, defining itself in terms of a revived, and largely imaginary, past. Nor did Irish revivalism suddenly emerge in the late nineteenth century to produce the organizations of Joyce's immediate cultural environment, like the Gaelic League (concerned with the language revival), or the Gaelic Athletic Association (concerned with sports revival), or the Literary Revival (concerned with a literature revival, in English). The construction of contemporary analogues with the

---

[2] In latter life, Joyce claimed that *The Book of Kells* was 'the most purely Irish thing we have, and some of the big initial letters which swing right across a page have the essential quality of *Ulysses*' (*JJ*, 545).

'Gael', 'Celt', 'Milesian', or 'Firbolg' has been a characteristic of Irish cultural history over a very long period of time. Indeed this paralleling or corresponding is arguably *the* process of Irish cultural history. The process of revivalism has been and continues to be a central strategy of Irish culture, deployed by Seamus Heaney and Brian Friel in the 1970s and 1980s, as it was by W. B. Yeats and J. M. Synge at the turn of the nineteenth century, and by Samuel Ferguson in the earlier nineteenth century. The longevity of revivalism is one reason why it has been a mistake for historians and Joyce critics to dismiss the enthusiasms of late nineteenth-century revivalists too readily. It is easy enough to laugh at, for example, Douglas Hyde's de-Anglicizing rhetoric. The crusading fervour of his attacks on barrel-organs and the wearing of 'English second-hand trousers'[3] does indeed look odd and cranky in the modern period. But the process of revivalism has been cumulative. Revivalism, in the broad sense, has been at the heart of the serious business of 'inventing Ireland', at least since the eighteenth century. There have been times in this long history when it has moved from the oddball cultural margins to take the centre stage. Indeed at some historical moments, revivalism has been crucial to the political agenda. That is to say, in the right context, it is possible for something which once appeared perhaps as juvenile faddism to become transformed into a compelling ideology of the moment. This happened in Ireland in the 1920s and 30s:

> The Irish nation is the Gaelic nation; its language and literature is the Gaelic language; its history is the history of the Gael. All other elements have no place in Irish national life, literature and tradition, save as far as they are assimilated into the very substance of Gaelic speech, life and thought. The Irish nation is not a racial synthesis at all; synthesis is not a vital process, and only what is vital is admissible in analogies bearing on the nature of the living Irish nation, speech literature and tradition. We are not a national conglomerate, nor a national patchwork specimen; the poetry or life of what Aodh de Blacam calls Belfast can only be Irish by being assimilated into Gaelic literature.[4]

---

[3] Douglas Hyde, 'The Necessity for De-Anglicizing Ireland', in *The Revival of Irish Literature*: Addresses by Sir Charles Gavan Duffy, Dr George Sigerson and Sir Douglas Hyde (London: T. Fisher Unwin, 1894), 155.

[4] Quoted in R. F. Foster, *Modern Ireland 1600-1972* (Harmondsworth: Penguin, 1988), 530.

Professor Timothy Corcoran, the author of the above, was an important figure in the formulation and articulation of education policy in the early Irish Free State. Here, in a classic exposition of revivalism, he places the revived Gael, the awakened Finn, at the very centre of his vision of the Irish nation. The vision, of course, was not his alone. Corcoran's essentialism is extremist, but it represents something fundamental to De Valera's new republic. Precisely to what extent the new state converged with cultural nationalism may be debatable, but it is certain that the Republic's promotion of, 'self-sacrifice, religious idealism, purity, respect for women and fear of external evils',[5] to say nothing of its educational policies, owed something substantial to revivalism. This, then, is revivalism at its most influential, confidently defining Irish culture, the Irish nation and Irish identity from a position of authority. The point is important, because it enables us to focus on a revivalism significant enough to be of major concern to the foremost novelist of the modern period.

Corcoran's statement is illustrative in further ways. Revivalism is by definition retrospective and it has usually produced a conservative nationalism. This may seem a wild generalization given the diversity in revivalist movements. In the heyday of modern revivalism, broadly the period between Parnell's fall and 1914, there were many revivalist organizations responding in very different ways to the dominant issues of Anglicization and modernization. There were notorious ambivalences in both Catholic and Protestant relationships to the 'new nationalism'. But whether the articulation was from Yeats or Moran, Gaelicism focused strong conservative perspectives in this period. Revivalist movements were by definition anti-modern. They were often puritanical, invariably anti-socialist and sometimes anti-trade union. Many were assimilated by the Catholic Church through its promotion of the Gaelic language and more guarded acceptance of Moran's extremely influential version of the Irish-Ireland movement. Certainly Corcoran's conservatism is apparent in his deep antagonism towards what he terms 'assimilation', but there is nothing particularly idiosyncratic about this in revivalist terms. The

---

[5] J. Hutchinson, *The Dynamics of Cultural Nationalism: The Gaelic Revival and the Creation of the Irish State* (London: Allen and Unwin, 1987), 288. Perhaps something of the impact of revivalism on the Irish State can be deduced from the fact that 69% of the post-independence republican élite served their time in the Gaelic League before entering revolutionary politics. See A.S. Cohan, *The Irish Political State*, quoted in Hutchinson, 298.

demonization of socialism which was characteristic of a revivalist rhetoric crossing a range of organizations, makes the point emphatically:

> For the past twenty years the Gael has been crying ... for help to beat back the Anglicization he saw dragging its slimy length along — the immoral literature, the smutty postcards, the lewd plays and the suggestive songs were bad, yet they were merely puffs from the foul breath of a paganised society. The full sewerage from the *cloaca maxima* of Anglicization is now discharged upon us. The black devil of Socialism, hoof and horns, is amongst us. [6]

By the 1920s the besieged Catholic/Gael was a dominant cultural identification, cementing a conservative alliance of the state, the nation and the Church.

Revivalism was also conservative in its eighteenth-century origins, but in a very different sense. Early revivalism was closer to High Toryism and established a set of identifications quite at odds to those of De Valera's Gaeltacht. Revivalism in the late eighteenth and the early nineteenth centuries emerged from a Protestant intelligentsia, and from Protestant institutions. These self-appointed guardians of the national culture were not attempting to construct a Catholic Ireland. On the contrary, they were attempting to preserve an Ascendancy Ireland, where traditional, feudal relations could be preserved from the onslaught of an alien modernity. This was the Protestant tradition of revivalism that was developed by Petrie, O'Curry, O'Donovan and, more radically, Samuel Ferguson and Standish O'Grady. It found its greatest champion in Yeats and his Literary Revival, and it was the literary culture which, until Joyce's intervention, held the most serious claim to be articulating not just the voice of Ireland but its very consciousness.

Revivalism was crucially a Protestant Anglo-Irish culture and one of the central arguments of *Joyce and the Anglo-Irish* is that it was understood as such by Joyce. Of course, Joyce was very much aware that his Catholic contemporaries were turning to Gaelicism in the League and the G.A.A., and a host of other revivalist organizations. He despised them for it, partly because he saw them as blindly following strategies which had been evolved by the old Ascendancy. Joyce takes some vicious swipes at the young 'Irishers' in the pre-*Ulysses* fictions, but, in the epic later work, his bigger target is the Literary Revival. The frontal assault, as

---

[6] From *The Catholic Bulletin*, quoted in F. S. L. Lyons, *Culture and Anarchy in Ireland 1890-1939* (Oxford: Oxford University Press, 1982), 96.

we shall see, is not against the imitators, but the progenitors and their descendants, the writers and intellectuals of a traditionally hegemonic class. It was through the agency of the late revivalists, Yeats, Synge, Lady Gregory and so on, that Anglo-Ireland continued to stake its monopolizing claim on Irish culture, to define the national culture, as it had done since the seventeenth century. In this sense the Literary Revival was not a new departure but the continuance of an old establishment. The argument here is that it becomes the dominant conservative culture against which Joyce redefines Ireland and Irishness.

This identification of revivalism as a conservative ideology suggests that Joyce's engagement is politically motivated. The idea that Joyce's response to revivalism is consistent with, or at least reinforced by, a radical politics will be developed in this study. But this does not mean that the identification of a coherent Joycean politics is centrally on the agenda here or even generally possible.[7] The Joycean text is related to revivalism, but not through deployment of an alternative discourse which is demonstrably 'socialist' or 'anarchist'. On the contrary, the Joyce text, for all its resistance to revivalism, is substantially within revivalist traditions. It imports revivalist discourses and, I will argue, is centralized in the post-colonial cultural issues which dominated revivalist Ireland. These issues had important political implications and articulations of cultural nationalism did, of course, consolidate around political positions and take political forms. But, despite the syncretic claims of Yeats's 'Unity of Culture', there is no doubt that revivalist formulations were characterized much more substantially by the complex mix of class and ethnic identities which were embedded in a heterogeneous colonial culture than by neat political positions and affiliations. In a flashpoint of revivalism, such as the *Playboy* riots, (which Joyce, incidentally, was so angry at missing),[8] it is perceived racial and class identities which are most obviously engaged, not political theories. Particularly in these post-Parnell years, defining the

---

[7] Joyce's political interests, particularly in socialism and anarchism have been well researched, most notably in Dominic Manganiello, *Joyce's Politics* (London: Routledge & Kegan Paul, 1980), and some Joyceans, like Colin McCabe in *The Revolution of the Word* (London: Macmillan, 1978), have postulated a political metonymy operating in Joyce's texts. But a Joycean politics has never been convincingly articulated.

[8] 'I feel like a man in a house who hears a row in the street and voices shouting he knows but can't get out to hear what the hell is going on' (*Letters II*, 212).

national culture was *the* burning issue for the Dublin intelligentsia. All interactions with cultural nationalism implied historicizations and historicization inevitably exposed social and cultural allegiances. Thus in the one extended account of Irish cultural history that Joyce produced, the Triestine lectures (1907),[9] Joyce's claim that he writes as an 'unprejudiced observer' (*CW*, 163) is everywhere compromised by such controversial and problematic statements as 'Ancient Ireland is dead just as ancient Egypt is dead' (*CW*, 173); by the characterization of Gaelic as being a 'harsh and guttural tongue' (*CW*, 156); by the caricature of a Gaelic League, whose members 'write to each other in Irish, and often the poor postman, unable to read the address, must turn to his superior to untie the knot' (*CW*, 151) and so on.

The suggestion here is that Joyce's encounter with revivalism engages something deeper, more visceral, than political persuasion. Such an argument implies a modernity of *Ulysses* which is recentred in Irish post-colonial contexts, because so much of the innovation of *Ulysses* will be presented here as responding to Anglicized traditions of Irish culture. In this broad sense, the current study joins ranks with recent scholarship that takes its bearings from the crucial importance of the colonial landscape in and for Joyce. At the same time there is an important distinction to be drawn between this study and a new Joyce incarnation that seems to be emerging. This new incarnation might be thought of as more the product of Irish scholars, which may be one reason for its historical sophistication. It has it origins, perhaps, in the admirable work of Seamus Deane, is evident everywhere in Emer Nolan's book, *Joyce and Nationalism* (1995) and, to some extent, operates in Declan Kiberd's *Inventing Ireland* (1995). The trouble with it is that it reconstitutes Joyce as a member of a 'family' of nationalisms which can indifferently include Yeats, Hyde and others in a broad cultural community. This Joyce incarnation erases or transcends the powerful contradictions and conflicts internal to his culture. That an Irish critic like Kiberd should wish to sustain such a view is understandable enough. But the view itself is problematic — above all in that it loses sight of the dynamic of Joyce's class consciousness and its central importance in his work. It is here, in insisting on the vital

---

[9] These lectures do discuss such matters as Irish politics, the role of the modern Catholic Church and so on, but Joyce makes clear his intention to deliver a history of Irish culture. This is apparent in his periodisation of this history into 'two large parts' and 'five sub-divisions'. He intended to cover the whole of this ground during the course of the three lectures that were planned. See *CW*, 176.

significance of the class question along with the colonial question, on their *inseparability,* that the historicizing approach to Joyce taken in this study parts company with that of the most interesting contemporary Irish Joyceans. The fundamental point of this study is that the antithesis between *Ulysses* and the culture of revivalism is formulated out of conflicting class and cultural identities.

One final introductory point. Historical materials have been used throughout this study. The materials have been used to contextualize the fiction, but I would stress that they have not been used to substantiate the 'truth' or otherwise of Joyce's interpretation of Irish history. I would argue that Joyce's version of things has validity by comparison to the wild historical fabrications promulgated by the Literary Revival, but this does not mean, of course, that Joyce's writing is objective history-making. It is mediated fiction and engages in its own distortions. To take a small, but illustrative example, I doubt that John Eglinton was really the idiot that Joyce depicted in *Ulysses* 9. Eglinton's own disputes with Yeats reveal a sharp mind, and it may be the case that Joyce owed a debt to Eglinton that he was not prepared to acknowledge. As early as 1899, Eglinton was arguing that a national literature based on old myths would fail because it would be out of touch with real life and 'modern sympathies'. He had strong doubts about an art which served the nation: 'in all ages', he wrote, 'poets and thinkers have owed far less to their countries than their countries have owed to them'.[10] He wrote of mechanical and scientific culture and its relation to art in terms that Joyce might well have approved of:

> The kinematograph, the bicycle, electric tramcars, labour-saving contrivances etc., are not susceptible to poetic treatment, but are in fact themselves the poetry, not without a certain suggestiveness of a scientific age, with which the poetry of Greek and Hebrew tradition vainly endeavours to vie. It is no wonder that an age which produced this concrete type of poetry should be content with an attitude of simple politeness towards those dreamers who talk with their heads in a cloud of vision.[11]

---

[10] J. Eglinton, 'What Should be the Subjects of a National Drama', in *Literary Ideals in Ireland* by John Eglinton, W. B. Yeats, AE, W. Larminie (Dublin: Maunsel, 1899), 13.

[11] J. Eglinton, 'National Drama and Contemporary Life', in *Eglinton* et al., *Literary Ideals*, 42.

The fact that Joyce should have turned this sophisticated writer, with whom he actually shared territory, into the fool of the National Library, to say nothing of the insults heaped on AE, damned for his 'vegetable verse' and 'vegetable philosophy' (*Letters II*, 28), and the liberties taken with just about every artistic precept deployed by Yeats, indicates that Joyce had a very considerable investment in historical reconstruction, a motivation that was powerful, committed, even raw. The final product, in *Ulysses*, may be deeply controlled, but something of the original rawness is certainly apparent in Joyce's blatantly self-dramatizing farewell to the 'mumming company' which included Russell ('he who once when snug abed/Saw Jesus Christ without his head'); Eglinton, who was apparently both puritanical and aristocratic (he, 'who will his hat unfix/Neither to malt or crucifix/But show to all that poor-dressed be/ His high Castilian courtesy'), and above all Yeats. Yeats, the architect of late nineteenth-century revivalism, was at the very centre of this 'motley crew', these dreamers of 'dreamy dreams', men of 'timid arses' who the young author of 'The Holy Office' intended to 'spurn for evermore'. The venom expressed in this invective, which has Yeats appeasing 'his giddy dames' frivolities/While they console him when he whinges/With gold-embroidered Celtic fringes' (*CW*, 149-52),[12] is surely suggestive of some deep class animosities. That the animosities cut both ways is apparent in some revivalist responses to Joyce and the publication of his book. George Moore found *Ulysses* 'boring', 'dirty' and derivative and identified its author as 'a nobody from the Dublin docks: no family, no breeding'.[13] J. P. Mahaffy described Joyce as 'a living argument in favour of my contention that it was a mistake to establish a separate university for the aborigines of this island — for the corner boys who spit in the Liffey'.[14] Once we accept that Joyce's engagement with history involves conviction and that there are social and cultural issues centrally at stake in his work, then a general distinction has to be drawn: a distinction between Joyce the so-called theorist of the *meaning* of history, who has featured so

---

[12] See also *Letters II*, 211 where Yeats is tellingly described as a 'tiresome idiot' who is 'quite out of touch with Irish people'.

[13] From B. H. Clarke, 'George Moore', in *Intimate Portraits* (1915), quoted in *JJ*, 529.

[14] From Gerald Griffin, *The Wild Geese: Pen Portraits of Famous Irish Exiles* (1938), quoted in *JJ*, 58.

largely in recent, post-structuralist accounts, and Joyce the combatant who is engaged in a furious war over cultural politics. This distinction will be developed throughout what follows, but I would just emphasize, here, that Joyce's engagement with Anglo-Ireland, which he essentially constructs as an engagement with cultural colonialism, is not, in my account, the pure, intellectual, theoretical affair that many recent writers on Joyce and history have suggested.[14] *Ulysses* is not a retreat into mythic historiography or philosophical relativism, or into a sealed world of endless verbal significance, but rather a vital and wildly comic production which is fundamentally engaged with the cultural conditions of its own making. It is John Eglinton who, again showing considerable insight, was perhaps first to place this engagement in the context of revivalism. He described *Ulysses* as a 'violent interruption of what is known as the Irish literary renaissance', and was certain about the social dimension embedded in this interaction, which is presumably why he read Ulysses as a expression of 'Celtic revenge'.[15]

---

[14] See, for instance, James Fairhall, *James Joyce and the Question of History* (Cambridge: Cambridge University Press, 1993), 38. In his opening chapter, Fairhall uses different accounts of the Phoenix Park murders and Joyce's own reconstruction of them in 'Eumaeus', to argue that, for Joyce, all history is subjective and therefore unknowable. He quotes Deane's view, which was also McCabe's, of Joyce working to 'find new relationships between author and audience through language, so that language (and author) could escape from history ... and yet at the same time be rooted in history.' See Seamus Deane, 'Joyce and Nationalism', in *James Joyce: New Perspectives,* ed. Colin McCabe (Brighton: Harvester Press, 1982), 137.

[15] J. Eglinton, *Irish Literary Portraits* (London: Macmillan, 1935), 42.

1 Opening Encounters

A historical perspective
There is a tradition, established by Yeats himself, which finds the origins of the Literary Revival in the friendship of Yeats and O' Leary. Their first meeting in the summer of 1885 becomes a genesis, a symbolic communion of age and youth, nationalist and one-time Unionist which liberates Yeats from the writing of Shelley and Spenser imitations and produces the Irish writer charged with the heroic task of reawakening a national imagination. This romantic scenario gained uncritical acceptance from historians of revivalism for a long time.[1] Yet it has no historical validity. Revivalism, conceived of as cultural nationalism, predates Yeats's birth by about a century and evolved not from a national consensus but, ironically enough, partly out of Catholic demands for social and political parity with Protestant Ireland. Although Celtic studies were already being co-ordinated by the Royal Irish Academy in the 1770s,[2] it was Catholic activists like Charles O'Connor and Thomas Wyse, founders of the Catholic Association (1760), who may have been the first to use romantic conceptions of pre-Norman or pre-Danish Ireland in an ideological way, stressing the heroism and morality of an indigenous Gaelic culture which the Ascendancy overlords had demolished in an orgy of greed and violence. The Catholic-Gael was an established figure in the political rhetoric already available to O'Connell in the 1820s, and he clearly realized its potency.

Initially, Anglo-Ireland was unimpressed by Catholic claims on a Gaelic past. It held a seemingly unbreakable authority over land, social status and political influence. Despite conflicts with Westminster, its position was underpinned by English arms and broad political policy and the Anglo-Irish retained English allegiances. The historiography of oppression was confidently contested by an epic of civilization battling against ignorance and barbarism. When the Royal Dublin Society and its band of Protestant antiquarians began to study Gaelic culture in the late eighteenth century, its purpose was far removed from any revitalization of the national spirit. The task was to preserve and catalogue the remnants of

---

[1] See, for instance, R. Fallis, *The Irish Renaissance* (Syracuse: Syracuse University Press, 1977).

[2] See Oliver MacDonagh, *States of Mind: A Study of Anglo-Irish Conflict, 1780-1980* (London: Allen & Unwin, 1983), 23.

a dead society, a task which implied the 'scientific' demonstration of the essential primitiveness of pre-plantation Ireland, thereby legitimizing the mockery of native 'Irishers' who were, after all, of an inferior race.[3]

Anglo-Irish revivalism, then, was an astonishing *volte face*. Ferguson's 'discovery' of a new Anglo-Irish nationality, and O'Grady's insistence that he himself was 'no rooted colonist of an alien earth' but a man engaged in linking 'his present with his country's past' to 'live anew in knowledge of his sires'[4] seemed to involve wild contradictions. But there was a powerful logic behind these developments. The Act of Union had seriously weakened Ireland's political independence and marked the beginning of an irreversible decline in the political power of Irish Protestants. As early as the 1820s, it was becoming apparent that England's loyalty to Anglo-Ireland, already badly compromised by the Rebellion of the 1790s, was provisional and entirely dependent on political expediency. Catholic Emancipation (1829) was to show that if Catholic demands were asserted with enough force, and in the right political circumstances, England would negotiate with Catholic Ireland. The process of Catholic political and social emancipation was, of course, a fundamental threat to the Ascendancy. During the 1840s, and in response to Catholic Emancipation, the Protestant intelligentsia produced an outpouring of revivalist literature, which included O'Curry's translation and publication of the Brehon laws; John O'Donovan's work on Irish grammar and his translation and annotation in seven volumes of *The Annals of the Four Masters*; the beginning of O'Grady's 'histories', and Ferguson's resurrection of the Cuchulain myths and the Red Branch of Ulster cycle. There was also a 'stream of popular essays on every aspect of Irish life and history, on Irish humour, Irish proverbs, battles, crops, crafts, literature and music',[5] many of them published in George Petrie's *Irish Penny Journal*.

---

[3] See, for instance, the Reverend Edward Lodowick's *Antiquities of Ireland* (1790) which operates a progress historiography entirely consistent with contemporary English historical reconstruction, reinforcing the hegemony of 'Anglo-Saxon' culture, by representing early Irish history as a dark age of ignorance and bloody tribalism.

[4] Samuel Ferguson, 'Mesegdra', in *The Lays of the Red Branch* (Dublin: Maunsel, 1897), 32-33.

[5] Hutchinson, *Dynamics of Cultural Nationalism*, 86.

Revivalism was thus created by an intellectual élite determined to identify a declining Anglo-Ireland with an 'authentic' Irish culture. The main objective of this activity was to 'recapture for the Protestant landlords the leadership of the Irish nation'.[6] The Whiggish progress version of history which had once been shared by the Protestant establishment was now replaced by a separatist formulation. Petrie, O'Curry, O'Donovan and, more radically, Samuel Ferguson and Standish O'Grady, all utilized Gaelicism in a passionate declaration of Ireland's spiritual superiority over England. They produced the essential texts which defined an empire of the spirit embattled with the inexorable materialism of the English.

By the end of the nineteenth century, what had been a threat for Ferguson had become the real world for Yeats and his contemporaries. It may be, as some contemporaries claimed, that the Anglo-Irish continued to 'maintain their yoke ... by the spirit of servitude which they have impressed on the national mind'. They certainly continued to hold the majority of landed property and dominated the 'business world and the liberal professions'.[7] On the other hand, the Catholic Church had grown massively in an expansion which had a potent and telling economic dimension. According to Emmet Larkin, Church expansion was pursued with 'an ingenuity, a perseverance and a confidence that would make the most hard-headed exponent of the Protestant ethic gasp'.[8] This expansion and Archbishop Cullen's drive promoted, amongst other things, an education revolution. Post-famine land legislation, notably the Encumbered Estates Act (1849), made it easier and more profitable for Catholics to acquire land, and in the latter half of the nineteenth century a new Catholic gentry emerged with its wealth based on dairy farming. A tenfold increase in the size of the Irish civil service was a product of modernization and bureaucratization which also boosted the Catholic middle class.[9] A blueprint of nation which excluded Anglo-Ireland

---

[6] Ibid., 90.

[7] L. Paul Dubois, *The Gaelic Movement in Contemporary Ireland* with an introduction by T. M. Kettle (Dublin: Maunsel, 1908), 93.

[8] Emmet Larkin, 'Economic Growth, Capital Investment and the Roman Catholic Church in Nineteenth-Century Ireland', *The American Historical Review*, LXXII/3 (April 1967), 864-65.

[9] Hutchinson sketches the growth of this process. There were four major

altogether was finding expression in the likes of D. P. Moran who thought Grattan's Parliament 'a fraud' in a 'disastrous epoch' and who vilified Young Ireland for bringing 'into life a mongrel thing, which they called Irish literature in the English language'.[10] It seems certain that Anglo-Ireland's colonization of a mythic past was the means by which a declining class attempted a last ditch preservation of its cultural and intellectual position, exercising a form of displaced landlordism through its romanticized conception of the peasantry and affirming an aristocratic code which scorned what Synge referred to as the 'rampant double-chinned vulgarity'[11] of the Catholic middle class — this being the class which had produced Joyce. Anglo-Ireland had certainly gone through some curious changes: landlords had become co-operatists; Protestants had become mystics; unionists had become nationalists. For all that, the Anglo-Irish intelligentsia still perceived itself as an aristocracy in spirit, however much its material fortunes might have declined.

There is no basis to the revivalist identification of a central, if 'hidden', cultural tradition which bonded Irish modernity to early and even pre-Christian times. The language issue apart, nationalist culture of the modern period had very little in common with the culture from which it claimed ancestry. Joep Leerssen's monumental study of pre-eighteenth-century literary culture in Ireland, *Mere Irish and Fíor-Ghael* (1986), confirms the great distance separating 'bardic culture' from modern Irish nationalism. Leersson shows, for instance, that the Gaelic clan system could not even have conceptualized, let alone generated, a nationalistic culture, because notions such as 'nation' and 'statehood' were completely alien to a culture structured around clans. In almost every respect imaginable, there is, as one would expect, a huge gulf between the Gaelic culture of antiquity and modern Irish nationalist culture. The culture

---

government offices created, the Land Commission (1881), the Congested Districts Board (1891), the Department of Agriculture and Technical Instruction (1899) and the National Insurance Commission. These required in addition to clerks, 'a technical staff of lawyers, medical officers, surveyors, engineers, scientists and instructors' (Hutchinson, *Dynamics of Cultural Nationalism*, 259). For a fuller account see R. B. McDowell, *The Irish Administration 1801-1914* (London: Routledge & Kegan Paul, 1964).

[10] D. P. Moran, *The Philosophy of Irish Ireland* (Dublin: Maunsel, 1905), 33-34.

[11] See A. Price, ed., *J. M. Synge: Collected Works, Vol. II: Prose* (London: Oxford University Press, 1967), 283.

which Anglo-Ireland claimed to have 'rediscovered', and which was presented as an authentic cultural tradition, was actually Victorian, 'translated', and popularized substantially by a Protestant intellectual establishment.

The Triestine lectures (1907)
The Triestine lectures, for all their contradictions and limitations,[12] together constitute the one non-fictional account of Irish cultural history that Joyce produced. For our purposes, the significance of Joyce's version of this history is its fundamental opposition to the influential Anglo-Irish account of cultural history propagandized by revivalism in the nineteenth and early twentieth centuries, although it is certainly Yeats's brand of revivalism to which Joyce was both most exposed and most responsive. The lectures suggest that, as far as Joyce is concerned, the Yeatsian incarnation is representative of the whole tradition. They constitute an attack on what Joyce regards as Anglo-Ireland's cultural pretensions and articulate an alternative account of Ireland's cultural history. It is for this reason that the lectures have a particular importance for this study.

The Triestine lectures challenge the Revival's cultural historiography on three main grounds. Firstly, there is the implicit charge that the Literary Revival's indifference to the achievements of the early Irish Church produces a false history, a thoroughly ideological construction. Secondly, Joyce makes a clear distinction between national culture and Anglo-Irish culture, thus refuting the Literary Revival's enunciation of its own ancestry. Finally, and perhaps most radically, Joyce challenges the view that an authentic national literary culture, protected and cultivated by the Anglo-Irish intelligentsia, had managed to survive and even flourish in adversity beyond the eighteenth century. For Joyce, the Gael was dead and beyond resurrection, except on his own highly idiosyncratic terms.

Anglo-Irish revivalism was determined to identify Protestantism with authentic Irish cultural traditions. It was partly for this reason that it ignored and sometimes refuted the cultural contribution made by the early Irish Church. Catholicism was represented as a foreign import which had tamed the wild Celtic spirit. The dialogues of Oisin and St Patrick imaged the eternal conflict between the heroic and the Christian ideal, and, in the

---

[12] As Mason and Ellsworth point out, the Triestine lectures are incomplete and were written with more than half an eye on the Irredentist audience that Joyce addressed at the Universita Popolare. See *CW*, 153.

opinion of Ernest Boyd, one of the earliest historians of the Literary Revival:

> the most distinguished of the Irish poets have always been on the side of Oisin. They have all made the same protest, and their work is tinged by regret for the joylessness of an age which is unfit to be compared with the great age of which the bards sang.[13]

In more than two hundred articles written during the heyday of Celtic propaganda, Yeats addressed every conceivable aspect of ancient Irish culture from Irish fairies to the tribes of Danu, and yet this huge production contained virtually no reference to the early Irish Church. 'Ireland, Island of Saints and Sages' is highly sensitive to this neglect and insists on asserting the centrality of the Church in the history of Irish culture. Pre-Christian Ireland — the age of heroism which germinated revivalist historiography and provided the inspiration for revivalist literature — is dispensed with in a single sentence. What follows is a catalogue of apostolic achievement in art, philosophy, history and science:

> Even in the first century of the Christian era, under the apostleship of St Peter, we find the Irishman Mansuetus, who was later canonized, serving as a missionary in Lorraine, where he founded a church and preached for half a century. Cataldus had a cathedral and two hundred theologians at Geneva, and was later made bishop of Taranto. The great heresiarch Pelagius, a traveller and tireless propagandist, if not an Irishman, as many contend, was certainly either Irish or Scottish, as was his right hand man Caelestius. Sedulius traversed a great part of the world, and finally settled in Rome, where he composed the beauties of almost five hundred theological tracts, and many sacred hymns that are used even today in Catholic ritual .... Fiery Columbanus had the task of reforming the French Church, and, after having started a civil war in Burgundy by his preaching, went to Italy, where he became the apostle of the Lombards and founded the monastery at Bobbio.
>
> (*CW*, 157-59)

The list of achievements continues with references to Frigidian, St Gall, Finnian 'the Learned', St Fiacre, Fursey, Arbogast, St Verus, Disibod, Rumold, Albinus, Kilian, Sedulius the younger, and to the heresiarchs John Duns Scotus, Macarius and Vergilius Solivagus. The offhanded

---

[13] Boyd, *Irish Literary Renaissance*, 62.

summary of the period as 'an unbroken record of apostleships, and missions, and martyrdoms' (*CW*, 158-160) does not cancel the obvious pride in figures like John Duns Scotus who 'according to legend ... listened to the arguments of all the Doctors of the University of Paris for three whole days, then rose, and speaking from memory, refuted them one by one'; or of Petrus Hibernus, 'the theologian who had the supreme task of educating the mind of ... St Thomas Aquinas, perhaps the keenest and most lucid mind known to human history' (*CW*, 161). Moreover, it is precisely this account of the early Church which, like O'Connell in the early days of the Catholic Association,[14] Joyce uses to justify the assertion that:

> the Irish nation's insistence on developing its own culture by itself is not so much the demand of a young nation that wants to make good in the European concert as the demand of a very old nation to renew under new forms the glories of a past civilization.
>
> (*CW*, 157)

The general sentiment would have been wildly applauded by revivalist Ireland, but the identification of a 'past civilization' with Catholicism made so emphatically by Joyce was precisely what the Literary Revival was determined to underplay.[15]

---

[14] Accursed be the day ... when the invaders first touched our shores. They came to a nation famous for its love of learning, its piety, its heroism [and] doomed Ireland to seven centuries of oppression .... In my daydreams I revive a brighter period of Irish history when Erin was the cradle of saints and science (M. O'Connell, ed., *The Correspondence of Daniel O'Connell* [Shannon: Irish University Press, 1974], Vol. IV, 87-88).

[15] There were Catholic revivalists who responded to Anglo-Ireland's attempted burial of Catholicism by focusing on St Patrick's role in 'fusing' Christianity and Celticism. Eoin O'Neill for instance, a key figure in the Gaelic League, argued that even by the fifth century

> the Irish nation had not been formed: divisions continued between Celt and pan-Celts, and like the peoples of Europe ravaged by war amid the collapse of the Roman empire, the Celts themselves were riven by internal strife. It was the miracle of St Patrick's arrival in Ireland in this universal darkness that brought into being the Irish nation. Fusing the Christian and Celtic cultures, he pacified the warrior Celts, united the Irish peoples, prepared the way for a national monarchy, and laid the foundations for the glorious outburst of Christian and classical learning in the Irish language in which the Irish led Europe.
>
> (Quoted in Hutchinson, *Dynamics of Cultural Nationalism*, 124)

In insisting on the civilizing influence of the early Church in Ireland, Joyce implicitly recognizes the Literary Revival as an attempted proselytizing of Irish culture. This insistence is a useful pointer to the actual complexity of Joyce's response to Catholicism and has an obvious bearing on his treatment of the Church in his work. Both Stephen's interest in the old schoolmen and his sense of being usurped, a dispossessed bard, operate within this historical context. There may be an element of self-mockery in the similarity he sees between 'the slow growth and change of rite and dogma' and 'his own rare thoughts, a chemistry of stars' (1.652-653), but there is also a genuine suggestion of cultural identification, and this promotes the suggestion that the 'genealogical' relationship existing between the 'priest of the eternal imagination' (*P*, 221) and 'the glories of a past civilization' (*CW*, 157) expresses a social consciousness, one which realizes itself in socio-cultural rather than political forms. The second chapter of this study, 'Usurper', will be concerned with Joyce's presentation of this social consciousness, with Stephen's articulation of the 'voice of Esau', with his identification with a dispossessed Catholic middle class in 'Aeolus' and with his direct interrogation of some of the Anglo-Irish makers of revivalism in 'Scylla and Charybdis'.

The reverse side of the Literary Revival's neglect of the Church's role in Irish culture was its emphasis on the part played by a handful of Protestant artists and academics in the reclamation of the old traditions. The fundamental contradiction of an Anglo-Ireland which had once implemented England's subjugation of the Irish now promoting national regeneration through Gaelicism was glossed over partly through the Revival's apotheosizing of O'Grady and Ferguson. For Yeats, O'Grady's 'histories' had fathered the Revival, and Ferguson, through his poetry, was the consubstantial son, 'the greatest poet Ireland ever produced' because he was 'the most Celtic' (Yeats, *UP1*, 103). It was Ferguson who had 'restored to us in *Deirdre*, a fragment of the buried Odyssey of Ireland' (Yeats, *UP1*, 92). His poetry was national, 'truly bardic, appealing to all natures alike, to the great concourse of the people' (Yeats, *UP1*, 101). In Yeats's view the very survival of Celtic culture depended largely on the work of these two writers. Their names echo through his promotion of the Revival. Joyce's sense of dispossession is further

---

This seems quite close to Joyce's view in 'Ireland, Island of Saints and Sages', except that for Joyce this past was irretrievable.

evidenced in his indifference to these progenitors of revivalism. In his account of Irish cultural history there is no place reserved for O'Grady and Ferguson. Indeed, in all Joyce's letters and critical writings, there is no reference to O'Grady and only one glancing allusion to Ferguson (*CW*, 85). His account of the cultural impact of Protestantism in 'Ireland, Island of Saints and Sages' may refuse any dogma of racial purity.[16] It nonetheless firmly challenges the revivalist view that Anglo-Irish literature represented a genuine extension of Celticism, and fully exposes Anglo-Ireland's complicity in the subjugation of a native Irish culture. Joyce argues that this culture began to die with the English invasion and that by the eighteenth century the process was all but complete. He is willing to claim the likes of Berkeley, Goldsmith, Swift, and Burke for Ireland, but he denies them any connection with what he calls 'the glories' of the 'old national soul' (*CW*, 173).

> From the time of the English invasion to our time, there is an interval of almost eight centuries, and if I have dwelt rather at length on the preceding period in order to make you understand the roots of the Irish temperament, I do not intend to detain you by recounting the vicissitudes of Ireland under foreign occupation. I especially will not do so because at that time Ireland ceased to be an intellectual force in Europe. The decorative arts, at which the ancient Irish excelled, were abandoned, and the sacred and profane culture fell into disuse.
>
> (*CW*, 161)

Of course, it could be argued that Joyce's version of Irish cultural history peddles its own myths. Ireland's monastic, artistic and literary culture did continue until the Penal Laws and the Act of Union. During the sixteenth and seventeenth centuries Irish families established universities, monasteries and schools of poetry in Ireland and Europe, including Louvain in Belgium. But this 'slippage' only confirms the ideological status of Joyce's account, an analysis in which the Anglo-Irish become no more than a hybrid to a Celtic/Catholic root. In a period of general cultural collapse they produced some exceptional writers, but these 'adopted the English language ... and almost forgot their native land' (*CW,* 170) and have little or no connection with anything that could be

---

[16] See *CW*, 162, where Joyce argues that 'to deny the name of patriot to all those who are not of Irish stock' would be an 'absurdity'. Of course, this raises the further issue of what precisely Joyce means by 'Irish stock'.

[margin note: → useful contradiction]

termed a national culture.

For Yeats, the nineteenth century marked the resurgence of a national culture; for Joyce it represented the final destruction of a native Irish culture. Yeats saw himself as the inheritor of traditions rediscovered in the nineteenth century; for Joyce there were no authentic literary traditions to be had from this long period of Ireland's history. This distinction between cultural historiographies is of central importance. Although nothing of the literary radicalism of *Ulysses* can be predicted from the Triestine lectures, or from any of Joyce's previous work, the sense of cultural displacement and usurpation which echoes through these lectures is certainly consistent with the damage that Joyce does to narrative traditions in *Ulysses*.

Anglo-Ireland's insistence on a syncretic cultural continuity struggling against adversity produced an aristocratic folk-culture of heroism, tradition and romantic retrospection, a culture which despised the modern in all its manifestations and which idealized the largely mythological past. Joyce, on the other hand, as the Triestine lectures make clear, operated in a different kind of continuity: the continuity of Anglicization, of cultural hegemony and cultural dispossession. From chapter 3 onwards, this study examines the textuality of *Ulysses* as a blatant reproduction of this dispossession which, far from obscuring its Anglicized origins, revels in the cultural conditions of its own making. Joyce's book is formulated out of such fabrics as English Victorian melodrama, Anglicized newspapers, English fashions, English women's magazines, Shakespeare's life and times, and the historical development of English literature. Anglo-Irish culture is garishly produced in *Ulysses* as a key constituent of this cultural colonization. In some episodes revivalist discourses and art forms are the target of extended pastiche. Standish O'Grady's extremely influential historiography lies centrally behind the interpolations of *Ulysses* 12 and the dramaturgy of the Irish Literary Theatre is uproariously let loose in *Ulysses* 15. In other episodes, the Revival's apocalyptic analysis of the modern world which was so inimical to art and which so threatened the Gaelic sensibility is allowed full rein, producing the bourgeois narrative of 'Eumaeus', for example, and the scientism of 'Ithaca'. The puritanism of Anglo-Irish revivalism is a constant target for Joyce's scorn, most startlingly perhaps in his interference with the poetics that produced a feminized iconography for the national culture, and a wild idealization of women in the process.

There is a further point of interest in the Triestine lectures which has to do with a notable exception to Joyce's deeply controversial view that

Ireland had no vital authentic literary culture to draw on, because one of the lectures is about Mangan, a Catholic poet and the only Irish writer of the nineteenth century in whom Joyce had any serious interest. A comparison of Joyce and Yeats's estimations of this poet is highly suggestive of the extent to which historical dynamics and social consciousness produced the antithetical positions that both writers adopted.

Like Yeats, Joyce wrote two pieces on Mangan (although in Joyce's case the second was only a reworking of the first). Both writers found Mangan's poetry inconsistent in quality, but beyond this very limited agreement there is little consensus. They differ considerably in their evaluations of individual poems, but the deepest source of dispute concerns the issue of Mangan's place in the national culture. In both his essays, Yeats is more concerned with the biographical than with literary appreciation. Indeed, the major interest of his second essay is in 'the kind of soul he [Mangan] had' and 'with the fashion in which he lived' and has nothing to do with poetry at all. Yeats is interested in establishing the existence of a love affair which many thought a metaphor and with announcing the true identity of Mangan's lover, a Francis Stackpole. According to Yeats, it was the failure of this affair that resulted in Mangan's artistic and physical deterioration, his 'rum-loving and, if Mitchel speaks truth, opium-eating habits' (Yeats, *UP1*, 196). Joyce probably had Yeats in mind (and perhaps Lionel Johnson and Charles Gavan Duffy) when he complained about the naïveté of Irish surprise at finding 'evidence of the poetic faculty in a man whose vices were exotic and whose patriotism was not very ardent' (*CW*, 180). This is not to say that Joyce rejects the biographical method; on the contrary, Joyce's use of biography is every bit as emphatic as Yeats's. But the two interpret biographical material in very different, in fact, antithetical ways. For Yeats, Mangan is a pathetic genius who is destroyed by his own misery. He utters 'a brute cry from the gutters of the earth' (Yeats, *UP1*, 117), and in Yeats's analysis this anguish becomes part of an expression of an intensely private abnormality:

> He never startles us by saying beautiful things. He does not say look at yourself in this mirror; but, rather, 'Look at me — I am so strange, so exotic, so different.
>
> <div align="right">(Yeats, <i>UP1</i>, 119)</div>

The manly combative vigour which Yeats thought so typical of the O'Grady/Ferguson tradition of Gaelicism is absent in Mangan. The latter's trademark becomes an intense, but essentially feeble introspection.

Joyce takes issue with this. His lecture reveals close personal identification with Mangan. Mangan the 'child of quiet and unresponsive manner ... preoccupied with religious matters', whose writings 'attracted the attention of the cultured, who recognized in him an exalted lyrical music and a burning idealism' (*CW*, 177), is obviously reminiscent of Joyce's fictional portrait of his own artistic temperament. But more than this, in Joyce's hands, Mangan's personal despair and dissipation become an embodiment of a racial consciousness, an echo of which may be found in *Portrait* where Davin is repelled by Stephen's sexual revelations and Stephen replies that, 'this race and this country and this life produced me .... I shall express myself as I am' *(P,* 203). Mangan was working 'without a native literary tradition' (*CW*, 182). But for Joyce, he nonetheless takes on the role that Yeats had reserved for Ferguson (a Protestant, a Unionist and an ex-Trinity man), as 'the most significant poet of the modern Celtic world' (*CW*, 179). Mangan 'sums up in himself the soul of a country' (*CW,* 184). One tonal characteristic of this national poetry is the expression of grief: 'this is the theme of a very large part of Irish poetry, but no other Irish poems are full, as are those of Mangan, of misfortune nobly suffered, of vastation of soul so irreparable' (*CW,* 184). Another feature was the spirit of revenge.

So the landless landowner regarded the one Catholic poet of any significance from this period as a rootless, self-destructive figure outside the mainstream of Gaelic culture. The churchless Catholic, on the other hand, presented Mangan as summing up Celtic dispossession, the last and most passionate representative of a dead culture. Joyce was to claim in later life that 'there is more intensity in a single passage of Mangan's than in all Swift's writings' (*JJ*, 545). 'With him' [Mangan], he writes in the Triestine lecture, 'the long tradition of the triple order of the old Celtic bards ended; and today other bards, animated by other ideals, have the cry' (*CW*, 174). Joyce's third and final lecture was to have been about these 'bards of today'. He never actually wrote this lecture, but the phrase 'animated by other ideals' perhaps indicates something of what Joyce intended. In 'Ireland, Island of Saints and Sages' he outlined the 'glories' of early Catholic culture. In 'Mangan' he restored Mangan to a national position and by implication robbed Ferguson and O'Grady of the national laurels which Yeats insisted should be theirs. It seems unlikely that Joyce would have had much to say in support of the Ascendancy's later revival. If Celtic culture had finally died with Mangan, then the highest position open to revivalists was that of keepers of the antiquities. Certainly Joyce would not allow them the voice of Ireland that they claimed was theirs.

'Ireland, Island of Saints and Sages' begins with the assertion that 'Nations have their egos, just like individuals' (*CW,* 154). In light of the Mangan essay, this is clearly more than just an incidental observation. For Joyce, there was a generic relation between racial and the individual artist's consciousness. Certainly this idea was to hold increasing fascination for Joyce. Stephen's maturation is concerned with his recognition of its truth, a truth that is arguably fundamental to the *Wake*. In any case, the Triestine lectures do not just describe a relationship of this kind with Mangan as example: they embody it through an analysis that reveals the racial and class dimension to Joyce's declaration of artistic independence, an analysis which must cast serious doubt on the view held for so long by Joyceans that Joyce's dispute with the Revival was anything as pure as a matter of aesthetics. For Joyce, the Literary Revival was a culmination of Anglo-Irish attempts to secure for themselves a remnant of the hegemony they had formally exerted over Ireland. The importance of the Triestine lectures is that they place Joyce in this context and suggest a crucial historical perspective for reading his work. They reveal a Joyce not divided from revivalist Ireland by a Promethean act of will, producing freakish Catholic offshoots to the 'real' national literature as H. G. Wells suggested, but rather a participant in what became known, in a crude simplification, as 'the battle of two civilizations'.

'You be Murphy and I'll be Smith': naming the state in *Dubliners*
The Gael was constructed by revivalism as a natural manifestation and Gaelic society idealized as an absolute congruency of culture and nature. The Gaelic community was bound together, not by materiality but by 'imaginative possessions, by stories and poems which have grown out of life, and by a past of great passions which can still awaken the heart to imaginative action' (Yeats, *Ex*, 213). There was an important corollary to this deification of the community and the land. Modern, urban life was anathematized as the antithesis of culture. The aristocratic virtues — nobility, tradition, beauty — could no more survive in modernity than the aristocratic class itself, and nationalism, which revivalism defined as an

aristocratic ideology, was similarly destined to wither on this bleak urban ground:

> Does not the greatest poetry always require a people to listen to it? England or any other country which takes its tunes from the great cities and gets its taste from schools and not from old custom may have a mob, but it cannot have a people.
>
> (W. B. Yeats, *Ex*, 213)

Far from engaging with revivalism, it could be argued that *Dubliners* subscribes at least to part of this agenda. There is nothing in Joyce's stories that endorses the conservative Gaelicism of the revival, but these city-tales do begin with actual and metaphorical disease. Joyce's Dublin is a 'centre of paralysis' and 'corruption' (*Letters II*, 122-23/134). The opening story revolves around a dead priest, representing the spiritual death of the city whose inhabitants are too servile and conventional to express their own natures — so often precisely Yeats's claim. The characters in this collection have made their pact with a thoroughly materialist and Anglicized society. These are the clerks and 'burghers' who value respectability, status and money above all else. Bob Doran throws away any chance of happiness to protect his good name. 'Culture' is a social and cash asset in 'A Mother'. The wayward Catholics in 'Grace' are advised to model their spiritual life on their manner of conducting business affairs. In 'Ivy Day', political support is bought for the price of a pint. Some of Joyce's creations, like Maria in 'Clay', put a brave face on matters and pretend that their life-denying environment is really 'quite nice'. Others, like Eveline, have more raw frustrations, but cannot assert themselves for fear of social condemnation. Those characters who do break convention, the parasites like Lenehan and Corley, are the most contemptible of all. Most of Joyce's Dubliners are unable to conceptualize their own need for redress or escape, and, ironically, those who most nearly approach an awareness of such needs — Little Chandler, Mr Duffy and Gabriel Conroy — are the most thoroughly bourgeois of this Dublin crowd, a crowd which clearly does not embody the values of Yeats's nation at all.

This conventional, mean-spirited, materialist Dublin, so different from the world of madcap dissenting brilliance produced in the memoirs of Joyce's contemporaries, could be seen as a confirmation of the revivalist account of things, although the relationship is not exactly one of agreement or concordance. It is more precisely a matter of Joyce correcting and outdoing the Revival. Where Yeats generalizes and sketches, Joyce specifies and picks over with great intimacy. Yeats's grandiose dismissal of urban bourgeois life, is displaced by the painstaking detail and accuracy of Joyce's reconstruction. Far from despising the urban environment as anti-art, Joyce reproduces it, to an elaborate and precise specification. He clearly and repeatedly announces the accuracy of this reproduction, advertising the sheer amount of knowledge that underpins his presentation of 'Irish life'. In Joyce's own estimation this authenticity becomes self-evidently a measure of the book's quality. He often contextualizes his 'expertise' with reference to revivalist ignorance. He regarded Moore's *The Untilled Field* (1903), for example, a book of short stories which had some influence on *Dubliners*,[17] as 'Damn stupid', precisely because it gets so many facts and details simply wrong.[18] This is reminiscent of Joyce's later criticism of James Stephens, whose 'knowledge of Irish life was 'non-Catholic' and

---

[17] This book was one of two revivalist fictions written by Moore. He had the stories translated into Gaelic with the revivalist market specifically in mind, but the Gaelic League refused to sell the volume, partly on the grounds of its blatant landlordism and anti-clericalism. The most important influence of *The Untilled Field* on *Dubliners* can be seen in final paragraph of a story called 'Home Sickness', which tells the story of an American Irishman who returns to Ireland on the advice of his doctor. He falls in love with an Irish woman, Margaret Dirken, but determines to return to New York without her and marries someone else. The story concludes:

> There is an unchanging silent life within every man that none knows but himself, and his unchanging, silent life was his memory of Margaret Dirken. The bar-room was forgotten and all that concerned it, and the things he saw most clearly were the green hillside, and the bog lake and the rushes around about it, and the greater lake in the distance, and behind it the blue line of wandering hills.
>
> (*The Untilled Field* [Gerrards Cross: Colin Smythe, 1976], 49)

There are obvious echoes of this in the lyrical ending of Joyce's 'The Dead'.

[18] 'I have read Moore's 'Untilled Field' in Tauchnitz. Damned stupid. A woman alludes to her husband in the confession-box as 'Ned'. Ned thinks etc.! A lady who has been living for three years on the line between Bray and Dublin is told by her husband that there is a meeting at Dublin at which he must be present. She looks up the table to see the hours of the trains. This on DW and WR [the Dublin, Wicklow and Wexford Railway] where the trains go regularly: this after three years. Isn't it rather stupid of Moore. And the punctuation! Madonna!' (*Letters II*, 71).

therefore 'non-existent' (*JJ*, 333). Joyce greatly surpasses the Revival in terms of veracity and this performance is effected partly in response to a moral imperative. 'He is a very bold man', writes Joyce, 'who dares to alter in the presentment, still more to deform, whatever he has seen and heard' (*Letters II*, 134). Of course, it is precisely the demands of realism that produce the principal challenge to revivalist aesthetics in *Dubliners*. Joyce theorized the art of *Dubliners* both as truthful reconstruction and as a European importation. Like Flaubert, who was also a Catholic, Joyce produces an art of immediacy, accuracy, and observation. It is the absolute antithesis of Yeats's hidden and remote world of the 'spiritual and the ideal' (Yeats, *Ex*, 166), an art which is deals in ideal essences and purports to be immune to analysis.[19] A comparison of the following two passages, one from Yeats's story, 'Red Hanrahan' and the other from Joyce's 'A Little Cloud' effectively illustrates the chasm separating revivalist narrative from the narratives of *Dubliners*. In the first passage, Hanrahan is about to leave a barn where some villagers are drinking:

> Some of the others came about him, pressing him that had been such a pleasant comrade, so full of songs and every kind of trick and fun, not to leave them till the night would be over, but he refused them all, and shook them off, and went to the door. But as he put his foot over the threshold, the strange old man stood up and put his hand that was thin and withered like a bird's claw on Hanrahan's hand, and said: 'It is not Hanrahan, the learned man and the great songmaker, that should go out from a gathering like this on a Samhain night. And stop here, now', he said, 'and play a hand with me; and here is an old pack of cards has done its work many a night before this, and old as it is, there has been much of the world lost and won over it'.
>
> (Yeats, *Myth*, 215-16)

A number of Joyceans, and notably Riquelme,[20] have argued that there are a range of similarities or parallels between the *Stories of Red*

---

[19] 'Sincere poetry' will contain 'the perfections that escape analysis' (Yeats, *Ex*, 164).

[20] See John Paul Riquelme, *Teller and Tale in Joyce's Fiction: Oscillating Perspectives* (Baltimore: John Hopkins University Press, 1983), and the response to Riquelme's 'exemplary' reading of 'The Dead' in Emer Nolan, *James Joyce and Nationalism* (London: Routledge, 1995). Riquelme 'presumes that the real meaning of 'The Dead' is entirely divorced from its literal sense' (Nolan, 30), which is precisely what Nolan finds so compelling for some reason.

Hanrahan and *Dubliners*. The usual suggestion is that a common body of symbolism from an implied syncretic 'Irish' culture unites the two. Though unconvincingly illustrated, accounts of this 'influence' have become widely accepted. It therefore needs to be stressed quite firmly and from the outset that *Dubliners* is, quite literally, a world apart from Yeats's mystical, supernatural and folk landscapes.

There are a number of obvious markers which make the above extract absolutely characteristic of the *Stories of Red Hanrahan* sequence. This passage has a very limited degree of cultural and social specificity. It is set in rural Ireland and the narrative purports to construct the rhythms and occasionally the idiom of rural Anglo-Irish speech. In terms of historicity, however, the passage is very non-specific. It has 'done with time' (Yeats, *Ex*, 163),[21] as all serious art must according to the Yeatsian aesthetic. The narrative is suggestive of popular romanticizations of oral tradition and, in this respect, appears to represent 'a return to the way of our fathers' (Yeats, *Ex*, 164). But the concept of 'tradition', here has no precise historical features. Like many of early Yeats's stories, 'Red Hanrahan' seems set in a mythical non-time. The most obvious characteristic of the passage, however, is that curious loading which gives meaning, significance and weight to every turn of phrase. Passing the 'threshold' is obviously portentous; the old man seems presageful; his 'withered' claw-like hand is ominous, as is the invitation to play at cards. The cards themselves, old and mysterious, do 'work'. What this work might be is not articulated, but the final line is appropriately grandiose. Mystification is central to the effect here and it derives not from genre, but from an aristocratic aesthetic. Yeats's 'laws of art' are 'the hidden laws of the world' (Yeats, *Ex*, 163). The artist is a highly privileged mediator. This is an art of 'wavering meditative organic rhythms, which are the embodiment of the imagination' (Yeats, *Ex*, 164). Yeats himself allows that such an art may sometimes be 'obscure' (Yeats, *Ex*, 164). But the obscurity, far from being intermittent, is pervasive and central. It is the most characteristic feature of Yeats's stories at this time. Indeed, mystification crucially shapes the disposition of revivalist culture generally in this period. For if the 'true' Ireland has all but disappeared under the tide of alien modernity, the art of revivalism becomes an art of 'the Unseen Life' and, according to Yeats, 'here in Ireland', there is much

---

[21] This escape from real time was characteristic of revivalism. For a political reading of this escape see below, 100.

'love of the Unseen Life' (Yeats, *Ex* 204).

This Platonic aesthetic has no place in *Dubliners*. In presenting his stories to the world, Joyce insisted on their realism, their faithful recording of what the author had 'seen and heard' (*Letters II*, 134). In exact opposition to the privilege afforded to the unseen by revivalism, exposure of the *seen* life is key to Joyce's early aesthetic. The letters to the publisher Grant Richards which explain the originality of *Dubliners* carry a hidden polemic in this respect. They deliver a clear challenge to the revivalist art that was achieving astonishing success as a national culture. The following extract from 'A Little Cloud', illustrates the essential distinction between a narrative which mystifies and a narrative which reveals. Chandler is on his way to meet Gallaher, and is feeling unhappy with his lot:

> Every step brought him nearer to London, farther from his own sober inartistic life. A light begin to tremble on the horizon of his mind. He was not so old — thirty-two. His temperament might be said to be just at the point of maturity. There were so many different moods and impressions that he wished to express in verse. He felt them within him. He tried to weigh his soul to see if it was a poet's soul. Melancholy was the dominant note of his temperament, he thought, but it was a melancholy tempered by recurrences of faith and resignation and simple joy. If he could give expression to it in a book of poems perhaps men would listen. He would never be popular: he saw that. He could not sway the crowd, but he might appeal to a little circle of kindred minds. The English critics, perhaps, would recognize him as one of the Celtic school by reason of the melancholy tone of his poems; besides that, he would put in allusions. He began to invent sentences and phrases from the notices which his book would get. '*Mr Chandler has the gift of easy and graceful verse*' ... '*A wistful sadness pervades these poems*' ... '*The Celtic note*'. It was a pity his name was not more Irish-looking.
>
> (*D*, 64-65)

There is, of course, a challenge to revivalism simply at the level of content in this passage. The Literary Revival is presented as a bandwagon, and a thoroughly sanitized and Anglicized one, with Chandler hoping for recognition from 'the English critics'. Celticism is portrayed not as the national destiny of Yeats's vision, but rather as a clique, a 'school'. Its essential characteristic is not the wild exhilaration of Yeats's middle period, but the melancholic tone, suggestive of an earlier incarnation which Yeats himself was later to discard as being too 'feminine'. 'Allusions', presumably to myth and fairy tale, like the melancholic tone, become necessary ingredients in the Celtic mix. Yeats's 'organic' culture is here reduced to faddism. The mockery is of revivalism as much as Chandler, but there are more substantial challenges in the style and manner of the Joyce passage. This text disputes with the mythic time of Red Hanrahan. 'A Little Cloud', like all the *Dubliners* stories, is historically specific; the story is very precisely set in turn of the century Dublin, a city in decline where children play like 'vermin' 'under the shadow of the gaunt spectral mansions in which the old nobility of Dublin had roistered' (*D*, 63). There is no attempt at quaintness in the turn of phrase here, that is, no attempt to identify nationality in terms of a language idiom deployed and privileged as narrative. Narrative in these stories generally is invariably self-consciously English-sounding. But the real challenge to revivalism is in what might be described as the rationalism of Joyce's narrative. Chandler's fantasy *is* of the unseen in the sense that it exists only in his private world, but, this is completely realized in the passage. There is no system of unseen and unknowable 'significance' here, as there is in 'Red Hanrahan'. On the contrary, Joyce's narrative, for all its appearance of cool detachment, knows that Chandler is a romanticizing, self-dramatist and allows the reader to know. This is the function of the irony.

This brief comparison of the narratives of *Dubliners* and the 'Red Hanrahan' stories is symptomatic of a gulf which can be measured in terms of aesthetics but is not *mere* aesthetics. Both writers are claiming to reproduce Ireland, but the Irelands they make are strikingly at variance. One constructs the essential Ireland as a timeless, spiritual and literally magical rurality. The other constructs a contemporary, material, urban space. The Revival acknowledges the reality of Joyce's Dublin, indeed it is precisely modern urbanism that places the true national identity under siege. But the Revival insists on identifying the city as alien territory. Urbanism is 'English', un-Irish simply by being modern. It houses deracinated, materialist city-dwellers; it cannot breed a race.

The city, then, has no place in the cultural nationalism of revivalism. Similarly, neither the romanticized rural community, nor the 'authentic' Irish identity invented by the Revival have a place in Joyce's short stories. In *Dubliners*, there is no real Ireland secreted somewhere behind the facade of a dull, dispiriting reality, except perhaps in Gabriel Conroy's head as he approaches sleep and imagines a snow-covered, western land inhabited by 'shades'. To be Irish in these stories is to be a contemporary product of colonial history. Frustration, materialism, obsession with legitimacy and respectability make up precisely the territory which is the legacy of colonialism, a legacy presented in intimate detail in *Dubliners*. In this Castle environment, backs must be watched and dues paid. This is a survivalist culture in which values like Bob Doran's 'honour' are a liability. Revivalism constructed identity in mystical terms of 'blood'. In *Dubliners*, it is fluid and often a matter of disguise and counter-disguise. Eveline plays at being a bohemian girl, Jimmy Doyle at being a 'merchant prince'(*D*, 36). The son of a police inspector, Lenehan poses as yachtsman cum 'toreador'(*D*, 42) and 'gay Lothario' (*D*, 44). Ignatius Gallaher fakes a European (and mostly French) identity. Duffy poses as a hard intellectual, although he is, when it counts, deeply conventional and respectable. Accents are assumed too. Celticism is adopted by Chandler and the Kearneys, when it suits them, but is brushed aside by Gabriel who writes under a pseudonym for the *Express* and is 'sick' of his 'own country' (*D*, 170). English accents have serious caché. Even the city wears a mask (*D*, 38). If there is a 'true' identity here, it lies somewhere within a dynamic which is implied by the narrator of 'An Encounter' as he plays truant with his friend Mahoney. The narrator presents himself as sensitive and cultured, and Mahoney as a wild, unruly and socially inferior boy. Uneasy in the presence of the curious stranger who is so interested in 'chastising boys' (*D*, 18), the narrator feels the need for disguise and quite spontaneously plugs into the colonial double-bind which ties colonized to the colonizer:

> — In case he asks us for our names, I said, let you be Murphy and I'll be Smith.
>
> (*D*, 18)

There are other challenges too, to revivalism in *Dubliners*. Joyce deploys and interrogates some of the traditions of allegory and symbolism that were characteristic of revivalist culture. Indeed, at least three of the *Dubliners* stories, 'Araby', 'Two Gallants', and 'The Dead', make conspicuous use of revivalist allegorizing and myth-making. In all three stories, female characters figure as emblems of a feminized nation.[22] They are variously adored, served, betrayed and defiled, evoking the historiographies of cultural nationalism. In all cases, Joyce's working of this material is heterodox and usually subversive of the cultural tradition it

---

[22] This issue of gender and nation is the subject of chapter 7.

appropriates. 'Two Gallants', for instance, contains a particularly overt representation of Ireland as feminized nation. But here Ireland is rudely disrobed, and the symbolism taken to an extreme. This is not just Ireland as woman, but Ireland also as the musical instrument which, in the popular imagination, is most traditionally Irish:

> His harp ... heedless that her coverings had fallen about her knees, seemed weary alike of the eyes of strangers and of her master's hands. One hand played in the bass the melody of *Silent, O Moyle*, while the other hand careered in the treble after each group of notes.
>
> (*D*, 46)

Far from offering a vibrant image of national identity, the symbolism here is tired, dull and overdone. Through Thomas Moore's parlour ballad which is much more Victorian than Celtic, Joyce's Mother-Ireland figure is also Anglicized and vulgarized: in *Portrait* Stephen regards Moore's statue as resembling 'a Firbolg in the borrowed cloak of a Milesian' (*P*, 180). The harp image does not lift the story. On the contrary, it is made consistent with the seedy deceit which is at the centre of 'Two Gallants'. This is an ironic travesty of the symbolic repertoire of cultural nationalism, one that is paralleled elsewhere in 'Dubliners'.[23] In 'Araby', 'Mangan's sister' serves as a crudely obvious image of Ireland as seductress or goddess, compromised again by incongruous and subversive associations. The seduction here is too blatant and the motives too self-serving to conform to the standard conventions.[24] Joyce grants no privilege to such images, symbols and motifs. They are part of and consistent with what the stories amply describe as a cultural environment

---

[23] This image is more than a detail in the Irish landscape. Betrayal and defilement are central to the story. The unnamed maid in 'Two Gallants', Corley's 'fine decent tart' (*D*, 45) could and has been constructed as a figure of the nation. At least one inventive reader has seen in Corley, the police inspector's son, a tribal chieftain. See The Rev. R. Boyle, ' "Two Gallants" and "Ivy Day" ', in *James Joyce Quarterly*, I/2 (Spring 1961), 3-8. The point to emphasize is that if the maid is another Ireland configuration, again the symbolism is highly idiosyncratic. This is Ireland with 'broad nostrils, a straggling mouth which lay open in a contented leer, and two projecting front teeth' (*D*, 47).

[24] See Harry Stone, ' "Araby" and the Writings of James Joyce' , in *The Antioch Review*, III (Fall 1965), 375-410. This is definitive on historical contexts to this story.

distinguished by its staleness.

It is Joyce's aesthetic of realism, howver, and the subsequent exposure of modern, urban colonialism as the Irish condition that attacks revivalism with most penetration. Joyce does of course acknowledge that his aesthetic owes a debt to European traditions, but there is no question that these influences are commandeered into an Irish cultural debate. There were times when Joyce had doubts about the quality and the accuracy of what he had achieved in *Dubliners*, but he was always certain that he had at least improved on the performance of his main competitors, the predominantly Protestant prose writers of the Literary Revival. So much is implied in his frequent mockery of the poor grammar and punctuation of writers like Synge, Moore and Yeats. He made the point absolutely clearly when he wrote to his brother, 'Do not think I consider contemporary Irish writing anything but ill-written, morally obtuse formless caricature' (*JJ*, 209).

'Are you Irish at all?': portraits of the artist

In both *A Portrait* and *Stephen Hero*, but with more insistence in the latter, revivalism is presented as a conservative cultural force. It is represented as a fad which allows the young Catholic intelligentsia, Stephen's 'tame geese' (*P*, 181), to play at being radicals before they settle down to a more secure and respectable conformist life. For Stephen, modern-day Gaels are hopelessly compromised:

> — ... Tell me how many of your Gaelic Leaguers are studying for the Second Division and looking for advancement in the Civil Service?
> — That's different. They are only civil servants: they're not ...
> — Civil be damned! They are pledged to the Government, and paid by the Government.
>
> — O, well, if you like to look at it that way.
>
> (*SH*, 69)

That it is accepted and even encouraged by the Church is the clearest indication of the actual harmlessness of the Gaelic League, at least as far as Stephen is concerned. Joyce's analysis here is highly controversial. Many historians would want to distinguish between the conformism of the League's hierarchy and a grassroots which could be shown to be independent of the Church and much more radical than Stephen allows.

However, the broad point about Church support for the League has been generally accepted and can easily be substantiated. Archbishop Walsh, for instance, felt unable to underwrite the League until firmly persuaded of its respectable character and innocuous intent. After some early stand-offs between parish priests and league branches, Walsh wrote to a prominent Gaelic Leaguer in 1897: 'I can now, I think, feel safe in again taking some share in the good work, as it seems to have passed out of the stage of meaningless contention.' He authorized 'any use you wish' of his name in connection with the League.[25] In *Stephen Hero* the priests make 'speeches of exhortation' (*SH*, 65) at the League branch which Stephen briefly attends in the hope of getting close to Emma Cleary. Father O'Growney's[26] photograph presides over the meetings. All of which gives May Dedalus some hope, for

> she thought that the superintendence of the priests and the society of harmless enthusiasts might succeed in influencing her son in the right direction.
>
> (*SH*, 55)

Stephen despises this 'working hand in hand with the priests' and predicts that it will eventually cause the movement's downfall. Although Madden, attempts to justify the complicity as strategic, a ploy used by the League to maximize support, Stephen's has doubts that the Church can be used in such a way:

> — Do you not see, said Stephen, that they [the priests] encourage the study of Irish that their flocks may be more safely protected from the wolves of disbelief; they consider it is an opportunity to withdraw the people into a past, literal, implicit faith.
>
> (*SH*, 58)

Here the League is presented as being used by the Church to slow the process of modernization. In glorifying the peasant and attempting to popularize an archaic culture, the League supports the Church's conservative objective of keeping Ireland shackled to a feudal past.[27]

---

[25] Quoted in David W. Miller, *Church, State and Nation in Ireland 1898-1921* (Dublin: Gill & Macmillan, 1973), 36.

[26] O'Growney was a leading figure in revivalism.

[27] According to David Miller, the Church had a different motive: 'Its [the League's]

This attack on the Gaelicism of Catholic Ireland is consistent with Stephen's Stockmann-like persona in *Stephen Hero*. His role, especially in this earlier portrait, is partly to expose the hypocrisy of a reactionary middle-class Ireland. As for the Literary Revival, both portraits seem comparatively quietist on this aspect of Dublin's cultural life. Whereas the language and sports revivals are constituents of the university culture reproduced, revivalist literature seems peripheral. In *Stephen Hero*, the 'modern school of Irish writers' is a 'subject' of which Stephen knows 'nothing' (*SH*, 153). His championing of 'the modern spirit', which he calls 'vivisective' and to which he contrasts 'the ancient spirit which accepted phenomena with bad grace' (*SH*, 190), effectively amounts to a dismissal of revivalist aesthetics, but this declaration is not presented in a revivalist context. Indeed, at a later stage in the book, far from disputing the aesthetics of the Literary Revival, Stephen is actually sustained by two of Yeats's stories. He admires 'The Tables of the Law' and the 'Adoration of the Magi' so much that he commits them to memory. He responds ultimately to 'the atmosphere of these stories' 'heavy with incense and omens' and above all to, 'the figures of the monk errants, Ahern [sic] and Michael Robartes' (*SH*, 183).

In *A Portrait*, however, there is no reference to these stories. But there is an interesting reference to Yeats's poem 'O'Sullivan Rua to Mary Lavell'[28] and Stephen does attend the very first production of the national theatre, a performance of *The Countess Cathleen*. He has memorized a verse from this play (see *P*, 225-26). Stephen is also interested in mysticism, and this too is suggestive of the Revival. He is a reader of Cornelius Agrippa and of Swedenborg (*P*, 224), as was Yeats. It is perhaps these interests, and the aristocratic undertones of his detachment, that leave his confused contemporaries unable to place him, and regarding

---

primary motive over the next few years would be to act as a popular pressure group whenever it should suit the Church's purpose to adopt a hostile attitude toward the State in educational matters' (Miller, *Church, State and Nation*, 43).

[28] See *P*, 251. This poem is alluded to in the distinction Stephen makes between himself and Michael Robartes: 'Michael Robartes remembers forgotten beauty and, when his arms wrap her round, he presses in his arms the loveliness which has long faded from the world. Not this. Not at all. I desire to press in my arms the loveliness which has not yet come into the world.' The distinction here is presumably between tradition and invention, although Stephen might have in mind the distinction between an established culture and a reality which has yet to be privileged as culture.

Stephen as kindred to the Protestant intelligentsia of the Literary Revival. Thus Emma Cleary thinks that Stephen must be 'a mystic or something' (*SH*, 192) and Davin, who at one stage wonders whether Stephen is Irish at all, advises him that Ireland must come first if Stephen is to be able to afford the luxury of indulging himself as 'a poet or mystic' (*P*, 203).

Neither *Stephen Hero* or *A Portrait* trades in the Gaelicism of the *Stories of Red Hanrahan* (1897) or in the ghosts, fairy tales and associated enchantments of *The Celtic Twilight* sequence (1893). Both novels, however, owe something to 'Rosa Alchemica', 'The Tables of the Law' and 'The Adoration of the Magi' (all 1897). In fact, the significance of these stories is greater than the brief allusion to them in *Stephen Hero* might suggest. In these medievalist stories, where Gaelicism and folk culture are particularly muted, there is a focus on exceptional rebels and outcasts who possess arcane knowledge. Aherne in *The Tables of the Law*, for instance, is a Catholic who refused the 'biretta', but remains 'half monk'. He has been a one time 'student in Paris' and possesses the secret books of Joachim de Flora (Yeats, *Myth*, 293-94). He gives 'the impression of a man holding a flame in his naked hand' (Yeats, *Myth*, 293). This is an iconoclast, an artist-rebel who believes that the 'beautiful arts were sent into the world to overthrow nations, and finally life itself, by sowing everywhere unlimited desires, like torches thrown into a burning city' (Yeats, *Myth*, 294). There are obvious connections between this characterization and Stephen Daedalus. Indeed, Stephen is quite substantially shaped by these strange figures who seem so outcast in the modern streets of Dublin. He reads both Aherne and Robartes as 'outlaws' whose morality is 'infrahuman or suprahuman'. Their speeches are 'like the enigmas of a disdainful Jesus' and 'they live beyond the region of mortality, having chosen to fulfil the law of their being' (*SH*, 183).[29] Whilst his contemporaries accept 'the tyranny of the mediocre because the cost of being exceptional is too high', Stephen refuses the life of 'a dull discharge of duties' and, in *Stephen Hero*, sees Yeats's characters as models of glorious rebellion. Aherne and Michael Robartes 'inhabit a church apart' (*SH*, 183), and confirm the nobility and the joy of Stephen's rebellion.

In *Stephen Hero,* Yeats's three stories quite explicitly provide Stephen

---

[29] The last phrase is actually from 'Tables of the Law' where, ironically, a beaten Aherne discovers that he 'could not sin, because I have discovered the law of my being, and could only express or fail to express my being' (Yeats, *Myth,* 305).

with role models. In *A Portrait* the stories are not alluded to at all, but their influence is even more substantial, if of a very different nature. In the later text, where there is greater narrative distance, the Yeats stories are not so much a confirmation of Stephen's outsider pose as they are an important source of a particular romantic rhetoric which Joyce deploys ironically. At key moments in *A Portrait*, invariably marked by a raising of emotional intensity, Yeats's stories are evoked in precisely the terms of this highly ornate rhetoric.

The Yeats's stories are all contemporary in setting, but the modern is a grey and shadowy background to rich, mysterious and medieval interiors which are very much removed from modern life. In 'Tables of the Law', Aherne is a figure who walks Dublin's streets, but most of the 'tale' is set in an old, catacomb of a building which, museum-like, houses beautiful, strange and powerful works of art. The modern world, however, is not just marginalized by these interiors. Modernity is despised as a spiritually empty shell. The characters in these stories are all in retreat from modern reality and searching for some kind of enlightenment. Thus transfiguration, removal from the dross of earth to something spiritual and, to use a Yeatsian word, 'impalpable', is a central idea in all three stories, as is transmutation. 'Rosa Alchemica', for instance, begins with a narrator indulging in a 'fanciful reverie' which has been inspired by a small book he has written on the transmutation of metals. He imagines a 'universal transmutation' which will turn everything into spirit and essence. Life will be transmuted into art. This 'vision' becomes a cry 'for the birth of that elaborate spiritual beauty which could alone uplift souls weighted with so many dreams' (Yeats, *Myth*, 267-70). Transfiguration in these stories means awakening the 'imaginative life', releasing the spirit and realizing the soul. The words 'soul' and 'spirit' have a special currency in these stories, just as they do in *A Portrait*, most famously in Stephen's 'speech' about the 'slow', 'dark' and 'mysterious' birth of the soul, and the nets which threaten to ensnare. Awakening into flight is also a figure in Yeats's stories, as it is in *A Portrait*. Indeed, this whole Yeatsian neo-Platonic landscape is evoked in *A Portrait*. For all his focus on Aristotelian process and structure, Stephen constantly adulterates it with Yeatsian romanticism.

Stephen understands both art and sexuality, for instance, as transfiguration and transmutation. Art is romanticized as a movement from dull earthbound corporeality to soaring spirit:

> ... he seemed to hear the noise of dim waves and to see a winged form flying above the waves and slowly climbing the air. What did it mean? Was is it a quaint device opening a page of some medieval book of prophecies and symbols, a hawklike man flying sunward above the sea, a prophecy of the end he had been born to serve and had been following through the mists of childhood and boyhood, a symbol of the artist forging anew in his workshop out of the sluggish matter of the earth a new soaring impalpable imperishable being?
>
> (*P*, 169)

This passage, with its visionary qualities, its mythologizing, its medievalism, its investment in prophecy and symbol and its romantic conception of art and artists, is typical of Yeats in the late 1890s, and especially suggestive of the three short stories. But there are many other passages which are similarly indebted to Yeats. Stephen's expressions of his own sexuality, for example, clearly involve Yeats. The overpowering sense of self-disgust which follows the retreat may belong to Catholic Ireland, but Stephen's idealization of sex mixes mariolatry with Protestant revivalism in about equal proportions. This is apparent in the closing scene of chapter 3. The fulfilment of sexual desire has already been constructed by Stephen as 'a moment of supreme tenderness' when he himself will 'fade into something impalpable' and become 'transfigured' in his lover's eyes (*P*, 65). The famous scene with the whore dramatizes this earlier image:

> He closed his eyes, surrendering himself to her, body and mind, conscious of nothing in the world but the dark pressure of her softly parting lips. They pressed upon his brain as upon his lips as though they were the vehicle of a vague speech; and between them he felt an unknown and timid pressure, darker than the swoon of sin, softer than sound or odour.
>
> (*P*, 101)

This rhetoric, which transforms a business exchange into a 'spiritual surrender' contains echoes of Yeats's stories. In 'The Tables of the Law' the narrator describes faces on frescoes in Sienna as expressing 'the incertitude, as of souls trembling between the excitement of the spirit and the excitement of the flesh' (Yeats, *Myth*, 295). In the same story, there is the description of the elect followers of Joachim de Flora 'who have no Father but the Holy Spirit'. These are the mystics who 'reveal that hidden substance of God which is colour and softness and a sweet odour' (Yeats,

Myth, 300). The contexts are very different to the Joyce passage, but the tones and associations are distinctly Yeatsian.

The scene in chapter five where Stephen wakes inspired and produces his villanelle provides another illustration of this intertextual relationship between *A Portrait* and the Yeats stories. Once again the imagery surrounding art manufacture in chapter five derives from religious ritual, but that in itself is precisely the Yeatsian project in the 1890s. The 'transmutation' of a material society into a spiritual community through cultural nationalism *was* the Revival's agenda and it was accompanied by an appropriation of a religious discourse. This is the practice of 'Tables of the Law' and 'The Adoration of the Magi', a practice theorized in 'Ireland and the Arts', for instance, where Yeats writes explicitly of artists as a priesthood long before Joyce so intricately conflated art and religion in *A Portrait*:

> We who care deeply about the arts find ourselves in the priesthood of an almost forgotten faith, and we must, I think, if we would win the people again, take upon ourselves the method and the fervour of a priesthood. We must be half humble and half proud. We see the perfect more than others, it may be, but we must find the passions among the people. We must baptize as well as preach.
>
> (Yeats, *E & I*, 203)

The artist-priest in the Yeats stories works with 'divine substance' to create a 'spiritual beauty' in an incense-filled atmosphere (Yeats, *Myth*, 270), and is possessed of visions and revelations. All this is incorporated in *A Portrait*. Thus when Stephen wakes inspired, 'a spirit filled him, pure as the purest water, sweet as dew, moving as music':

> An enchantment of the heart! The night had been enchanted. In a dream or vision he had known the ecstasy of seraphic life. Was it an instant of enchantment only or long hours and days and years and ages
>
> (*P*, 217)

The rose imagery here, where an 'afterglow' deepens to a 'rose and ardent light', develops from the rose imagery which runs through *A Portrait* and this too may articulate with Yeats's symbolism of this early period. The Rose, of course, was a national symbol for Yeats. Joyce appropriates it in *A Portrait*, Anglicizing the image in the red and white roses of York and Lancaster, and re-nationalising, as it were, in the image of Stephen's green rose which exists nowhere in reality.

Yeats is not the only revivalist to whom *A Portrait* refers, although his influence is most marked. The most direct borrowing is not from Yeats but from Synge's account of the Aran Islands, which, as Anthony Roche has shown,[30] offers a clear prototype for the girl wading on the beach at the end of chapter four of *A Portrait*. Almost all the details of the image in *A Portrait* appear first in Synge, except that Stephen's vision is more explicitly erotic. Here is the Synge account:

> ... and as I walk round the edges of the sea, I often come on a girl with her petticoats tucked up around her, standing in a pool left by the tide and washing her flannels among the sea-anemones and crabs. Their red bodices and white tapering legs make them look as beautiful as tropical sea-birds, as they stand in a frame of seaweeds against the brink of the Atlantic.[31]

In Roche's somewhat under-theorized view, Joyce's closeness to Synge in this instance, is evidence of a common culture which both artists draw on. But it is surely voyeurism rather than any ethnicity that connects the two writers here, with Joyce distinguished at least as the more intimate observer. Joyce's borrowing is also ironically aware of its context. What poses as 'natural' reportage in Synge becomes sheer rhetoric in Joyce. It is clearly marked as determined by the provisional enthusiasm and romanticism of a young man. Synge, on the other hand, assumes the objective detachment of the anthropologist, not very convincingly.

It is hardly necessary to demonstrate the existence of irony in *A Portrait*, but it is important to register how such irony is deepened by recognizing the extent to which Joyce is reacting against the Literary Revival. Stephen's fierce individualism is not only 'supersaturated' in Catholicism. It is also a compound of religious and secular mysticism derived from both the Catholic Church and the Protestant Revival. The aestheticism which apparently so clearly individuates Stephen so dramatically, actually identifies him as steeped in the neo-Platonic aesthetic of early Yeats, as well as in Aristotle and Church scholasticism. The Stephen thus produced is even more contradictory, more entrapped in what he sees as the avoidable 'nets' of his culture, than Joyceans have

---

[30] Anthony Roche, ' "The Strange Light of Some New World": Stephen's Vision in *A Portrait* ', *James Joyce Quarterly* (XXV/3), Spring 1988, 323-32.

[31] Synge, *Collected Works*, Vol. II, 77.

thought. Stephen scorns cultural nationalism, yet his aristocratic demeanour is highly suggestive of the aristocrats, fallen and otherwise, who were making Ireland's cultural renaissance. What many readers have found most distasteful about Stephen, his romanticism and self-dramatisation, finds many echoes in the Literary Revival which becomes an kind of unaccredited model for some of Stephen's key positions and the rhetoric which narrates them. Precisely at the moments when Stephen seems most keenly engaged in expressing his own nature he is, quite often, configured through one of the characteristic romanticising rhetorics of the Revival.

This then, in outline rather than definitive detail, is the nature of Joyce's handling of revivalism in these pre-Ulysses texts. The discussion of the pre-*Ulysses* texts is limited to broad outline here, partly because some critical work has already been done in contextualising these against nineteenth and early twentieth century revivalist cultures.[32] But primarily this treatment results from the fact that the pre-*Ulysses* texts simply do not engage the Literary Revival with anything like the imperative of *Ulysses*. *Dubliners, Stephen Hero* and *A Portrait* construct an Irish life which is in total opposition to the romantic mythopoetics of Yeats and Co. But they do so with only limited reference to the aristocratic culture they oppose. *Ulysses*, on the other hand, is a vivid exposure of a dynamic relationship with revivalism. The attack on Literary Revivalism penetrates into the very design of *Ulysses*. It shapes the Ulyssean aesthetic and is centrally on display in the book's textuality. It is for these reasons, and the general neglect of the importance of revivalism both in and to *Ulysses*, that the rest of this study focuses exclusively on this later text.

---

[32] See, for example, Roy Gottfried, ' "Scrupulous meanness" reconsidered: *Dubliners* as stylistic parody' in Vincent J. Cheng and Timothy Martin (eds), *Joyce in Context* (Cambridge: Cambridge University Press, 1992), 153-171 hereafter Cheng and Martin; Fairhall, especially chap. 3, 64-111.

2 Usurper

This chapter examines six early episodes of *Ulysses*, 'Telemachus', 'Nestor', 'Proteus', 'Aeolus', 'Scylla and Charybdis' and 'Wandering Rocks'. Between these episodes there are obvious textual discontinuities, a fragmentation of 'styles' which distinguishes the acceleration of interior monologue in the 'Telemachia' from, for example, the headline interruptions of 'Aeolus'. There are further disruptions within episodes. 'Scylla and Charybdis', as I suggest below, is comprised of a range of narrative interventions which constitute a microcosm of textual unorthodoxy and diversity in *Ulysses* generally. With the exception of the opening of 'Aeolus', Stephen Dedalus holds the central position in five of these six episodes. In a broad sense he is, for all the Protean drifts, a counter-balance to discontinuity, fragmentation and diversity.

The analysis here is concerned firstly with identifying the nature of the imperatives that drive Stephen, compelling the dispossessed Joycean artist to reconstruct himself as the 'father of all his race'. But I am also concerned to demonstrate how the narrative disruptions of these early chapters collude with and reinforce Stephen's articulation of the 'voice of Esau', the voice of dispossession. For all the heteromorphic shifts in the narrative, there is a sense in which these chapters stand by and underwrite Stephen's alienated perception of a colonial culture, where both 'authentic' traditions and the new wave of cultural nationalism is compromised by deep ideological contradictions. A discussion of 'Wandering Rocks' is included here precisely because this episode so clearly illustrates the collusion between book and character. 'Wandering Rocks' moves on decisively from Stephen's consciousness, but the representation of the city at large in this episode nonetheless confirms the Dedalian world-view.

The buckeen and the dogsbody: aspects of history and culture in the Telemachia

The central action of 'Telemachus' is that bitter piece of business between Stephen and Mulligan which culminates in the word 'usurper' (1.744). What happens between these two characters has often been seen in terms of a conflict between the romantic artist 'rebellious, outcast, haunted, feeding on resentment bitterness and remorse' and the mocking pragmatist who 'claims the artist's Ivory Tower'.[1] In such readings, 'Telemachus' becomes focused on how a purist defines himself, in knowingly self-dramatizing terms, against a compromising changeling. Thus the 'Joycean Telemachus *insists* on being dispossessed'.[2] There is a perceived pathology to Stephen's sense of being displaced which is entirely consistent with Joycean biography. Ulick O'Connor writes that Joyce himself had 'a priest-like vocation to his art':

> He could have seen Gogarty very well as somebody who wanted to have it both ways. Gogarty was undoubtedly a poet. But he remained on in Dublin, he became a successful surgeon, he married a rich woman ... he settled for an easy life .... In addition there is no doubt that Joyce had a pathological obsession with betrayal — an almost voluptuous desire to be betrayed.[3]

In this remark an uneasy attempt to rationalize Joyce's feelings about a usurping Gogarty eventually collapses, which is precisely what has happened in some attempts to explain why Stephen designates himself as a usurped figure.

It is obvious that Stephen does construct his own world, but to argue that his perception is a product of 'emotional confusion'[4] is at once to disenfranchise him and is therefore deeply problematic. Indeed, a reading which understands Stephen's landscape of usurpation and dispossession

---

[1] Charles Peake, *James Joyce: The Citizen and the Artist* (London: Edward Arnold, 1977), 112.

[2] Bernard Benstock, 'Telemachus', in Clive Hart and David Hayman, eds, *James Joyce's 'Ulysses': Critical Essays* (Berkeley and Los Angeles: California University Press, 1974), 12.

[3] Ulick O'Connor, 'Joyce and Gogarty — Royal and Ancient, Two Hangers-On'. in Augustine Martin, ed., *James Joyce: The Artist and the Labyrinth* (London: Ryan Publishing, 1990), 343.

[4] E. P. Epstein, 'Nestor', in Hart and Hayman, *James Joyce's 'Ulysses'*, 27.

in terms of personal obsession comprehensively depoliticizes a context where even an embarrassed Haines can see that 'history is to blame' (1.649). The text itself demands something quite different. From the beginning, there is an insistent and complex representation of divided class and racial identities, and it is this division which lies at the heart of the tension between Mulligan and Stephen. Stephen is an Irish Catholic. Mulligan is an Anglo-Irish Catholic who has had the advantages of a Protestant education and feels himself to be a natural member of an Ascendancy which in historical reality was no longer exclusively Protestant but was still upper class, retaining the values and attitudes of a hegemony even when its material fortunes were on the decline. These class identifications are not part of any 'background' to 'Telemachus'. On the contrary, the articulation of class consciousness is very much to the foreground of the episode. When Mulligan blesses gravely 'thrice the tower, the surrounding land and the awaking mountains' (1.10-11), he asserts a confident landlordism and simultaneously mocks the Catholicism which in its perceived 'native' variety invests Stephen with inferior status. The physical details of characterization imply both social distinction and class antagonism. Mulligan is suave and flashy in dress; Stephen is dowdy and wears cast-offs. Mulligan has expensive dental work; Stephen has rotten teeth, a characteristic according to Mulligan of the primitives who inhabit the 'bogswamp' (1.413). The word 'plump' is repeatedly associated with Mulligan (1.1, 31, 125, 729) and is reinforced by related qualifiers like 'sleek' (1.742). This opulence of physique becomes juxtaposed to the shabby poverty of the 'jejune jesuit' (1.45) and is another indicator of Mulligan's social advantage over Stephen:

> Across the threadbare cuffedge he [Stephen] saw the sea hailed as great sweet mother by the wellfed voice beside him.
>
> (1.106-07)

Mulligan's attitude towards Stephen is most typically patronizing and paternalistic. Stephen is the 'poor dogsbody' (1.112), that is, the servant or the undistinguished whom Mulligan magnanimously provides with handouts: 'I must give you a shirt and a few noserags. How are the secondhand breeks? .... You look damn well when you're dressed' (1.5/112-13/118-19). In a similar vein, Mulligan exercises a cultural superiority over Stephen: '*Epi oinopa ponton*. Ah, Dedalus, the Greeks! I must teach you. You must read them in the original' (1.78-80). The barb in this remark derives partly from the use of Stephen's surname. He is the Greek who knows no Greek, the fraud, the pretender.

The significance of Mulligan's assertion of social superiority deepens with a certain grammatical feature of 'Telemachus'. Sentences which contain the word 'tower' (in popular traditions the round tower is, of course, as emblematic of Ireland and Irish culture as harp or wolfhound) usually have Mulligan as a subject, never Stephen. So that it is Mulligan's voice which sings 'from within the tower' (1.281); in 'the gloomy domed livingroom of the tower', it is Buck Mulligan's 'gowned form' which moves 'briskly to and fro' (1.313-14). The effect of this grammatical precedence, one reinforced by Mulligan's insistent claims to rightful ownership of the key to the tower, is to emphasize Mulligan's sense of being ensconced, of a natural right of occupancy.

At a time when, with all their traditional aristocratic *hauteur*, Joyce's Anglo-Irish contemporaries were formulating a syncretic view of Irish culture and society, of the 'Unity of Culture', (Yeats, *Auto*, 355) the harmonizing of the 'noble and the beggarman'[5] which Yeats promoted in the pre-Rising years, Joyce insists on conflict and bifurcation in the Telemachia, and not just in the relations between Mulligan and Stephen. The embarrassing scene with the old milk woman underlines the unbridgeable gulf between the intelligentsia and the people. Stephen's envy of his rich Anglo-Irish charges in 'Nestor' (see 2.6) punctures the syncretism that was characteristic of the Revival's ideology. So does the emphasis on the massive cultural gap which operates between the Unionist Deasy and Stephen. The following exchange illustrates a decidedly tense social environment which is apparent everywhere in these opening episodes:

> Laughing again, he brought the mirror away from Stephen's peering eyes.
> — The rage of Caliban at not seeing his face in a mirror, he said. If Wilde were only alive to see you !
> Drawing back and pointing, Stephen said with bitterness:
> — It is a symbol of Irish art. The cracked lookingglass of a servant.
> (1.141-46)

The immediate cause of Stephen's bitterness is Mulligan's jibe that he is

---

[5] See 'The Municipal Gallery Revisited', in Yeats, *CPO,* 369.

like Caliban. In *The Tempest*, Caliban is 'a salvage and deformed slave',[6] occupier of 'an intermediate position in the moral scale, below man, just as angels were above him'. He is 'the link between ... the settled and the wild, the moral and the immoral'.[7] Mulligan's remark and the manner of Stephen's response to it recalls centuries of cultural imperialism which had stamped on English minds an indelible image of native Irish primitiveness. The Catholics of Ireland, wrote Froude, were 'more like tribes of squalid apes than human beings'.[8] A similar analogy occurred to Charles Kingsley who wrote of 'white chimpanzees ... if they were black one would not feel it so much, but their skins, except where tanned by exposure, are white like ours.'[9] At one level, Mulligan draws a joke parallel between Wilde's elegant dandyism and Stephen's cheap dishevelment, but his words also carry a sharp reminder of the Anglo-Irish domination of Irish culture. Behind them lies a pantheon which in Yeatsian tradition included the names of Swift, Berkeley, Goldsmith, Congreve, Burke, and Grattan, and to which one could add the names of those most eminent in revivalism: O'Grady, Ferguson, Yeats himself, Synge, Russell, T. W. Rolleston, Douglas Hyde, Lady Gregory, Eglinton, William Larminie. All were Anglo-Irish. George Moore, a wealthy Catholic landowner, was the major exception and his part in revivalism was short-lived. The effect, and presumably the intention, is to make Stephen's artistic ambitions ridiculous, not just because he does not look the part (as Mulligan himself most obviously does), but because the 'badge of inferiority' of native Catholicism throws him beyond the cultural pale, robbing him of reflection in the mirror that is Ireland's culture (a mirror which Mulligan, in an obvious usurpation motif, has stolen from a 'plainlooking servant' (1.139). Stephen's angry response

---

[6] Caliban is so described in the 'Dramatis Personae' of *The Tempest*.

[7] L. Edwards, 'The Historical and Legendary Background of the Wodehouse and Peacock Feast Motif in the Walsokne and Brauche Brasses', *Monumental Brass Transactions* (VIII/7, 300-11), cited by Frank Kermode in his introduction to the Arden edition of *The Tempest* (London: Methuen, 1954), xxxix.

[8] J. A. Froude, untitled in *The Times*, December 3 1880, 3.

[9] Charles Kingsley, *His Letters and Memories of His Life: Edited by His Wife* (London: H.S. King, 1877), II, 107. See also Vincent Cheng's account of race and racism in his *Joyce, Race and Empire* (Cambridge: Cambridge University Press, 1995).

reveals a sensitivity to all these implications. The cultural tradition which Mulligan would ennoble becomes worthless, with Mulligan himself a 'dogsbody' pandering to English tastes and fashions and a 'jester at the court of his master' (2.44).

The refusal to serve and the apparently contradictory sense of being predetermined by history to serve echoes throughout these first three chapters with particular force, and is a measure not of some fin-de-siècle artistic credo, but rather the clearest possible evidence of Stephen's colonial status. He might be 'privileged' in terms of intellect and education, but this itself is part of the dialectic of dispossession which shapes Stephen as a Hamlet figure, who is humbled in Deasy's study before the 'princely presence' of a portrait of Edward the Seventh (2.299). He determines that he can break the 'nooses' that tie him to working for a Unionist headmaster in an Anglo-Irish school (2.234), but for all his fierce independence he *is* in service.[10] When Deasy doles out the 'sovereigns' that are Stephen's payment, Stephen's response shows a servant sensibility. He gathers 'the money together with sly haste' and puts 'it all in a pocket of his trousers' (2.223-24). Everyday details collude to create a colonial landscape. In the protean world of *Ulysses* 3, the dog on the beach (a literal dogsbody specifically aligned with Stephen and his riddle at 3.361-64) is a cur 'brought skulking back to his master' (3.354-55). Similarly, the woman on the beach is seen in feudal terms, as a follower of 'her lord, his helpmate, bing awast to Romeville' (3.374-75). Secrets become 'tyrants' waiting to be 'dethroned' (2.172). Stephen asserts that he 'will not be the masters of others or their slave' (3.295-96), but equally asserts that he *is* the servant of three masters. He runs Deasy's errands and wears Mulligan's shoes. His identity, as it is constructed in clothes, is tied up with both the Parisian bohemian and Catholic servitude: 'my cockle hat and staff and hismy sandal shoon' (3.487-88). At the very point when he makes the decision not to return to the tower, he images the effect of his departure in master/servant terms: 'in the darkness of the dome they wait, their pushedback chairs, my obelisk valise, around a board of abandoned platters. Who to clear it?' (3.274-75). These are just a few examples of the exercise of a colonial lexicon in which words connected with power, servitude and dispossession carry emphatic currency and

---

[10] It is often pointed that many of Joyce's characters are unemployed. One might add that many of those that *are* employed work for the state, or for Protestant employers.

which powerfully circumscribe Stephen's feelings about his mother's death. The idea of history being 'a nightmare' from which Stephen is 'trying to awake' (2.377) is not abstract, theoretical or 'modern' in a general sense. It refers to something very real and tangible: a colonial history which so shapes Stephen that even his expression of 'proud intellect' is, as he well knows, the product of a dialectic.

In the relations between Mulligan and Stephen, Joyce exploits social divisions between what was then a relatively new Catholic hierarchy, divisions which were determined by much older class distinctions. Although Joyce's text is far from indifferent to economic injustice (one might refer here to Deasy's ownership of a 'tray of Stuart coins, base treasure of a bog' (2.202-03), or to Stephen's images of his family's poverty, of his mother's 'shapely fingernails reddened by the blood of squashed lice from the children's shirts' — 1.268-269), the confrontation the novel exploits focuses most precisely on the issue of cultural dispossession. It is primarily in this sense that Stephen as prototype artist is displaced and usurped. The fact that he has no desire to 'yoke himself' in another kind of servitude to Egan the old Fenian does not at all alter his sense of himself as dispossessed. The following extract is further illustration of this point. Here Mulligan proposes joining forces with Stephen for the purpose of 'Hellenizing' Ireland:

> — God, Kinch, if you and I could only work together we might do something for the island. Hellenise it.
> Cranly's arm. His arm ...
> — What have you up your nose against me? Is it Haines? If he makes any noise here I'll bring down Seymour and we'll give him a ragging worse than they gave Clive Kempthorpe.
> Young shouts of moneyed voices in Clive Kempthorpe's rooms. Palefaces: they hold their ribs with laughter, one clasping another. O, I shall expire! Break the news to her gently, Aubrey! I shall die! With slit ribbons of his shirt whipping the air he hops and hobbles round the table, with trousers down at heels, chased by Ades of Magdalen with the tailor's shears. A scared calf's face gilded with marmalade ...
> Shouts from the open window startling evening in the quadrangle. A deaf gardener, aproned, masked with Matthew Arnold's face, pushes his mower on the sombre lawn watching narrowly the dancing motes of grasshalms.
> To ourselves .... new paganism .... *omphalos*.
>
> (1.157-76)

Mulligan is flaunting his social advantage again by advertising his Oxford education (in historical reality, Gogarty had met Samuel Chenevix Trench, the model for Haines, at Oxford). Stephen's image of an Oxford of privilege, stylized effeminacy, and ritualized violence is in part a response to that flaunting, but it is also a bitter and sarcastic framing context for Mulligan's proposal. The concept of 'Hellenization' owes nothing, of course, to any Irish cultural heritage and everything to one of Oxford's most famous sons, Matthew Arnold. It was Arnold of course who used the word, most forcibly in *Culture and Anarchy*, to describe the process by which what he saw as the stiff-necked, materialist English middle-class would become linked to 'the best culture of their nation'.[11] Arnold adored Oxford as the centre of cultural perfection. It was the city which 'by her ineffable charm, keeps ever calling us nearer the true goal of all of us, to the ideal of perfection'.[12] One function of Stephen's caricature is to puncture a famous idealization. Thus Arnold is relegated to the position of a somnambulant grass-cutter who is deaf to the fun and games of a Magdalen dusk.[13] But the primary purpose of this resentful little scene is to further establish Mulligan's entrenchment in the culture of aristocratic England. His high-sounding invitation to Stephen to 'do something for the island' becomes an offer to participate in a traditional Anglo-Irish cultural orientation. Stephen's 'To ourselves .... new paganism .... omphalos' is a non-sentence punctuated by ellipses which actually express his sensitivity to the paradoxes behind Mulligan's apparently altruistic urge to be a cultural patriot.

The final word of 'Telemachus', 'usurper', draws its authority and conviction from this social context and from the immanence of a history that has shaped and determined the relations between the dogsbody and the buckeen ('buck' was a well known derivative of the Anglo-Irish word

---

[11] Matthew Arnold, 'The Popular Education of France', reprinted in *Democratic Education*, ed. R. H. Super (Ann Arbor: University of Michigan Press, 1962), 22.

[12] Matthew Arnold, 'Oxford', in *Essays in Criticism* (1865); reprinted in *Arnold: Poetry and Prose*, introduction and notes by E. K. Chambers (Oxford: Oxford University Press, 1939), 151.

[13] This college may have been chosen with deliberation. It was Wilde's. In an article written in 1909, Joyce had said of Wilde that 'in the tradition of Irish comedy that runs from the days of Sheridan and Goldsmith to Bernard Shaw, [he] became, like them, court jester to the English' (*CW*, 202).

'buckeen', meaning a young man who apes the manners of the wealthy).[14] But it is not only in the soured relations between Dedalus and Mulligan, and other characters, that class and racial identities conflict. 'Telemachus' seems designed around the historiographical in a more general sense. Its characters are representative of broad socio-cultural forces, or even — as in the case of the old milkwoman — cultural emblems, and 'Telemachus' draws much symbolism from a popular patriotic culture which itself dealt in the propagandizing of a version of history and which Joyce identified as Anglo-Irish in origin and development.

'Telemachus' is very clearly related to popular revivalist culture, a culture which, much to Yeats's irritation, was always transmuting the 'authentic' vital expression of the national consciousness into a new vulgarized orthodoxy. In its enlistment of the allegorizing tendencies of romantic nationalist literature, 'Telemachus' draws on the popular traditions in obvious ways. It is a chapter of round towers and emerald gems. It has its 'wandering crone' (1.404). Haines is the visiting 'Sassenach' (1.232), a modernized representative of the 'stranger' or the 'Saxon' figure, whose father 'made his tin by selling jalap to Zulus' (1.156). All this raises particular expectations about Stephen in the role of islander and Mulligan as patriot. It is significant that, in reality, Samuel Chenevix Trench came from an old Anglo-Irish family. That Joyce transforms him into a 'Saxon' suggests that he is consciously producing a trio that will give him all the ingredients of a classically nationalist recipe. There is the suggestion of a specific poem of popular nationalist cultural traditions, Thomas Moore's 'Let Erin Remember the Days of Old':

> Let Erin remember the days of old,
> Ere her faithless sons betrayed her;
> When Malachi wore the collar of gold,
> That he won from the proud invader,
> When her kings with standard of green unfurled,
> Led the Red-Branch Knights to danger;
> Ere the emerald crown of the western world
> Was set in the crown of a stranger.

---

[14] See E. J. Walsh, *Ireland Sixty Years Ago*: 'among the gentry of the period [i.e. the late eighteenth century] was a class called 'Bucks', whose whole enjoyment and the business of whose life seemed to consist in eccentricity and violence' (17). This book was reprinted as *Rakes and Ruffians: The Underworld of Georgian Dublin* (Dublin: 1847; reprinted New Jersey: Totowa Press, 1977).

> On Lough Neagh's bank as the fisherman strays,
> When the clear cold eve's declining.
> He sees the round towers of other days
> In the waves beneath him shining;
> Thus shall memory, often, in dreams sublime,
> Catch a glimpse of the days that are over;
> Thus sighing, look back through the waves of time
> For the long faded glories they cover.[15]

Stephen quotes from the song at 'Proteus' line 302-03, but 'Telemachus' owes a much more substantial debt to this text. It mirrors Moore's song, but the reflection is a distorted one. Joyce uses some of the more familiar features, but in defiance of the significance they traditionally held. His Haines clearly evokes Moore's stranger, for instance; he possesses the 'green stone' set in a cigarette case (1.616). But a relatively straightforward humorous allusion also involves a more complex dramatic displacement, because Joyce, who insisted on an orderly priority for his enemies,[16] refuses Haines the status of villain. This basically innocuous Englishman is a Hibernophile. Ironically, he is also the only competent Gaelic speaker allowed between the covers of *Ulysses*. Similarly, Mulligan is linked to Moore's poem by his given name, by the transposition of gold collar into gold teeth, and by a local act of bravery. But he is then robbed of heroic status in all other respects. Most startling of all is Joyce's transformation of the round tower. This traditional image of Irish culture and its survival in the national consciousness becomes not only truncated, but an utterly Anglicized edifice. Its builder is not Cuchulain, but 'Billy Pitt' and its present tenants pay rent to 'the secretary of state for war' (1.543/540). There may be further points of contact between Moore's and Joyce's texts. As Stephen looks into the waves, what he sees reminds him not of a glorious cultural past, but of his mother's agonized death (see 1.248-53). He later imagines a drowned man in the sea (1.675). Stephen is the dreamer of 'Telemachus' and what he dreams is hardly sublime (see 1.103-10). The general significance of

---

[15] Thomas Moore, 'Let Erin Remember the Days of Old', in *Irish Melodies* (London: Longman, 1869), 148.

[16] See, for instance, his comment in 'Ireland, Island of Saints and Sages': 'I do not see what good it does to fulminate at English tyranny while the Roman tyranny occupies the palace of the soul' (*CW*, 173).

Joyce's interference with Moore's poem is therefore clear. We are not dealing here with simple comic intertextuality. The closing word of 'Telemachus' can be read in a number of ways, but is clearly no joke. 'Telemachus' transforms the symbols and images which typically expressed a historiography of patriotism and the effect of that transformation is to deny authenticity to such a historiography. The aristocratic culture of Anglo-Ireland, which had reserved to the landed classes the dual role of hero in the face of English injustice and benevolent guardian over both an ancient Celtic culture and a native simplicity, is demythologized. It need hardly be pointed out that Joyce had no particular quarrel with Moore. In fact, he had a strong liking for Moore's *Melodies* in their musical settings. He chooses this particular poem presumably for its representative qualities, and perhaps because he could not resist the dark irony of a title which exhorts the nation to remember what never happened. Nevertheless it is worth pointing out that Moore was a Catholic, one of the first Catholics to be allowed through Trinity's gates. Before his work was taken up in middle-class drawing rooms, he was also hugely popular with the Anglo-Irish gentry. The first number of his *Irish Melodies* was dedicated to 'the Nobility and Gentry of Ireland'.[17] In Joyce's terms, he was a servant.

When we look at Moore's poem 'Let Erin Remember', it becomes perfectly clear that despite its would-be national status, there is actually nothing natively Irish about it. Its tone of dignified resignation, its versification and the language in which it is written are all English exports. The loss of an Irish culture of antiquity, which is thematic here, is everywhere enacted in the poem's manner. Not that this relationship between matter and manner is intentional stylization on Moore's part. On the contrary, the relationship is actually a paradox over which Moore exercises no control.[18] The poem is a product of cultural imperialism, but

---

[17] See the 1807 edition of *Irish Melodies*. In later editions Moore honoured specific individuals. The Longman edition of 1869 is dedicated to the 'Marquis of Lansdowne'. See Behan's comment on Moore and aristocrats in the following footnote.

[18] Moore's *Melodies* are illustrative of cultural imperialism in another way, because he stole the tunes for most of his poems from much older Irish songs. The tune for 'Let Erin Remember', for example, was stolen from a tune called, in English, 'The Red Fox'. Dominic Behan, who writes with some passion about Moore's complicity with the English, quotes Byron's comment that 'Tommy dearly loves a lord'. Behan

since it purports to be patriotic, it cannot reveal itself as such. In this sense it perfectly embodies the contradictions that faced cultural nationalists. At its centre is a silence about the conditions of its own making, and it is this silence that is loudly articulated in Joyce's round tower, a tower which echoes with allusions to the products of English and Anglo-Irish minds: to Shakespeare, Wilde, Nelson, Captain Marryat, Swinburne, Locke, Yeats and so on. It is these names that establish the cultural orientation of Joyce's Telemachia, an orientation complicated only by Stephen's heroes of Europe, and, more emphatically, by his catalogue of Church schoolmen and heresiarchs, their 'horde of heresies fleeing with mitres awry' (1. 656).

The treatment of Moore's poem in 'Telemachus' suggests a textual collusion with Stephen's articulation of the 'voice of Esau'. This is the first Ulyssean assault on revivalist art and its nationalist claims, and it is a relatively muted one. For the most part, however, the focus of attention in the 'Telemachia' is on Stephen, not on any narrative intervention. It is Stephen's consciousness, as Joyce represents it, rather than exposed textuality, which identifies forms of cultural hybridity and conveys a sense of cultural dispossession. Joyce's engagement with revivalist culture here has found preliminary formulation as the servant's revenge on the servants of empire. But before Stephen's most direct encounter with the Anglo-Irish Revival, there is, in 'Aeolus', an interesting interlude in the newspaper office where Stephen meets up with the products of a failed Catholic middle-class nationalist movement. That 'Aeolus' comes before the library scene is a question of deliberate strategy and will have an important impact on how we read 'Scylla and Charybdis', the episode where Stephen confronts representatives of the group of men who claimed to be formulating the new national consciousness.

---

discusses Moore's violation of 'the sanctity of the songs he took from Ireland's folk lore and so bowdlerized'. See Behan's *Ireland Sings* (London: Tro Essex Music Co., 1973), 4.

Pisgah sights: the national press and the Catholic middle class in 'Aeolus'

The resurgence of Anglo-Irish revivalism in the late nineteenth century was synchronous with the defeat of a powerful middle-class nationalist movement. Although this movement was led by a landlord, Parnell, and characterized by high levels of rural support, it was essentially meeting the aspirations of a dynamic Catholic middle class. There is a romantic historical tradition, which maintains the idea that Irish nationalism was one movement of continuous resistance, albeit in different forms. But in Ireland, as elsewhere, decolonization was always characterized by conflicts between competing nationalisms representing different social and political interests. The defeat of Parnellism left a gap which conservative forces of various kinds, Church, State and Irish Protestant, were quick to exploit. Anglo-Irish revivalism was one of these conservative forces. In the following analysis I shall argue that Stephen Dedalus does not so much identify with the ideology of Catholic middle-class nationalism as he anatomizes the fact of its collapse at the hands of reactionary forces. In Stephen's terms, this represents another form of usurpation.

'Aeolus' is usually seen as further example of Stephen Dedalus outfacing and overcoming those 'nets' which threaten his artistic vocation, and as an extension of the Telemachia in this sense. The men in the *Evening Telegraph* office are 'idle', 'futile', 'losers', 'scroungers', 'cronies'[19] — indistinguishable in fact, in the general perception, from Irishmen in, say, 'Sirens' or 'Cyclops'. The aim of these men is to 'pressgang' Stephen into servitude, although service to what has not been made clear. An invitation to write journalism is easily refused and hardly seems to amount to much of a threat. The main design features of the episode, the captions, the rhetorical figures and the littering of expressions related to the wind are apparently there to reproduce the debased rhetoric of city culture in general and of the press in particular. Stephen's dry 'parable of the plums' is invariably seen as a sarcastic antidote to this debasement.

There are times, of course, when Stephen *is* unreservedly iconoclastic, notably in 'Scylla and Charybdis', where he confronts the Anglo-Irish

---

[19] Most of these descriptions can be found in, for example, Stanley Sultan's account of 'Aeolus' in, *The Argument of Ulysses* (Ohio: Ohio State University Press, 1964), 111.

intelligentsia, and in 'Oxen of the Sun' and 'Circe', where he engages more intimate ghosts and demons. But his response to the social context established in 'Aeolus' is rather more complex and equivocal. For all his wariness, he seems emphatically drawn to this group of men. He understands them, and there is some evidence to suggest that they understand him. Both McHugh and Crawford at least are keen to encourage Stephen, and to protect him from the bitter cynicism of J. J. O'Molloy[20] — a cynicism which seems to be presented as a common fate for members of the Irish Catholic intelligentsia.

The origin of this empathy is in both a shared social status and a shared historical consciousness. There is a clannishness about the men in the *Telegraph* office which is not just a matter of acquaintance or friendship. They are a gathering, a gathering of failure and unfulfillment, which is partly why the energetic Bloom is so famously excluded. In the 'Omnium Gatherum' section, Stephen, McHugh, Crawford, O'Molloy and Lenehan are elevated to the status of a quintet of high performance talent. They represent literature, the classics, the press, the law and 'the turf' (7.604-07). But the ironies of these designations are obvious. In reality, these are the underachievers, and wasted potential is not simply a matter of personal dissipation. The relevant historical context, here, is the collapse of a dynamic middle-class Catholic nationalism, a collapse which frames everyone in the group, including Stephen, whose sensitivity to the eclipse of Catholic radicalism is perhaps best seen in his brief meditation on O'Connell and the huge meetings held at Mullaghmast and Tara. However ambiguous Stephen's words may be in content, they are decidedly, and beautifully, lyrical in cadence. They are reminiscent in this respect of the 'Proteus' passage where he imaginatively identifies with a 'people' and a history of 'Famine, plague and slaughters. Their blood is in me, their lusts my waves' (3.306-09).

> Hosts at Mullaghmast and Tara of the kings. Miles of ears of porches. The tribune's words, howled and scattered to the four winds. A people sheltered within his voice. Dead noise. Akasic records of all that ever anywhere wherever was. Love and laud him: me no more.
>
> (7.880-83)

There is more than a touch of the Pisgah in the rhythm and sound of this,

---

[20] There are many occasions in 'Aeolus' when O'Molloy is silenced, or when his comments provoke angry responses. See, for instance, the exchange at lines 540-48.

which makes Stephen here consistent with a chapter where defeat is imaged, over and over again, by the Pisgah motif.

Stephen's 'parable of the plums', then, is far from being the only Pisgah vision in 'Aeolus'. Much of the narrative detail of the episode revolves around miscarriage, ineffectuality and disappointment. Even Bloom's lively canvassing in the end comes up against Myles Crawford's crude obstruction. Similarly, Stephen's publishing mission gets as far as Crawford's pocket, but there is serious doubt as to whether Deasy's article on the politics of foot and mouth disease will ever actually see the light of day (although it does actually appear in the evening edition of *The Telegraph*). J. J. O'Molloy can express only a vain hope that Stephen 'will live to see it published' (7.906). O'Molloy himself is a 'mighthavebeen' (7.303), a man who, like J. F. Taylor, and Moses, has 'a great future behind him' (7.875-876). Unfulfillment characterizes O'Molloy's status in immediate time also, because in this episode he is struggling to get a loan and is refused by both Crawford and Ned Lambert. There are other characters who have failed to reach potential, or who have declined in social status, or who have sold out in various ways. There is Stephen's father, of course, but also professor McHugh and the mildly crazy Crawford. The latter 'began on the *Independent*' (7.307-308) which was originally a committed publication set up after the Parnell scandal to espouse the views of Parnellites, but now he is editor of *The Evening Telegraph*, a right-wing rag. Even Ignatius Gallaher, the 'daddy' of journalists, according to Crawford, has gone the same route. At one time he wrote for T. P. O'Connor's radical newspaper, *The Star*, but he now works for R. P. Blumenfield, who in 1904 was editor of the Tory *Daily Express*.[21] Interestingly, the men in the newspaper office understand that they are themselves partly to blame for their position. On at least two occasions, this is articulated as an example of colonial doublebind, the complicity that ties the colonized to colonial institutions: Professor McHugh calls Myles Crawford 'the sham squire' (7.348; the reference is to Francis Higgins, who reputedly betrayed Edward Fitzgerald). Crawford later responds by referring to McHugh as, 'You bloody old Roman empire' (7.374), and referring to him in the terms of a song:

---

[21] The owner of the *Express* was Alfred Harmsworth, an influential Tory figure in the publishing world.

> — *'Twas rank and fame that tempted thee*
> *'Twas empire charmed thy heart*
>
> (7.372-3)

There may also be a continuation of the Pisgah motif in the failure to complete narrative, as when O'Molloy begins but never finishes the story 'about chief Baron Palles. It was at the royal university dinner. Everything was going swimmingly ... ' (7.503). Or when Myles Crawford begins to, but never actually does, throw some light on his own wild comments about 'Maximilian Karl O'Donnell': 'I'll tell you how it was ... A Hungarian it was one day ...' (7.549-50). There is even uncertainty about the closure of Stephen's narrative, with Crawford asking if he has finished. The sense of the unfinished, incomplete and disappointed is very strong in the chapter.

These personal failures are harmonized in 'Aeolus' with a wider context of cultural and political failure and displacement which is imaged in a range of narrative detail. Like the detail of the newspaper boys squatting 'on the doorstops' of the *Telegraph* office playing 'We Are the Boys of Wexford', which was once a rallying call of nationalism, on a mouth organ.[22] But the suppuration of the civic world is reflected above all in the perceived degeneration of journalism and oratory, the two key cultural forms which fashioned and reflected Irish public opinion in the late nineteenth and early twentieth centuries. The powerful oratory of J. F. Taylor has 'gone with the wind' (7.880), to be replaced by 'Doughy' Dawson's[23] sentimental drivel. O'Connell's speeches at mass rallies in the

---

[22] Ironically, this was always a song of failure. The last verse goes: 'My curse upon all drinking — 'twas that that brought us down;/ It lost us Ross and Wexford, and many another town./ And if for want of leaders we lost at Vinegar Hill/We're ready for another fight and love our country still.' See Ruth Bauerle, *The James Joyce Songbook* (New York & London: Garland Publishing Inc., 1982), 287-88.

[23] All the orators alluded to in 'Aeolus' existed and have been identified, with the exception of 'Dan' Dawson. It may be that Joyce had in mind here a Charles Dawson, an important figure in the Irish industrial movement, which aimed at reviving Irish industry. Dawson's flowery and wildly inflated rhetoric is reminiscent of the Citizen's talk, but also of 'Doughy' Dawson's more literary endeavours. Speaking before the Limerick Industrial Association in April 1904, Dawson explained his plans for a national exhibition of Irish industries which would serve to:

heyday of the Catholic Emancipation movement are now 'dead noise' for Stephen. Irish radicalism is linked by McHugh with 'the catholic chivalry of Europe that foundered at Trafalgar' (7.556), as well as with the 'empire of the spirit' (7.567), but is now a 'lost cause'. The Pisgah sight becomes the central Irish perspective, partly through J. F. Taylor's (and Bloom's) parallelism between Ireland and Israel; partly through Dawson's sickly prospect of *'our lovely land'* (7.271), but also through McHugh's assessment of Ireland in the modern world which has 'Lord Jesus' usurped by 'Lord Salisbury', the English aristocrat:[24]

> — We were always loyal to lost causes, the professor said. Success for us is the death of the intellect and the imagination. We were never loyal to the successful. We serve them. I teach the blatant Latin language. I speak the tongue of a race the acme of whose mentality is the maxim: time is money. Material domination. *Domine!* Lord! Where is the spirituality?
>
> (7.553-57)

Myles Crawford takes up the same issue of cultural decline, although from the newspaper angle, when he argues that the fire has gone from Irish journalism:

> industries, to create new ones, to search for and develop the boundless resources which a beneficent providence has spread around on every side — resources which lie buried in the fertile womb of earth, in the rivers and mountains, in the rapid rivers which wash our coasts, in the forces of Nature, lately replenished by the unchained giant of electricity, the motor of many industries already, and the destined source of countless to come which will ere long awake the silent streets of town and village, and fill the air with the hum of industry all over the land.
> (From a speech quoted in *The Freeman's Journal*, and many other Dublin newspapers, on April 7th 1904, 7)

At the very least, Dawson's speech is a good example of a contemporary Irish oratory described by T. M. Kettle as 'wallowing in a trough of dismal rectitude'. He continued, 'as in the culmination of the *Dunciad*, universal dullness covers all' (T. M. Kettle, *Irish Oratory and Orators* [London: T. Fisher Unwin, nd.], viii).

[24] The 3rd Marquis of Salisbury (1830-1903), who was violently opposed to Irish Nationalism. According to Weldon Thornton, the McHugh who is 'mainly interested in uses of 'Lord .... has chosen his example randomly but well'. It seems highly unlikely, given the context of this speech, that McHugh's exemplification can be fortuitous. See Weldon Thornton, *Allusions in 'Ulysses'* (North Carolina: The North Carolina University Press, 1961), 115-16.

— Grattan and Flood wrote for this very paper .... Irish volunteers. Where are you now? Established 1763. Dr Lucas. Who have you now like John Philpot Curran? Psha!

(7.738-40)

Stephen's parable functions, then, as the climax to a pattern of references to underachievement and unfulfillment. Whatever difficulties there may be in interpreting the precise details of his allegory, there is a sense in which he speaks for the episode, albeit in a highly idiosyncratic voice, and for the Catholic men who constitute the Aeolian company. They have been blown off-course and, interestingly and possibly uniquely in *Ulysses*, they both encourage and appreciate Stephen's intervention. McHugh 'sees' with 'pleasure' (7.1061) the general point of Stephen's mocking parable and is 'tickled' with the allusion to the 'one-handed adulterer' (7.1072) that is to Nelson, the hero of empire who is to be distinguished from the Irish two-handled adulterer whose statue 'is not'. Myles Crawford joins in with the joke. McHugh in particular shows a real understanding of Stephen point:

— You remind me of Antisthenes ... the sophist. It is said of him that none could tell if he were bitterer against others or against himself.

(7.1035-37)

In fact, the newspaper office is one of the very few social contexts in *Ulysses* in which Stephen seems welcome, accepted and moderately comfortable. The most revealing comparison is surely with 'Scylla and Charybdis. In the library scene, Stephen is excluded. He is bitter and on the attack. His ideas are disdained, unappreciated and even openly ridiculed, especially by AE. The essential difference between these two episodes is that, in 'Scylla and Charybdis', Stephen is encountering the Anglo-Irish intelligentsia who are in the process of formulating what they see as a dynamic, new cultural nationalism which will culminate in the Protestant production of 'our national epic'. In 'Aeolus', on the other hand, the social context concerns the failure of Catholic, middle-class, constitutional nationalism. It is a context which Stephen apparently understands and identifies with at a level which is deeper than the intellectual, as his uncontrollable physiological response to Seymour Bushe's 'grace of language' suggests (see 7.776).

Joyce's setting of this wreckage of potentiality in the world of newspapers is entirely designed. The Irish press had played a central role in the development of a nationalism which threatened the collapse of the Anglo-Irish world, in political, social and cultural senses. It is not too much to say that journalism had been the major shaper of national consciousness. The demise of the nationalist movement, seemingly at the very point when it was on the verge of achieving so much of its political agenda, was exactly synchronous with the commercialization and almost complete Anglicization of the mainstream Irish press. In fact, the fortunes of the Irish press are paradigmatic of the fortunes of Catholic political nationalism and the disarming of what had once been a radical Catholic activism.

Catholic newspapers did not begin to emerge in Ireland until the early nineteenth century. Before that time, the Castle controlled all Irish newspapers, through seditious libel legislation, cash grants and subsidies for newspaper owners, or prohibitive pricing. Readership was exclusively Protestant for much of the eighteenth century and most of the serious content was lifted wholesale from London despatches. The emergence of a Catholic press was to quite a large extent a product of O'Connell's emancipation movement, which was crucially supported by new radical newspapers like *The Morning Register*, *The Belfast Vindicator*, *The Cork Examiner* and *The Nation*, and which, above all, produced a new owner for *The Freeman's Journal*. In 1854, Sir John Gray, a friend and political ally of O'Connell, committed the *Freeman's* to constitutional nationalism and the Catholic cause and, for much of the remainder of the century, this newspaper was the most influential publication in Ireland. It began to lose popularity when it deserted Parnell and never again recovered its former status, which is why at the beginning of 'Aeolus', Bloom is wondering whether the current owner, William Brayden, 'our saviour', can 'save the circulation' (7.71). It is from John Gray's 'pavement island' that McHugh peers 'aloft at Nelson through the meshes of his wry smile' at 'Aeolus', lines 1067-68, in what turns out to be yet another Pisgah perspective.

Of necessity, journalists for the Catholic press during the heyday of Catholic radicalism were political activists. They were engaged in a battle with right wing publications like *The Irish Times*, *The Dublin Daily Express* and *The Dublin Evening Mail*. Founded in 1823, the last of these was initially full of 'virulent anti-Catholic bigotry'.[25] Moreover, the Catholic Press was forced to flout a barrage of publishing restrictions,

---

[25] Hugh Oram, *A History of Newspapers in Ireland 1649-1983* (Dublin: Mo Books, 1983), 49.

with the result that 'the mandatory training of many Irish journalists then was jail'.[26] It is partly this link with political nationalism that confers so elevated a status on journalists of the past in 'Aeolus', at least, as far as O'Molloy is concerned. O'Molloy argues that the current corruption of journalism is a product of the times: 'Sufficient for the day is the newspaper thereof' (7.736). The implication is that political commitment and quality of writing are closely connected. An editorial from the first edition of *The Nation* (1842) will give the flavour of the journalistic style of a radical press that had vanished by the end of the century:

> With all the nicknames that serve to delude and divide us — with all their Orangemen and Ribbonmen, Torymen and Whigmen, Ultras and Moderates and Heaven Knows What Rubbish besides, there are in truth, but two parties in Ireland: those who suffer from her national degradation and those who profit by it. To a country like ours, all other distinctions are unimportant. This is the first article of our political creed; and as we desire to be known for what we are, we make it our earliest task to announce that the object of the writers of this journal is to organize the greater and better of those parties, and to strive, with all our soul and all our strength, for the diffusion and establishment of its principles. This will be the beginning, middle and end of our labours.[27]

Beyond this acknowledgement of a historically distant golden age of Irish journalism and political activism, however, many of the fictional characters in 'Aeolus' are of a generation that participated in the further resurgence of the Catholic press that accompanied Parnell's nationalist movement in the 1870s and 1880s. This generation would also have experienced the collapse of a popular radical Irish press that followed Parnell's disgrace.[28] It is this cycle that is mostly responsible for the nostalgic retrospection of 'Aeolus'. A dynamic Catholic middle class has become a servant class; or, as in McHugh's analogy, developed from the J. F. Taylor speech, just as Stephen's parable is, 'the masters of the Mediterranean are fellaheen today' (7.911).

---

[26] Ibid., 81.

[27] *The Nation*, October 15th 1842, 1.

[28] There is some simplification in Joyce's presentation here, if not distortion. Papers like *The Shan van Vocht*, the *Northern Patriot,* and the *Irish Citizen* continued radical traditions.

The fragmentation of the Irish Nationalist Party and the death of Parnell were accompanied by a determined and highly successful attempt by the establishment to gain full control of the Irish press. Firstly, key publications were bought out by right-wing Protestant families. The Guinness family and Alfred Harmsworth built up a press empire which included *the Daily Mail, The Dublin Daily Express, The Morning Mail* and the *Weekly Warden*. The association between the press and barrels of Guinness at *Ulysses* 7, lines 21 and 44 is suggestive of the Guinness family's interest in newspaper ownership. The 'Chapelizod boss', Harmsworth, is referred to at line 733. The conservatism of newspaper ownership is also implied in the description of William Brayden, the *Freeman's* owner, which evokes both Church and State. Brayden is a 'stately figure' who passes 'statelily up the staircase' and has a face 'like Our Saviour' (7.42/45/49).

Secondly, the Catholic Church took the opportunity of Parnell's fall politically to emasculate nationalist publications. Most infamously, the Church took over ownership of *The Nation*, which became *The Irish Catholic and Nation*.[29] By 1892 this once powerful political organ was almost exclusively reporting the doings and sayings of the Catholic hierarchy, so that the headlines for Saturday, 9th June 1892 read 'The Bishop of Ossory Amongst His People'; 'Forty Hours of Adoration at Rathmines'; 'St. Patrick's Catholic Benefit Society' and so on. The books reviewed are about Catholicism and there are adverts for 'The Irish Catholic Packets' at 3d each. Packet number 6 contains '12 Benedictine Saints' Images and Mottoes'. The edition includes dire, moralistic short stories and poems and the one political item in the edition for Saturday, 2nd June is an attack on Redmond, the man who 'cast aside his duty to his country for the sake of his personal obligations to one [i.e. Parnell] who had betrayed his native land for the most unholy of human ends'.[30] This clerical intervention in the press is referred to several times in 'Aeolus'. At the *Freeman's* offices, for instance, the foreman panics about the possible loss of 'the archbishop's letter' which is 'to be repeated in the *Telegraph*' (see 7.181).

---

[29] The insignia for the new *Irish Catholic and Nation* were interesting: a harp in a circle, with two crossed keys and, in the circle, a bishop's mitre, crook and vestments.

[30] *The Irish Catholic and Nation*, Saturday, 2nd June 1892, 1.

Above all, the Irish press became 'modernized', both in terms of technology and content and layout, which meant a commercialization, and a 'non-partisan approach' that had 'a devastating effect on the rest of the newspapers, including *The Freeman's Journal*'.[31] The key mover in this process was William Martin Murphy, owner of *The Irish Independent* and notorious chairman of the Dublin Tramway Company.[32] His 'two legacies to Ireland were *The Irish Independent* and an efficient public transport system in Dublin',[33] which may explain why trams and a technologically modernized press are so associated at the beginning of 'Aeolus'. Certainly the new style of reporting, with abundant photographs (see Bloom's comment about the new press 'M.A.P. Mainly all pictures' at 7.97), reader competitions and flashy headlines, the sort of stuff 'goes down like hot cakes' (7.338) according to Bloom, owed a great deal to Murphy's new commercialism. Headlines like 'Lass that Loved a Sailor' (for a breach of promise case), 'Dying Like Flies' (about infant mortality in Dublin) and 'What Did He Do With It?'[34] (a story about Asquith's government having a disposable budget surplus of £3 million) represented a significant change in caption style. As Stuart Gilbert pointed out, this change is reflected in the 'Aeolus' headlines:

> It will be noticed that the style of the captions is gradually modified in the course of the episode; the first are comparatively dignified, or classically allusive, in the Victorian tradition; later captions reproduce, in all its vulgarity, the slickness of the modern press.[35]

---

[31] Oram, *A History of Newspapers*, 102.

[32] It was W. M. Murphy who refused to employ members of the Irish Transport and General Workers Union in his United Tramways Company in 1913. This issue proved to be a flashpoint in the strikes and lockouts of 1913. Yeats wrote an attack on the same W. M. Murphy in his splendidly titled poem, 'To a Wealthy Man Who Promised a Second Subscription to the Dublin Municipal Gallery if it Could be Proved the People Wanted Pictures'.

[33] Oram, *A History of Newspapers*, 102.

[34] These headlines are all taken from editions of *The Irish Independent* published between May and June 1904.

[35] Stuart Gilbert, *James Joyce's 'Ulysses'* (London: Faber & Faber, 1952 edn), 178 fn.1.

In this way a history of the press is built into the very structure 'Aeolus', and this history is firmly linked to the collapse of radical Catholic nationalism and to the process of colonial modernization which helped to produce that collapse.[36] Thus the earlier headlines are not simply 'comparatively dignified': they carry cutting political irony. The first Aeolian section illustrates a modern transport system passing through a colonized urban topography (the terminus is at 'Nelson's pillar' and a tram starts for 'Palmerston Park') and has 'IN THE HEART OF THE HIBERNIAN METROPOLIS' as its caption. The second caption, 'THE WEARER OF THE CROWN', continues the satirical note. The 'joke' is not just a matter of comic inflation. The mail car which wears the crown, parked suggestively in North Prince's Street, is a piece of colonial street furniture which serves a colonial institution, the Royal Mail. 'HOUSE OF KEY(E)S' (7.141) works in a similar way, because the caption heads a section on the commercialization and displacement of nationalism through an advertisement which carries an 'innuendo of home rule' (7.150). The apparently innocuous 'NOTED CHURCHMAN AN OCCASIONAL CONTRIBUTOR' (7.178-79) has an ironic edge, and so does 'HIS NATIVE DORIC' (7.326), a caption for 'Doughy' Dawson's verbiage which is about as far from 'Doric' or 'native' as is conceivable. 'O, HARP EOLIAN!' (7.370) works similarly, because here the promise of a nationalist symbol (already once stolen from Greek culture) is comically displaced in reality by the twang of dental floss. 'LOST CAUSES/NOBLE MARQUESS MENTIONED' (7.551-52) produces some delightful savagery at the expense of the English aristocrat who did most to oppose Home Rule and who was 'a minor anti-Christ for the Irish'.[37]

The flashy modern captions, on the other hand, are about tricksy intonation, silly innuendo and titillation and are emptied of any political significance: 'SOME COLUMN — THAT'S WHAT WADDLER ONE SAID'; 'DIMINISHED DIGITS PROVE TOO TITILLATING FOR FRISKY FRUMPS. ANNE WIMBLES, FLO WANGLES — YET CAN YOU BLAME THEM' (7.1006/1069-71). Both kinds of headlines lie or distort, but in very different ways. In the

---

[36] The English connection was powerful amongst the new press owners. Harmsworth was raised to the peerage as Baron Northcliffe in 1905 and became the chief proprietor of *The London Times* in 1908. It was widely thought in Dublin that Murphy's journalists were exclusively English. As for the Catholic Church, it continued to milk the English connection for all it was worth.

[37] Thornton, *Allusions in Ulysses*, 116.

earlier ones, distortion is very often politically engaged. In the later captions, it trivializes.

These changing captions are a startling typographical delineation of how the Irish press, at one time the voice of nationalist aspiration, had become commercialized and sanitised. It was reduced to advertising, to harmless and often trivial entertainment and to the all-important racing results. The political energies of Catholic activism have been displaced in 'Aeolus' by an anodyne modernity — a modernity which was characterized by a profound right-wing shift in Irish political life and by a concerted restoration of the conservative forces of Church and State which had been so threatened by Parnellism. Almost uniquely in nineteenth-century Europe, the Irish middle class failed to gain the political ascendancy, and it is this historical process which conditions much of the substance of 'Aeolus', the chapter in which Dan Dawson writes in hopelessly sugary terms of 'our lovely land' and where Bloom asks the pressing question: 'Whose land?' Professor McHugh rams the point home. 'Most pertinent question ... With an accent on the whose' (7.273-75).

Much of the characterization in 'Aeolus', which many commentators have misread as a moralistic indictment of native indolence, is actually a product of historical dynamic. The seedy search for the price of a pint, the nostalgic retrospection, the failure to achieve, the sell-outs, the pseudo-scholarliness (as when McHugh's unconsciously echoes Mulligan's pretentious allegiance to things Greek: 'Kyrios! Shining word! The vowels the Semite and the Saxon know not. Kyrie! The radiance of the intellect' — 7.562-63). These are not symptomatic of some generic Irish trait of dissipation, but rather the constituents of what it is to be colonized. Perhaps the most poignant signs of the times are Myles Crawford's mad historical confusions, which have the rousing tone of radical discourse, but hopelessly muddle centuries, and allegiances, and get failures mixed up with victories.

There are, of course, less disturbing and less ugly products of the colonized mind in 'Aeolus'. There is the wit and the venom, for instance, most delightfully on show in the attack on Dan Dawson's gutless, coffee-table brand of nationalism. There is the self-mockery and, above all perhaps, the self-knowledge:

> — *Imperium romanum*, J. J. O'Molloy said gently. It sounds nobler than British or Brixton. The word reminds one somehow of fat in the fire.

Myles Crawford blew his first puff violently towards the ceiling.
— That's it, he said. We are the fat. You and I are the fat in the fire. We haven't got the chance of a snowball in hell.

(7. 478-82)

There is even a compelling energy, a refusal to lie low. Crawford, in particular, and despite his occasional pessimism, rails against the emptiness of modern political life and maintains a commitment to the remedial will. 'Foot and mouth disease' and reports on the 'great nationalist meeting in Borris-in-Ossory', are 'all balls', he maintains, 'Bulldosing the public!' The imperative is to 'give them something with a bite in it. Put us all into it, damn its soul. Father, Son and Holy Ghost and Jakes McCarthy' (7.619-21).

In fact, to pay attention to questions of class and political and cultural history is to turn the standard view of 'Aeolus' on its head. The men in the newspaper office are not the hypocrites of post-Parnellism, but rather the products of reaction. The design characteristics of 'Aeolus', the setting, the headlines and the deployment of rhetorical figures, establish both a history of conservative reaction and reproduce the new era in which language is corrupted because it is divorced from meaningful communal action. Stephen himself is not scornfully detached from the community of failure. He clearly sees the trap of going the same way as a J. J. O'Molloy, an unemployed member of a profession which once produced O'Connell and many other figures in radical Catholic nationalism. Yet Stephen does not disown his community. The real point about his contribution to its culture of dispossession is that it functions as a confirmation of their historical experience. His 'parable' is an indictment of a conservative Ireland which has defeated liberal Catholic nationalism — which is one reason why 'the parable of the plums' contains so much sexual innuendo. In part, it offers a direct challenge to the straight-laced morality of the post-Parnellite period. Ireland is represented by two feeble old women, old sows who, in their consumption of 'brawn' and 'plums', also eat their own male farrow. They are deeply conservative, struggling up an imperial phallus to pay homage to Nelson, and they are terrified lest 'the pillar will fall' (7.1010). Their allegiance is to the Crown and, of course, to the Catholic Church. There is nothing here to offend Stephen's companions. They themselves can and do take credit for the idea about 'the promised land'. McHugh, at least, gleefully appreciates the ironic contrast between the imperialist adulterer whose statue is still standing and his hero Parnell, whose statue has yet to be constructed. Crawford also picks up on the sexual innuendo that establishes the all-important parallel between sexual and political domination, a parallel which was standard in Irish culture, but which has been widely ignored in readings of 'Aeolus'. There is clearly a sense in which the so-called deracinated artist has imaged for McHugh and the others their story of defeat. In some measure, at least, he has articulated their consciousness.

'Normans, but bastard normans': culture and nationalism in 'Scylla and Charybdis'

In 1961, S. L. Goldberg published *The Classical Temper*, an influential book about the aesthetics of *Ulysses*. Goldberg admired the realism of *Ulysses*, but had problems with the Joyce who broke all the rules. His book was nonetheless important in helping to establish Joyce's texts as paradigms of both romantic individualism and modern relativity. Like earlier Marxist critics, Goldberg thought there was little to say about Joyce and historical consciousness, except that as an exemplary modernist, Joyce deployed a mystificatory myth-based historiography. For Goldberg, Joyce's 'social insight' was uncertain. Compared to his contemporaries — 'Lawrence, Mann, Eliot even' — his 'grasp of the underlying conditions and causes of the twentieth-century nightmare' was 'not particularly impressive'.[38] But the earlier episodes of *Ulysses*, (from 1 to 10; episode 11 is the real turning point in the technical innovation which caused Goldberg difficulties), the very chapters which Goldberg thought of as an 'aesthetic' triumph, are fundamentally located in historical, cultural and social issues. In fact, 'aesthetics' itself is crucially a social and cultural matter for Joyce, and, if there are any doubts about the issue, 'Scylla and Charybdis' resolves them.

Episode 9 of *Ulysses* dramatizes a debate amongst intellectuals. The participants make a show of conducting the debate courteously but, as the super-polite responses suggest, this is a courtesy that is contrived, and there are occasions when Stephen's Anglo-Irish contemporaries become openly irritated by what he has to say. His preference for Aristotle over Plato makes Eglinton's 'blood boil' (9.80). His critical method is seen as crude sensationalism. With appropriate Anglo-Irish disdain, AE regards

---

[38] S. L. Goldberg, *The Classical Temper: A Study of James Joyce's 'Ulysses'* (London: Chatto & Windus, 1961), 303-05.

Stephen's biographical approach to reading Shakespeare as the work of an intellectual menial, 'interesting only to the parish clerk' (9.184). The Shakespeare debate, however, is not itself the source of antagonism in 'Scylla and Charybdis'. It is but one episode in a history of conflict, a history that finds its strongest expression in the hostility and resentment of Stephen's asides, but which also includes Stephen's review which slates Lady Gregory's literary efforts, the accusation that he pissed on Synge's halldoor, and the rumour that Synge is out to 'murder' him. There is clearly more at stake here than the relative merits of Aristotle or Plato, more behind the 'dialectic' enacted than an academic 'examination into the truth of an opinion'. Intellectual disagreement is not enough to explain why George Russell, the visionary thought by many young Dublin intellectuals to be a 'saint and a genius' and described by Yeats as 'the one masterful influence among many young Dublin men and women who love religious speculation, but have no historical faith' (Yeats, *Auto*, 240) should become the ridiculous 'Buddh under plantain' of 'Scylla and Charybdis', worshipped by female acolytes, 'their pineal glands aglow' (9.283-84).

The fundamental issue in this episode, one which underlies the antagonism between protagonists and will determine the direction of the debates on aesthetics and Shakespeare, is the legitimacy of Anglo-Ireland's claim to be forging from nothing more than an appropriation of Irish myth and folk-tale nothing less than the consciousness of a nation. The intellectuals with whom Stephen debates in the library are Anglo-Irish (and were — one can look them up in the *DNB*, which means that their fictionality is maginalized, as if Joyce wants to insist, as Stephen does, on historicity. They both want to get the facts right). Much of the talk which interrupts Stephen's Shakespeare exposition is about the Revival, and many key revivalist figures and texts are referred to. At least three revivalist plays are mentioned or quoted from: AE's *Deirdre* (9.191), Yeats's *Cathleen ni Houlihan* (9.38) and Synge's *In the Shadow of the Glen* (9.38). There are allusions to many revivalist poems, half a dozen of Yeats's alone. These include 'A Cradle Song' (9.28), 'The Wanderings of Oisin' (9.578), 'King and no King' (9.67) and 'The Song of Wandering Aengus' (9.1093). Jubainville's *Le Cycle Mythologique Irlandais* is referred to at line 93. This was a force in revivalism well before Best's English translation in 1906. Larminie based a poem on it in 1889, and, according to Phillip L. Marcus, it was an important influence on Yeats's *The Secret Rose* and *The Wind Among the Reeds*.[39] George Sigerson, the Gaelicist who produced the influential *Revival of Literature* (1894) and *Bards of the Gael and Gall* (1894) is alluded to at line 309. Douglas Hyde, of course, was a key figure in both the language and literature revivals. His major contribution to the latter was his *Literary History of Ireland* (1899) and *The Lovesongs of Connacht* (1899). The last title is referred to several times in 'Scylla and Charybdis'. Yet another revivalist scholar, the Reverend Patrick S. Dineen, actually comes into the library at line 968. He published an Irish-English dictionary in 1904, wrote plays and edited the four volumes of George Keating's *History of Ireland*. It seems highly likely that the 'Irish nights entertainment' referred to at line 1105 recalls Ferguson's *Hibernian Nights' Entertainment*, a collection of tales first published in 1834 but reissued in a new edition in 1904. These stories are told in Dublin castle by prisoners of the British: 'its associations are thus with story-telling or, more generally, art in a hostile place ... and subjection to England.'[40] In addition, there are references to minor revivalist figures, like T. Caulfield Irwin and Louis H. Victory, for instance (see 9.283). The point is that revivalism is *the* cultural environment of the episode. Despite minor disagreements between themselves, and even the occasional piece of self-mockery, Stephen's adversaries believe themselves to be collaborators in an important enterprise. They claim to be reconstituting Ireland. The new generation of poets are 'Our young Irish bards' (9.43) and bards were conspicuously significant in revivalist historiography. Revivalism understood the new bards to be a privileged élite. Like their forerunners in Gaelic Ireland before the plantation, they were to be 'entrusted with the preservation of the history and literature of our country'.[41]

The cultural renaissance is stimulating other literary forms. 'Our players' are in the process of making a new Irish theatre (9.1130); a novel with an Irish Don Quixote who 'must speak the grand old tongue' (9.311)

---

[39] See Phillip L. Marcus, 'Notes of Irish Elements in "Scylla and Charybdis" ', *James Joyce Quarterly*, X/3 (Spring 1973), 312-19. This interesting essay was, to my knowledge, the first time that revivalist 'elements' had been noticed at all in 'Scylla and Charybdis'.

[40] Ibid., 315.

[41] Standish O'Grady, *History of Ireland: The Heroic Period,* (London: Longman, 1878), I, 50.

is only a matter of time away. 'Scylla and Charybdis', however, produces a sustained dismantling of these grandiose claims, written not according to the Olympian indifference of a modish, Europeanized intellectual, but at ground level, by a Catholic Irishman whose presentation of revivalism was profoundly conditioned by his exposure to Anglo-Irish culture generally and by his understanding of the ideological determinants behind the most recent incarnation of that culture.

This context makes the setting of the ninth episode of *Ulysses* nothing if not ideologically significant. The National Library of the nation which in 1904 had no legal existence, evolved from Anglo-Irish institutions. Its antiquarian collection was a gift from the Royal Dublin Society. Membership of the first antiquarian committee was drawn from the aristocracy and the Protestant Church and included the Bishops of Cloyne and Derry and Lord Moira. The first librarian of the Royal Dublin Society was the Rev. Dr. John Lanigan and, when Dr Daniel Murray, Catholic Archibishop of Dublin in the 1830s, applied for membership, he was refused. Stephen's sense of the National Library as alien ground, of himself as an Irish-Jew in a colonized Egypt-Ireland reflects a Catholic sensibility (see 9.352-355).

Stephen's reception in the library has to do with an established social division and the animus that was its consequence. When Eglinton (who has 'a sire in Ultonian Antrim', 9.818) and Russell (who was reared in 'the northeast corner', 9.203) snigger at what they see as Stephen's uncouthness of mind, and when Stephen is pointedly excluded from Russell's gathering of Dublin luminaries, we witness a class consciousness that is evident everywhere in the episode. There is a snobbery in 'Scylla and Charybdis' that constantly reminds Stephen of his place. Thus when he enlists the help of Aquinas to the cause of his theorizing, Mulligan interrupts with this:

> — Saint Thomas, Stephen began ...
> — *Ora pro nobis*, Monk Mulligan groaned, sinking to a chair.
> There he keened a wailing rune.
> — *Pogue mahone! Acushla machree!* It's destroyed we are from this day! It's destroyed we are surely!
> All smiled their smiles.
>
> (9.772-777)

Here a Catholic intellectual drawing on Catholic theological traditions becomes a priest-ridden primitive in a dialectic that is immediately understood by all. 'All smiled their smiles' is not innocuous. It is a bitter narrative intervention and marks the social and racial gap between Stephen and the rest.

The same background explains why Stephen identifies revivalism as a variant on an old theme of usurpation. His opposition *is* partly a matter of personal choice, but it is also a matter of historical predetermination. In any case, the distinction between the two hardly matters because for Stephen, 'condemned to do' (9.849) as he does, personal choice and historical fate always conflate and collude. Like Shakespeare who 'found in the world without as actual what was in the world within as possible' (9.1041-42), Stephen finds his personal deracination ratified by usurpation in the real world. Historically predetermined to stand on usurped ground, he reads his exclusion from the mapping of Ireland's literary future as a form of cultural apartheid and his contemporaries' claim to be articulating the voice of the nation as a form of cultural dispossession.

> — They say we are to have a literary surprise, the quaker librarian said, friendly and earnest. Mr Russell, rumour has it, is gathering together a sheaf of our younger poets' verses. We are all looking forward anxiously.
> Anxiously he glanced in the cone of lamplight where three faces, lighted, shone.
> See this. Remember.
> Stephen looked down on a wide headless caubeen, hung on his ashplanthandle over his knees. My casque and sword. Touch lightly with two index fingers. Aristotle's experiment. One or two? Necessity is that in virtue of which it is impossible that one can be otherwise.
>
> (9.289-297)

Even before the direct *Hamlet* reference, there is a perception of an Elsinore-like quality in the library, a friendly innocuous surface compromised by a conspiratorial trio of faces in 'lamplight'. If the Aristotelian experiment is an attempt by Stephen to detach himself from his feelings of being a usurped king/dispossessed son, it is an attempt that does not come off:

> Listen.
> Young Colum and Starkey. George Roberts is doing the commercial part. Longworth will give it a good puff in the *Express*. O, will he? I like Colum's *Drover*. Yes, I think he has that queer thing genius. Do you think he has

> genius really? Yeats admired his line: *As in wild earth a Grecian vase.* Did he? I hope you'll be able to come tonight. Malachi Mulligan is coming too. Moore has asked him to bring Haines .... Our national epic has yet to be written, Dr Sigerson says. Moore is the man for it .... We are becoming important, it seems.
> Cordelia. *Cordoglio.* Lir's loneliest daughter.
> Nookshotten.
>
> (9.300-15)

The comments between Stephen's thoughts appear to come from one voice but they actually represent a composite voice, a voice which pays condescending lip service to Gaelic culture — the new fictional hero of Ireland's 'national epic' will have to wear 'a saffron kilt' (9.310-11) — but a thoroughly Anglicized voice. It speaks of working through English and Anglo-Irish institutions and reserves the national honours for a Catholic writer, but a wealthy landed Catholic whose sense of his own Irishness was a particularly uncertain affair and whose reputation was built on writing English novels for an English audience. Stephen's initial response to this excited vision of Ireland's cultural rejuvenation is a maudlin sense of himself as a Hiberno-Cordelia figure, but this self-indulgence is immediately moderated by the word 'nookshotten', a Shakespearean coinage which occurs only in *Henry V* and which is used in that most patriotic of plays to vilify England and the invading English. The speech is worth quotation:

> Duke of Bourbon:Normans, but bastard Normans, Norman bastards!
> *Mort de ma vie!* If they march along
> Unfought withal, but I shall sell my dukedom
> To buy a slobb'ry and a dirty farm
> In that nook-shotten isle of Albion.
>
> (*Henry V*, III.V.10-14)

Stephen's appropriation of this word announces the racial origins of these revivalists and implies a course of action. The historical victim who is the product of 'Famine, plague and slaughters' (3.306) and a servant of Church and State, intends to retaliate. His performance in the National Library will enact the cunning revenge of a usurped Catholic and will represent a step towards repossession of the round tower of Irish culture, albeit on his own highly idiosyncratic terms. 'They list', he thinks, 'And in the porches of their ears I pour' (9.465).

Stephen may not believe in his own theory, but he is nonetheless eager that his performance should be a dazzling one. Irrespective of the question of critical validity, his 'mixture of theolologicophilolological' (9.761-62) is, by any standards, an astonishing display of erudition and intelligence, but it positively shines against the inane mysticism, dull-witted naïveté and artificial formality of the supporting *dramatis personae*. The brilliance of the exposition is a deliberate strategy responding to and negating stereotypes of Catholic inferiority and inverting a typical scenario of revivalist romanticism where a noble, courageous and self-effacing aristocrat (like, say the Countess Cathleen or Patrick Sarsfield in Lady Gregory's *The White Cockade*) devotedly protects charming native simplicity against the corrupting forces of the invader. Moreover, Stephen's intellectual pyrotechnics owe a considerable debt to traditions of medieval Scholasticism, the very tradition which Anglo-Irish culture either ignored or denigrated. Stephen creatively commandeers the theology of a Church which in revivalist historiography had been responsible for promoting an intellectual authoritarianism that had effectively extinguished the imaginative spirit of the Gael.[42] His first debts are to Aristotle, whose thinking permeated Catholic theological strategies, and to Aquinas. His theory proper begins according to Jesuitical precept, opening with 'Composition of place' (9.163), as Ignatius Loyola prescribed in *Spiritual Exercises*. His expresses most approval of Catholic theologians like Sabellius ('subtlest heresiarch of all the beasts of field', 9.862) and again for Aquinas 'with whom no word shall be impossible' (9.863-64). When he attempts to negotiate the difficult space between the life of the artist and the art that is begotten, not made, he does so with concepts and in a language derived from the fundamental tenets of Catholicism doctrine. The Athanasian Creed lies at the heart of Stephen's conception of art as mediating between the actuality of 'the world without' and the 'possible' of 'the world within' (9.1041-42), as a begetting of the artist's 'consubstantial' image. This passage from the Creed indicates something of the nature of the indebtedness:

> The Father is made of none, neither created nor begotten. The Son is of the Father alone, not made, nor created, but begotten. The Holy Ghost is of the

---

[42] See O'Grady, *History of Ireland*, where it is claimed that the Church 'ruined' Gaelic culture and 'ended the golden age of bardic composition' (I, 24).

Father and of the Son, neither made, nor created nor begotten, but proceeding. So there is one Father, not three Fathers, one Son, not three Sons, one Holy Ghost, not three Holy Ghosts.[43]

The Catholicism of Stephen's exposition again seems a conscious strategy, a blasphemous plundering certainly, but one which interrogates notions of Catholic inferiority and implicitly insists on restoring Church scholasticism to a meaningful place in Ireland's intellectual tradition.

The performative aspects of Stephen's exposition are clearly determined by cultural history as it is perceived by a mind that repeatedly returns to the practice of historicization, conflating time, not so that past and present become interchangeable, but rather to emphasize the continuance of the past in the present. Thus Stephen sees Socrates poisoned by the 'archons of Sinn Fein' (9.239) and Shakespeare's histories sailing 'fullbellied on a tide of Mafeking enthusiasm' (9.753-54). But what of the Shakespeare theory itself, a complex psychodrama which might seem far removed from Stephen's Celtic revenge and quite resistant to any process of historical contextualization?

In fact, the 'voice of Esau' gets its most insidious articulation through Stephen's lurid demystification of England's literary giant. Consider the scenario in its broadest sense. A Catholic dispossessed initiates and sustains a debate among Anglo-Irish intellectuals in Ireland's National Library on England's greatest literary figure. There is something deeply subversive in this set-up. It is as if Stephen is forcing down the throat of Anglo-Ireland a recognition of its cultural origins. His rough handling of the bard is designed to produce demonstrations of a continuing commitment to those origins. His image of Shakespeare as 'an old dog licking an old sore' (9.475-76) is partly self-mockery aimed at his own refusal to let the issue of dispossession go, but it also produces, as he knows it will produce, a sterling round of Shakespeare idolatry and a stern reminder from Russell of the aesthetic which the Revival had adopted in an attempt to negotiate the contradictions of its history and its relationship to the empire that produced it. In other words, it is through his theory that Stephen challenges the credentials of an Anglo-Ireland that purports to speak for Ireland.

Russell essentially removes art from real time, and thus undermines one of the essential characteristics of Stephen's perception of the world

---

[43] Quoted in George Brantl, ed., *Catholicism* (London: Prentice-Hall, 1961), 70.

as a place where the past is presently active. Russell's neo-Platonic conception of art as a revelation of 'formless spiritual essences' (9.49) and a communion with 'the eternal wisdom' (9.52) locates him firmly in a revivalist orthodoxy. The same basic view is echoed throughout revivalist writings, and it is a view which raises one of the central contradictions of revivalism. Despite its general retrospectiveness and apparent synchronicity with an ancient past, revivalism was utterly ahistorical in its approach to literature. Dismissive of all aspects of modern society — 'the sixshilling novel, the music-hall song', the 'corruption' of Mallarmé (9.107-08) — revivalism liberated a pre-time, a mythic ideality when the Gael performed heroic deeds, spoke the language of Gods and 'relinquished to the base-born excessive zeal concerning wealth and its distribution'.[44] The ostensible purpose of this *entrelacement* was precisely to halt the process of crass materialism and reinvigorate the land with an all but lost spirituality. As Yeats put it, the 'national' literature was to 'make Ireland, as Ireland and all other lands were in ancient times, a holy land to her people.'[45] But as O'Grady's remark about the nobility of the acceptance of social injustice shows, this denial of history was deeply ideological. It allowed a side-stepping of history which was, to put it mildly, convenient. A real history of racial conflict and cultural imperialism was displaced by a mythology of syncretism. According to Russell:

> the idea of our national being emerged at no recognizable point in our history. It is older than any name we know. It is not earth born, but the synthesis of many heroic and beautiful moments, and these it must be remembered are divine in origin.[46]

Here we see again that characteristically compelling revivalist use of the word 'remembering'.

It is precisely this escape from history that Stephen blocks. His investigation into Shakespeare's life and times is not the simple voyeurism that Russell takes it to be. It is an attack on the revivalist view

---

[44] Ibid., 171.

[45] W. B. Yeats, 'A Note on the National Drama' in Eglinton et al., *Literary Ideals*, 19.

[46] AE, 'Nationalism and Imperialism' in Augusta Gregory, ed., *Ideals in Ireland*, (London: Longman, 1907), 14.

that culture is plugged into divine wisdom, an attack that implies a thorough understanding of the historical fabrication which this Platonic aesthetic supports.

> — Not for nothing was he [Shakespeare] a butcher's son, wielding the sledded poleaxe and spitting in his palms. Nine lives are taken off for his father's one. Our Father who art in purgatory. Khaki Hamlets don't hesitate to shoot. The bloodboltered shambles in act five is a forecast of the concentration camp by Mr Swinburne.
>
> (9. 130-35)

This muscular declaration is more accusation than biographical footnote, and what makes it accusatory is the creative historicism which allows Stephen to fuse the hobnailed brutality of *Hamle*t Act V with contemporary English revenge inflicted on the Boers. This is a violent invasion of Russell's historical void. The timeless wisdom which he sees rising from the pages of the Shakespearean text is ousted by Stephen's conception of a macho Shakespeare whose family background in the art of butchery nicely conflates with his later incarnation as a poet of empire. In complete antithesis to revivalism, Stephen insists on interaction between literature and the historical conditions of its making, and one of the things he produces from the interaction is a red, white and blue Shakespeare. The texts that for Russell 'commune' with divine knowledge, for Stephen pulse with all the confidence of a powerful, wealthy and expansionist culture. Stephen's Shakespeare has accumulated great personal wealth:

> He was a rich country gentleman ... with a coat of arms and landed estate at Stratford and a house in Ireland Yard, a capitalist shareholder, a bill promoter, a tithefarmer'.
>
> (9.710-712)

This accumulation makes him a model self-made man, an icon of Elizabethan prosperity, and his art reflects material abundance. It is an 'art of surfeit' (9.626):

> — Twenty years he lived in London and, during part of that time, he drew a salary equal to that of the lord chancellor of Ireland. His life was rich. His art ... is the art of surfeit. Hot herringpies, green mugs of sack, honeysauces .... Sir Walter Raleigh, when they arrested him, had half a million francs on

his back including a pair of fancy stays.

(9. 623-629)

Here a connection between surfeit and empire is buried in the allusion to the infamous pirate of empire and in the sarcastic comparison of Shakespeare's finances to the finances of the highest paid judicial functionary of a colonized country. Elsewhere there is a more direct sense of the plays resonating with the patriotism, the prejudices and the expansionism of England's golden age:

> — All events brought grist to his mill. Shylock chimes with the jewbaiting that followed the hanging and quartering of the queen's leech Lopez ... *Hamlet* and *Macbeth* with the coming to the throne of a Scotch philosophaster with a turn for witchroasting. The lost armada is his jeer in *Love's Labours Lost*. His pageants, the histories, sail full-bellied on a tide of Mafeking enthusiasm .... The *Sea Venture* comes home from Bermuda and the play Renan admired is written with Patsy Caliban, our American cousin.

(9. 748-757)

The images of Shakespeare as capitalist landowner, the idea of the histories ringing with English jingoism, of *Hamlet* and *Macbeth* pandering to the intellectual pretensions and exotic vices of James I, and, above all, the perception of 'Patsy Caliban' in *The Tempest*, a conflation which links Amerindia with Catholic Ireland in a common history of cultural invasion, express the historical consciousness of an Irish Catholic. They exemplify a theoretical determinist position held by Stephen about the relationship between art and the history it must come out of. Just as Shakespeare's art has to be an 'art of surfeit', luxurious, but riddled by 'the sense of property' (9.74) which fears dispossession as much as it prizes accumulation, so Stephen's reading of Shakespeare must be the reading of a dispossessed Irishman. This theoretical position, however, is not just theory. It comes from real lived experience and expresses a historical consciousness. As for Anglo-Ireland, the implications are clear. It cannot hear the resonance of imperialism in Shakespeare because it is a product of English imperialism itself. It produces an ahistorical aesthetic because to face history would mean facing intractable contradictions. At which point it may be worth pointing out that the Elizabethan history which Stephen so vividly instates is of particular importance to Irish history because it was during Elizabeth's reign that the foundations were laid for a centralized form of government and a plantation economy that would finally subjugate Gaelic and Catholic society to English rule, at least for the following three centuries.

Stephen's debunking of Shakespeare has very little to do with the question of literary value. He does not reject Shakespeare; he appropriates him, and in more senses than one. The John Bull Shakespeare is under the ownership of an Irish critic; the cuckolded Shakespeare, whose works are powered by feelings of resentment and bitterness, is the creation of an Irish artist, one who, having refuted the authenticity of revivalist culture, proceeds to signal his own intention to make art from the ignobility of usurpation. This, I take it, is Stephen's final intervention in the politics of culture.

Throughout the delivery of his theories, Stephen makes obvious connections between himself and Shakespeare's life and Shakespeare's heroes and villains. For instance, his reconstruction of Shakespeare playing the part of King Hamlet rewrites, as it were, 'Telemachus'. As Stephen wears the clothes cast off by Mulligan, so Shakespeare 'comes on under the shadow, made up in the castoff mail of a court buck' (9.164-165). Similarly, at line 150, Shakespeare's journey to London becomes Stephen's journey to 'corrupt Paris'; at line 220 Ann Hathaway's death is aligned with May Dedalus's death, and so on. This parallelism is often seen as the product of wild egoism, and no doubt some point is being made here about Stephen sharing in the genius material that makes a Shakespeare. But what Stephen and Stephen's Shakespeare most obviously share is the sense of dispossession. What Stephen hears in the Shakespeare production is 'the note of banishment, banishment from the heart, banishment from home', which 'sounds uninterruptedly from *The Two Gentleman of Verona* onwards till Prospero breaks his staff' (9.999-1002). Just as 'the voice of Esau' echoes through Stephen's exposition, so it does in Shakespeare's writing: 'the theme of the false or the usurping or the adulterous brother or all three in one is to Shakespeare, what the poor are not, always with him' (9.997-99). Now the false or usurping brother is not a bad metaphor for Stephen's perception of Anglo-Ireland (which gives this remark from Best a significance which he himself fails to realize: 'that's very interesting because that brother motif, don't you know, we find also in the old Irish myths' — 9.956-57), and from this we can begin to see how Stephen's Shakespeare theory constitutes an elaborate allegory in which Anglo-Ireland is represented by Dick and Edmund Shakespeare, the two usurping brothers; Ireland's entrenchment in English culture by Ann Hathaway's infidelity; Ireland's dispossession by a body of work which rings with the sound of dispossession. Of course, put crudely in this way, the beautiful insinuation of the allegory is lost, but the point of the exercise should at any rate be clear. Shakespeare's art has nothing to do with Russell's 'divine wisdom'. It is made from the ugly fabric of human pain, insecurity and anger. The allegory implies that Stephen can work from the same materials and in the process reconstruct himself as 'the father of all his race' (9.868-69).

There are two further points I want to make about 'Scylla and Charybdis'. Firstly, just as, in 'Telemachus', there is textual collusion with Stephen's dispossession, notably in the interference with Moore's song, so in 'Scylla and Charybdis' narrative intervention collaborates with Stephen's theorizings. *Ulysses* is a designed debunking of Anglo-Irish culture, antithetical to revivalism in almost every conceivable way: its aesthetic, its realism, its pseudo-mythologizing, its obsessive insistence on the now, all turn the revivalist conception on its head. It is also possible to read *Ulysses* as an invasion of the cultural territory which Anglo-Ireland itself attempted to appropriate. Joyce's exhuberant, transgressive interference with the English language and with English cultural forms suggests a liberation from a culture which continued to define Anglo-Ireland. The technical innovation of *Ulysses* also functions to retrieve from a history of Catholic persecution, not an ideology of Catholic nationalism, but a brilliantly assertive art of the dispossessed. As if to suggest that 'Scylla and Charybdis' holds a special place in this enterprise, this episode is given a curious heterogeneity which seems to point forward to later chapters of the book of which it is part. The narrative occasionally breaks into Elizabethan parody, which clearly has an intrinsic function but which is also suggestive of the 'Oxen' technic. At line 500, there is a sudden appearance of musical notation, which suggests the 'fuga per canonem' of 'Sirens'. Similarly, at line 893, the episode becomes a play, as if pointing towards 'Circe'. These narrative disturbances of the ninth episode involve a kind of forecast of the rest of a book that effectively wrecked Anglo-Ireland's cultural ambitions. The narrative, then, like Stephen's theories, constitutes a kind of warning.

Finally, I would emphasize the obvious. For all the concentration on Stephen Dedalus in the early chapter, even here, *Ulysses* is continually moving out in the direction of wider social contexts. Dispossession is not simply a private obsession of Stephen's, but a glaring fact of life which operates in the social world of the school, in the newspaper office, and the library. Dedalus is constructed by his culture and is representative of it. His consciousness, however much it resists determination, is a colonial product, and the chapters here examined are sequenced in a way that continually deepens the implication of history in the making of Joyce's artist. The chapter which follows 'Scylla and Charybdis', and which precedes the wholesale shift in the novel towards discursive and stylistic aberration, is 'Wandering Rocks'. It is an episode which in very dramatic ways, serves to underscore, the fact that Stephen's 'Voice of Esau' is an articulation of a dispossessed culture.

Moving in times of yore: historiographies in 'Wandering Rocks'
'Wandering Rocks' has been most typically read as *the* chapter of modernity. In the 1970s, Clive Hart's classic essay established the chapter as operating a kind of aesthetics of urban 'nowness'. The simultaneity of actions; the close control of the relation between clock time and distance in space; the often strained and even wilful juxtapositions and intercalations — these were read by Hart as creating an image of generic, modern, urban culture. In Hart's analysis, 'Wandering Rocks' becomes not just representative of Dublin. It reconstructs the dynamics of modern urban life. The narrator here possesses an 'urban mind'.[47] The narrative functions like the mind of the city. The fact of modern mechanisation is implicated in the very compositional method behind the episode, which was apparently constructed like a time and motion study, mathematically designed with a map of Dublin in one hand and a clock in the other. Hart established 'Wandering Rocks' as a literally 'calculated' piece of writing, reproducing 'the working parts of a physical and social machine of great intricacy',[48] and most subsequent commentators have followed this reading. In fact, relatively little has been added to our understanding of 'Wandering Rocks' since Hart's pioneering work.

This episode undoubtedly deals in a dynamics of modern urbanism, but the Dublin reproduced here is not just any city. For one thing, this city is emphatically a colonized place. The famous positioning of Church

---

[47] Clive Hart, 'Wandering Rocks', in Hart and Hayman, *James Joyce's 'Ulysses'*, 190.

[48] Ibid., 201.

and State at the beginning and end of the chapter contextualizes Dubliners on the streets in relation to the same conservative ascendancy that frames the men in the newspaper office. Like 'Aeolus', the episode is, as Hart himself pointed out, full of missed opportunities, trivial Pisgah sights.[49] Characters miss trams and boxing matches, fail to connect, leave stories incomplete and so on. Moreover, for all the modernism of this episode, the Dublin of *Ulysses* 10 is historically defined in ways which makes it completely consistent with the episode that immediately precedes it. 'Wandering Rocks' extends the library debate about cultural politics into the streets by reproducing a colonized urban landscape.

One way of registering this historical fabric is simply to catalogue the historical figures alluded to in the episode: Cardinal Wolsey; Mary, Queen of Scots; Lord Aldborough (who was an eighteenth-century nobleman); Lord Talbot de Malahide (an admiral); Lord Molesworth and Robert and Mary Rochefort, who were the Earl and Countess of Belvedere. That particular group of aristocratic names figures in just one particular section of 'Wandering Rocks', the Father Conmee section, and Father Conmee has a particular interest in the past, so this section could be regarded as a special case. Except that it is not only the Catholic priest who is, moving in 'times of yore' (10.174). One of the readerly things that 'moving in times of yore' involves in 'Wandering Rocks' is the recognition of a historical roll-call which is not just confined to the Conmee section but is actually sustained throughout the whole of the episode, with a number of concentrations of such material in particular passages. The roll-call includes Nelson, the hero of empire who is alluded to in the savagely ironic line from 'The Death of Nelson', 'For England, home and beauty' (10.232/235).[50] Grattan and Silken Thomas are featured on the list. The latter was a Fitzgerald, a family which is highly profiled in 'Wandering Rocks'. Besides Silken Thomas, Lord Edward Fitzgerald of the eighteenth century is present, and so is 'mor Fitzgerald', the so-called

---

[49] Ibid., 189.

[50] Dublin had a contemporary reputation for being a very musical place, and music carried the romanticism and quite often the national aspirations of the country. In 'Wandering Rocks', a chapter of the city which is aural in some very precise ways, the only music you hear is that line bitterly growled out by a man who has lost his leg in the navy: '*For England, home and beauty*.' This line strikes a keynote which resounds in the historical fabric here outlined.

'great Fitzgerald' of the late fifteenth and early sixteenth centuries. There are references to buildings once owned by the Fitzgeralds and to streets named after them. Emmet is alluded to and 'the sham squire', Francis Higgins, and Major Sirr, and Sir Jonah Barrington, the eighteenth-century constitutionalist, and Guy Fawkes and Wolfe Tone, 'whose statue' — like Parnell's 'was not' (10.178) — these last two being particular examples of presence by absence. There is also Dilly Dedalus who in a curious monarchical transposition, is described as having 'a Stuart face of nonsuch Charles' (10.858), which Thornton[51] identifies as a reference to Catholic lost causes. Again 'Wandering Rocks' reads backwards to 'Aeolus'.

History is present everywhere, not only in reference to historical figures, but in street names and places and statuary, like Mountjoy Square, and Aldborough House. Great Charles's Street, William Street, George's Quay and James's Street, form an evocative quartet of English monarchs. Trinity College is prominent in the episode, but not University College. There are references to the old bank of Ireland, the Irish parliament in the eighteenth century and to St Mary's Abbey, which is a key location in the episode. According to Ned Lambert, this building marks 'the most historic spot in all Dublin' (10.409). There are also references to Kildare Street, Sir John Rogerson's Quay, Pembroke Quay, O'Connell Bridge, London Bridge Rd, Bedford Rd, Castleyard Gate, Lord Edward Street, Essex Gate, Parliament Street, Merrion Square, Bloody Bridge, the statue of King Billy's horse and Queen's Bridge. The list could go on to include the Empire music hall and the offices of the Patriotic Insurance Company. These latter are ironic additions to the more serious point of this catalogue, which is certainly not a commemorative celebration of a past cultural vibrancy and energy. Conmee sees the past in this way, and compares it to what he regards as a moribund contemporaneity. But these personages and street names actually commemorate something quite other than a vibrant national culture. They are the markers of an imperial history which has its presence stamped very firmly over the stones of a modern urban landscape. These markers carry a historical dynamic: the dynamic of colonization. The frequency of monarchs' names and the names of both English and Anglo-Irish landed families make a topographical delineation of plantation status. They are an attempt at a kind of authentication, registering not just material

---

[51] Thornton, *Allusions in 'Ulysses'*, 234.

ownership, but ownership of the historical process itself. It might be argued that dissent and resistance are also registered in the streetnames and historical personages of 'Wandering Rocks'. Moreover, the overwhelming emphasis is on Anglo-Irish resistance to the metropolis and especially Anglo-Irish resistance of the eighteenth century. However, that resistance was ambiguous, to put it mildly, in both nationalist terms and on the issue of Catholic emancipation. In any case, here, the process of historical commemoration in public places is by definition a process of assimilation. This is history made ritual, made safe, turned into civic ceremonial or romantic adventure, just as history-making, if Father Conmee has anything to do with it, is a safe occupation for mild-mannered gentlemen, and a vice-regal cavalcade the ritualization of historical process. A more dangerous history, a history of Tone and Parnell perhaps, is shadowy in terms of civic acknowledgement — the statues are not there. Of course, some kinds of history are completely invisible. There is no Whiteboy Square or Fenian Arcade or Famine Avenue in 'Wandering Rocks'.

History in 'Wandering Rocks', then, is ideologically reconstructed in the labelling of the cityscape and, in characters' minds and it is a thoroughly Anglicized history that we read. The colonial fabric of 'Wandering Rocks' functions as a context for modernization inasmuch as the fabric insists on the colonial past out of which the modern Irish city is built, and identifies modern Irish urban life itself as a colonial construction. This list of historical personages, streets and buildings is not some accidental by-product of Joyce's so-called encyclopedism. It is compiled in collaboration with the central design characteristic of this episode, which has the Church and State featuring famously at both ends. Moreover, the imperative demand that we read the Dublin of 'Wandering Rocks' as a colonial construction is reinforced by the fact that Dubliners, as well as the city itself, talk history. They reconstruct history and they deploy historiography.

Many of the Dubliners in 'Wandering Rocks' narrate historical events, as in the case of Ned Lambert, who tells the story of the Fitzgerald who fired Cashel Cathedral and informed an aggrieved English monarch, *'I'm bloody sorry I did it ... but I declare to God I thought the Archbishop was inside'* (10.445-56). Or like Tom Kernan who delivers reconstructions of Emmet's death, and Lord Edward Fitzgerald's escape from Major Sirr, and the arrest of Francis Higgins (see the section from lines 718 to 799). As if to confirm that the past is fundamental to a reading of the contemporary urban landscape, two of Joyce's Dubliners in 'Wandering Rocks' are in the business of actually writing history. One of them in actuality did write something which purported to be history. Both are clergymen and, interestingly, one is a Catholic and the other a Protestant. Hugh C. Love is a Protestant minister (see line 948) with 'a refined accent'. Love is both a 'visitor' (10.237) and a landlord who has 'distrained for rent' (10.943). If anything his Protestant status is overdone. He and Conmee both come from different sides of the fence. Yet they are also history writers who collaborate with one another, for they both utilize a similar historiography, and this suggests both a collusion between Church and State and the ideological importance of the control wielded by authority over historical meaning.

Hugh C. Love, a man who is 'well up in history' (10.439), is writing a history of the Fitzgeralds, and there is some indication of the kind of history-making in which he is engaged. Like Conmee, he seems temporally displaced, not quite of his time as he imaginatively reconstructs himself in the company of his heroes, picturing himself 'attended by Geraldines, tall and personable' (10.929-30). His historical research will undoubtedly testify to the greatness of this family. In both choice of family and the implication of treatment, Love's project becomes part of an Anglo-Irish tradition which flourished in the late nineteenth and early twentieth centuries to produce plays like *Gerald of Kildare* and Terence Flood's *Silken Thomas* (1906). There were also epic poems such as 'Silken Thomas or St Mary's Abbey' and the five cantos of a poem called 'Gerald Fitzgerald: A Tale of the Sixteenth Century'. There were histories, too, like *The Great Earl of Kildare* by Donagh Bryan, a Trinity College graduate who dedicated his book to 'the Lady Nesta Fitzgerald and to all who are descended from the Great Earl'.[52] The interest generated in this important landed family produced a flurry of publications, all of them identifying the Fitzgeralds as representing a heroic, patriotic tradition of Anglo-Irish selflessness and honour, and all of them linking fifteenth and sixteenth-century Anglo-Ireland, quite falsely, with Celticism and the national cause. Thus in Flood's play Silken Thomas, who declared against Henry VIII in St Mary's Abbey in 1534, has this to say on his arrest:

---

[52] Donald Bryan, *The Great Earl of Kildare* (Dublin and Cork: The Talbot Press, 1933), dedicatory page.

> The struggle between the Saxon and the Celt is not yet ended; for be assured that, as long as the fire of patriotism burns in the soul of a nation, it cannot be extinguished by men of your type and character, nor even by men who shall be rightly considered your superior.[53]

Behind Bryan's history is a similar attempt to identify 'the Great Earl of Kildare', 'the most completely Irish man in Ireland',[54] as a unifying nationalist. His rule, according to Bryan, was:

> neither Norman nor Gaelic but an organic compound of both, in that it represented all the then existent elements of Ireland. The Great Earl tried to make the Deputyship [that is rule over the Lordship] hereditary in his family. It is likely that before long the English lordship in Ireland would have been repudiated, the Mayors of the Palace would have become Kings and by the same process as took place in other countries, Ireland would have become united under a strong national government.[55]

United, one might reasonably add, under a strong national government which would have concentrated political power in the hands of a landed élite and consigned Catholic Ireland to perpetual serfdom. Needless to say, modern historiography conclusively refutes these crudely ideological versions of Fitzgerald history which were produced by Anglo-Ireland. According to Stephen Ellis, writing in 1985, the Fitzgeralds were 'a family of empire'.[56] In his relationship with successive English monarchs, the 'mor Fitzgerald', for example, head of the senior English Pale family, was scrupulous in his *protection* of the English monarchy's interest, particularly during his ten year period of governorship, which started in 1496 with a promise to 'defend the land from the king's enemies, rebels and traitors and to observe Poyning's Law'.[57] That law forbade the holding of Irish parliaments. It was described by a historian contemporary

---

[53] Terence Flood, *Silken Thomas* (Kilkenny: The People's Printing and Publishing Works, 1906), 36.

[54] Bryan, *The Great Earl of Kildare*, ix.

[55] Ibid., xi.

[56] Steven G. Ellis, *Tudor Ireland: Crown, Community and the Conflict of Culture 1470-1603* (Harlow: Longman, 1985), 62.

[57] Ibid., 82.

with Joyce as 'gagging a small Parliament' and 'enslaving a nation'.[58] Gerald was pre-eminent in Irish politics at this time precisely *because* he enjoyed the king's confidence and 'unparalleled colonial support'.[59] His policies served 'the colonialists' common interest even when directed to private ends'. Attempts to see Kildare's expansion as extending 'Ireland's' interest at the expense of the Crown' are Ellis says, 'entirely false and anachronistic'.[60] All of which means that there is a point to Joyce having a Protestant minister serving up this chapter of fabricated Irish history, and a further point to Ned Lambert apparently joining Love in the lionization of this colonial family as Irish patriots, rebels and iconoclasts, 'hot members' (10.448) as Lambert puts it. Lambert's own comments on the Fitzgeralds and his deference to Hugh C. Love and to Love's historical expertise suggest that historical fabrication has become accepted at street level as historical fact.

History in 'Wandering Rocks', then, is not only colonial history registered in the fabric of the city. History is also quite specifically a colonial history distorted and dominated by Protestant and Anglo-Irish interpretations. Thus Tom Kernan, famously Protestant by birth, identifies with the 'fine dashing noblemen' (10.788) of late eighteenth-century Ireland. Even if the likes of Sir Edward Fitzgerald and Emmet were, according to Kernan, 'on the wrong side' (10.789-790) they were nonetheless, authentic gentlemen careering through rollicking times as chronicled in Sir Jonah Barrington's *Personal Sketches and Recollections of His Own Times*. This book — which Kernan expresses a desire to re-read — was written by an aristocrat who described himself as 'a sound Protestant without bigotry and a hereditary royalist without ultraism. Liberty I love; democracy I hate; fanaticism I denounce.' [61] *Personal Sketches* promotes another historiography common in Anglo-Irish writing, this time focusing on the mid-to late eighteenth century, establishing the age which culminated in Grattan as a period of aristocratic rafishness, —'every estated gentleman in the Queen's County

---

[58] W. A. Conor, *History of the Irish People* (London: John Heywood, 1886), 114.

[59] Ellis, *Tudor Ireland*, 89.

[60] Ibid., 89.

[61] Sir John Barrington, *Personal Sketches and Recollections of His Own Times* (London: Cameron and Ferguson, 1876), viii.

was honoured by the gout'[62] — Protestant selflessness and gentlemanly 'good sense' and, perhaps above all, as a period of paternalistic social cohesion:

> At the Great House all disputes amongst the tenants were ... settled, — quarrels reconciled — old debts arbitrated: a kind Irish landlord reigned despotic in the ardent affections of the tenantry, their pride and pleasure being to obey and support him. But there existed a happy reciprocity of interests. The landlords of that period protected the tenant by his influence.[63]

In 'Wandering Rocks', the only exception to history being defined by the Anglo-Irish establishment is the Catholic Church's version of the past, as exemplified in Father Conmee's historical musings. But this hardly constitutes a challenge. On the contrary, Conmee confirms both Barrington's and Love's distortions. Despite living at the end of a century which saw virtual civil war, the mass mobilization of Catholics in political movements, the Famine and the struggle over land, Conmee manages to maintain a smiling, 'cheerful decorum' and a sycophantic deference to the Irish aristocracy. His reconstruction of 'old worldish days', 'loyal times in joyous townlands' and 'old times in the barony' (see 10.159-60) establishes, like Barrington's *Personal Sketches* and the Anglo-Irish presentation of the Fitzgeralds, another crudely ideological vision of a harmonious past in which everyone knew their place and was grateful for it. The distortion is entirely consistent with the booklet that Conmee produced in reality, *Old Times in the Barony*, which was published by the Catholic Truth Society in 1902. This offering, which is utterly unconscious of the irony of its title, is a Catholic elegy to Protestant landlordism. Located somewhere vaguely in the nineteenth century, Conmee writes of a time before modernity when 'homely practices of piety prevailed',[64] when society was bound by 'ties of kinship';[65] when there was an 'absence of any contention between classes or creeds'. This construction of social cohesion, which, like Barrington, Conmee thinks of

---

[62] Ibid., 4

[63] Ibid., 3.

[64] The Very Reverend John S. Conmee, *Old Times in the Barony* (Dublin: The Catholic Truth Society, 1907), 12.

[65] Ibid., 13.

as 'the most delightful characteristic'[66] of the past, had an obviously ideological implication. In this sentimental confection, the past is robbed of its dynamic and resistance to authority is silenced. Typical of the distortion is Conmee's comments on the military contingent which at one time was based in the barony of Luainford: 'In military matters, as in others, Luainford has sadly fallen from its high estate', writes Conmee:

> Fifty years ago it was the headquarters of a General; and large numbers of cavalry and artillery as well as of infantry, contributed in no small degree to the local colour of the streets and general attractiveness of the town .... the General himself, it was awesomely whispered, 'had fought agin Boney'. From such things grew the goodwill with which the Tommy Atkins of those times was greeted by the public when he appeared in the local festivities of the Barony.[67]

It is worth pointing out that, of course, the word 'Barony' signifies the domain of a Baron. But the word took on a particular meaning in Ireland, from about 1596, in the heyday of the plantation drive. From this time 'barony' specifically meant the division of an Irish county; whereas in Scotland, for example, it referred to something different, a 'large freehold estate, even if held by a commoner'.[68] For Conmee, the word conveys an 'old worldish' charm. But its historical dimension actually refers us precisely to the period when the Tudor colonial drive in Ireland took on a new and decisive forcefulness.

If we were to push precision further, however, we might want to distinguish between Hugh C. Love's production of heroic Protestant nationalism and Conmee's more genteel vision of a cultural syncretism when both rulers and ruled knew their place and lived in happy contentment. But these historiographies, the one from a Protestant minister and the other from a Catholic priest, substantially overlap and are broadly reconcilable. Symptomatic of this consistency is that fact that both Conmee and Love use the archaic, poeticizing and romanticizing word 'yore' for the past. Conmee moves 'in times of yore' and, as he notices the viceregal cavalcade, Love becomes 'mindful of lords deputies

---

[66] Ibid., 12.

[67] Ibid., 25.

[68] *Shorter Oxford English Dictionary*, 159.

whose hands benignant had held of yore rich advowsons' (10.1203-04). This historiographical concord is one obvious example in 'Wandering Rocks' of Church and State working hand in glove. That they do so is Stephen Dedalus's contention and, of course, it is a contention structurally built into 'Wandering Rocks' and signalled at the end of 'Scylla and Charybdis' in the missing lines of the closing quote from *Cymbeline* which read:

> Laud we the Gods;
> And let our crooked smokes climb to their nostrils
> From our blessed altars. Publish we this peace
> To all our subjects. Set we forward; let
> A Roman and a British ensign wave
> Friendly together.[69]

The historical support for this view, that by the end of the nineteenth century the Catholic Church establishment and the English state had done a decisive reconciliatory deal is overwhelming. The massive growth in the power, position and material prosperity of the Church had been achieved with the support of the English State, and the Church hierarchy understood that fostering the 'English connection' had produced a slow but sure process of Catholic emancipation which was infinitely safer than the more unstable, explosive material of secular nationalist activism. Conmee's deference to MPs and aristocracy and the quality of his historical imaginings are not idiosyncratic but symptomatic.

In 'Wandering Rocks' the colonial past is continued in the colonial present. The continuity can be measured partly in the topographical survivals, the streetnames and statuary, partly in the representation of the vice-regal cavalcade, a clear survival of empire street theatre, and partly in terms of the historiographies which in various ways distort the past in ways which romanticize Protestant culture and are silent about Catholic oppression and resistance. The impact of this colonial past on contemporary Dubliners is not a simple matter of the way in which Joyce's citizens respond to the dazzle of colonial cavalcade. The colonized consciousness is articulated in a maze of detail, in divided loyalties, ambiguous gestures, and in subtle deferences. Colonial history is also present, as we have seen, in silences and absences. Indeed, as Clive

---

[69] *Cymbeline*, V.v. 476-481.

Hart suggests, absence is at the centre of the episode insofar as Joyce's divided urban landscape has no 'common conceptual basis' which might 'hold the city together'.[70] In place of a shared culture, there is suspicion, intrigue and a web of strained and often spurious 'connections'. The most obvious material link between the sections of 'Wandering Rocks' is, in fact, money. Coins are dropped from a window in charity; Boylan jangles 'merry money'; 'four shillings, a sixpence and five pennies' are chuted from Conmee's 'plump glove palm into his purse' (10.116-17). There are price lists and talk about prices. Dilly Dedalus admires curtains which cost five shillings and tries to get her dissolute father to cough up for more essential commodities. Bloom reads *'All the dollarbills her husband gave her', 'were spent in the stores'* (10.608-09). Kernan remarks that 'where there's money going there's always someone to pick it up' (10.736-37) and indeed there is. In an earlier scene Molly's runaway coin is retrieved by an 'urchin' (10.255). These are some of the many references to money in 'Wandering Rocks' — money lost, spent, gambled, needed. The image is not of McHugh's 'empire of the spirit', but of a society materially poor, struggling to make ends meet in more ways than one, and this too is contextualized in 400 years of colonial history.

Such then is the nature and centrality of usurpation in these chapters of *Ulysses*. Literary culture, historical culture, the one-time nationalist press, the new wave's attempt at Ireland's cultural rejuvenation, all are Anglicized and dominated by the Anglo-Irish. One of the obvious results of this reading, is that these chapters take on a new coherence in terms of their relationship to each other, a coherence which derives quite simply from what the episodes are about. Textual strangeness, what Shklovsky termed *ostranenie,* which might be thought to delineate boundaries between the episodes, is circumscribed by this coherence. As I have indicated, much of the textual energy and innovation of these early chapters derives from a narrative collusion with Stephen's mode of thinking history. The inverted symbolism of 'Telemachus', Stephen's interior monologue, the newspaper headlines of 'Aeolus', the episodic structuring of 'Wandering Rocks', to one extent or another, these all collaborate with Stephen's articulation of the 'voice of Esau'. Another result of this reading, is that Stephen Dedalus becomes firmly located in Irish cultural contexts, and much more racially and socially determined

---

[70] Hart, in Hart and Hayman, *James Joyce's 'Ulysses',* 193.

than he has been represented in previous readings. If we regard Stephen as a late nineteenth-century 'apotheosis of individualism', who comprehensively rejects all 'social and religious obligations', as many Joyceans have done, then his talk of 'usurpation' does indeed become 'melodramatic',[71] if not incomprehensible. Many Joyceans have been left wondering, like 'Buck' Mulligan (who knows, but refuses to say) exactly what drives Stephen. Read as a dispossessed Catholic, a representation of the colonized mind, he becomes knowable. Stephen cannot be neatly squeezed into any simple nationalist camp, but he has been essentially configured by empire history. The servant who refuses to serve has displaced the narrator of *A Portrait* to become his own best ironist. He is analytical, engaged in the world, and in most respects fairly cool-headed. There is a sort of courage to Stephen too — the courage to articulate the dishonour that the culture avoids or about which it preserves a stony silence, or laughs away in embarrassment, and to face the crisis in identity that is the most obvious product of the colonial relationship with the 'motherland'. Stephen's protean world is not a philosophical abstraction, but a condition of a culture which is everywhere defined by its relationship to the metropolis — where it most conforms, where it rejects, even, perhaps especially, where it rebels.[72]

Joyce himself indicated that there was little more that he could do with Stephen after these early chapters in *Ulysses*. But the 'shape' that 'could not be changed' has frequently been read too closely in relation to *Portrait*. What has not been fully appreciated in the past is just how far Joyce *did* get with the Stephen of *Ulysses*, how far the perimeters had advanced from the earlier incarnation in the *Bildungsroman*. It is certain, however, that Joyce had no intention of developing his handling of cultural usurpation through some kind of conventional plot development.

---

[71] See Arnold Kettle, *An Introduction to the English Novel*, (London: Hutchinson University Library, 1951), II 135-51.

[72] I suspect that Stephen Dedalus may be partially responding to Horace Plunkett's analysis of Ireland's problems in his influential book, *Ireland in the New Century* (London: John Murray, 1904). In Plunkett's profoundly racist version of things, Ireland's problems were largely the result of 'the Irish character', by which he meant, the Irish Catholic character. For Plunkett, Irish Catholics had 'many an inheritance of [the] epoch of serfdom' (105). 'The impartial observer' he went, on 'will, I fear find amongst the majority of our people a striking absence of self-reliance and moral courage' (110).

It is equally certain that in the book which lets nothing go, the handling of cultural usurpation, so centrally established on the agenda, had to be developed in some way. Between 'Wandering Rocks' and 'Ithaca', Stephen does not really change at all. His strategies, by and large, have been exhausted. In the second part of this study, I shall be arguing that the book itself now takes over from where Stephen has left off. The process begins with Bloom who, placed in the context of Irish literary culture is not so much the moral Everyman of critical tradition as a literary intervention, a cartoon misfit. As such he is just as functional in the so-called 'battle of two civilizations' as, for example, the interpolations of 'Cyclops'. But from 'Sirens' onwards, it is the narrative itself which displays, in the most extraordinary ways, the distortions of Anglicization and cultural hybridity. Unlike revivalism, which kept a determined silence about the cultural conditions of its making, *Ulysses* revels in self-exposure, and from 'Sirens' onwards the strategy of exposing the cultural conditions of its own making becomes a central driving force.

3 Corresponding with the Greeks

The encounter between Joyce and the Literary Revival, if it was restricted to the story of Stephen Dedalus, would be interesting but of limited significance. The larger claim made here is much more substantial, that *Ulysses* is constructed in opposition to revivalist historiographies and aesthetics. The national culture thus becomes exposed in *Ulysses* as an ideology, and as a cultural appropriation faking authentic ethnicity. This exposure penetrates to the basic design elements and structural principles of *Ulysses*. I would stress at this point that Joyce's assault is not a rejection of nationalism *per se*,[1] but rather a displacement of very specific nationalist forms that are, in Joyce's reproduction, both reactionary and Anglicized. At the same time, revivalist culture does permeate *all* the nationalist discourses available to Joyce — from Yeats, through Griffiths, to Moran. In this sense, Irish national culture, however much it was redefined by new generations of Catholic intelligentsia, remained an invention of landlord consciousness, as far as Joyce was concerned.

To demonstrate the intimate implication of revivalism in the fundamentals of Ulyssean design, this chapter reads the *Ulysses's* blueprints, the schema, as the formulation of a literary strategy which engages the conservative and Anglicized nature of revivalism. These elaborate plans seem to insist on the epic status of Joyce's book, apparently authenticating its canonical status by establishing relationship with the premier text of the premier Western culture. In the reading that follows, however, Homeric correspondence, both as a scheme and as it is executed in *Ulysses*, will be presented as an satirical abduction of a traditional cultural practice. This practice united revivalist Ireland with Victorian and Edwardian England and so provides a very clear illustration of the Anglicized terms in which the Literary Revival expressed itself.

On the other hand, there were significant distinctions between Hellenization in English and Irish cultures. Whilst Gilbert Murray at

---

[1] It is perhaps worth pointing out that the rejection of nationalism in the early decades of the twentieth century, was, for obvious reasons, a much less problematic position than it is in the post-colonial present.

Oxford applauded Greek civic excellence, and Matthew Arnold elevated Greek creative spontaneity, Yeats and O'Grady reconstructed Homeric epic in gigantist terms as a culture of passion, action and heroism. The second part of this chapter reads Leopold Bloom as a literary strategy, deployed in Joyce's hilarious version of corresponding with the Greeks as the exact antithesis of the revivalist hero.

An overview of *Ulysses* as an Irish epic

Homeric correspondence is absolutely central to the design of *Ulysses*. It is explicit, if problematized, in the Romanized title of the book, and embedded in the various columnar schemes[2] which Joyce made available to key figures in the very early days of Joyce studies: to Herbert Gorman, the first Joyce biographer; to Stuart Gilbert, who wrote the first full length study of *Ulysses*; and to Carlo Linati, the Italian critic. In these schema, the tripartite division of Joyce's book into Telemachia, Odyssey and Nostos is, of course, Homeric. Each episode of Joyce's novel corresponds to an Odyssean event. All the columns in the schema are referred in some way to the prototype text, with the single exception of an anti-epic column denoting the time of day at which each episode takes place. In the 'symbol' designations, the symbol for 'Telemachus' is 'heir'; for 'Nestor' it is 'horse'; for 'Proteus' 'tides'; and for 'Calypso' 'nymph'. Some of the 'art' designations are similarly Homeric: the art of 'Circe' is 'magic', for instance. Likewise the 'organ' listings, which have 'lungs' representing 'Aeolus' and the 'ear' representing 'Sirens'. The 'technic' designations include 'gigantism' for 'Cyclops' and 'narcissism' for 'Lotuseaters'. The 'correspondence' column itself, which was omitted in the version published in Gilbert's *James Joyce's 'Ulysses'* (1930), but restored in Kenner's *Dublin's Joyce* (1955), is particularly insistent on Homeric linkage. This column identifies both the transparent, that Stephen corresponds to Telemachus and Mulligan to Antinous, for instance, and the ingenious, like the resonant correspondences in 'Wandering Rocks' between the Bosphorus and the Liffey, the Viceroy and 'the European Bank', and Conmee and 'the Asiatic Bank'. All in all, the columnar scheme insists on a central intertextuality, driving *Ulysses* at a very wide range of levels. This elaborate ghosting has been read in many

---

[2] These schemas have been published many times. The one referred to in this account is the composite which appears in Peake, *Citizen and the Artist*, 120.

ways, and there is still no real agreement about the overall effect of its execution in *Ulysses*, about whether this 'epic' is entirely mock or whether there is a genuine mythopoetic waiting to be discovered. Some critics have regarded Homeric correspondence in purely formalist terms as a 'scaffold' or a 'framework' on which to peg modernist material that is incompatible with traditional structuring.[3] The precise meaning of 'correspondence' is by no means established, but it should uncontentious that Homeric epic is essential to *Ulysses*, if only because the schema with their compelling provenance insist on this much.[4]

The concern here is not with any further identification of Homeric parallels in *Ulysses*, but rather with an understanding of how Joyce recognizes and interrogates Homeric correspondence as a cultural practice. The focus is not on the reproduction of Homer in *Ulysses*, but on *Ulysses* as a self-conscious participant in the *process* of Homeric correspondence. If we take Homeric analogy as a synecdoche for correspondence with classical Greek culture generally — and the schema, with their wider references to Plato and Aristotle are partially consistent with such a view — then Joyce's diagrammatic becomes in some sense an exposed product of the paramount status which classical Greek culture has in Western historiography. Joyce's schema are in relation to Gerty McDowell's 'Greekly perfect' mouth and to the statuary of shapely goddesses so admired by Bloom: 'curves the world admires' (8.921). The Joycean diagram itself is the sort of cultural object which might hold Bloom's attention, precisely because of its

---

[3] This was Pound's view and Eliot's. The latter's remark about Joyce using myth to impose aesthetic order on the chaos of contemporary reality has influenced formalist accounts of Homeric correspondence in *Ulysses*. Eliot's remark, however, said more about *The Waste Land* than it did about *Ulysses*. Joyce's novel has very little difficulty in establishing ordering principles, mythic or otherwise and it effectively banishes urban angst to the realms of metropolitan liberal faddism. See T. S. Eliot, 'Ulysses, Order and Myth', *The Dial*, LXXV (1923), 480-83.

[4] Perhaps even more than the provenance, the importance of the schema is underwritten by the simple fact that they show how Joyce somehow could reduce the 644 pages of his huge book to a meaningful diagram. These schema are more than working notes. With their obsessive ordering and structuring, the insistent intertextuality, their notification of narrative shifts and discontinuities, the schema do indicate something substantial about what *Ulysses* amounts to, and perhaps about what kind of an 'epic' the book is.

pseudo-classicism. Bloom could identify with Joyce's schema, just as he identifies with the bedroom print of 'The Bath of the Nymphs'. This 'giveaway' from *Titbits* is not mere titillation, but a prestigious 'masterpiece'. The 'naked nymphs' are, in Bloom's lame justification, evocative of 'Greece: for instance all the people that lived then' (3.372). For Bloom, as for Mulligan and Professor McHugh, classical Greek is 'the language of the mind'. It carries the very 'radiance of intellect (7.563-65). It gives us arcane words like 'metempsychosis', a word which is not just Greek but 'from the Greek' (3.341-42). Like many characters in *Ulysses*, Bloom has his own manner of establishing correspondence with the Greeks (indeed, he reminds himself to write 'Greek ees' in his secret correspondence with Martha Clifford, partly as disguise, but partly to impress — 11.860). This, apparently, is the sure sign of a cultured man — although Mulligan's suggestion that Bloom is 'Greeker than the Greeks' (9.614-15) carries very different connotations. Conversely, the barbarian is identified in terms of distance from the Greek prototype of civilized culture, which is why Stephen's surname is, in Mulligan's estimation, a 'mockery': 'Your absurd name, an ancient Greek! (1.34). In *Ulysses*, the culture of classical Greece provides the model of civilization. Characters aspire to embrace it, however peripherally, and they contextualize their own social status and even their physical appearance with reference to it.

Hellenization can easily be identified as a cultural process which is ridiculed as pretension in *Ulysses*. At the same time *Ulysses* is loudly announced as an overdone exemplification of the very correspondence it ridicules. For those readers who think that by shadowing Homer, *Ulysses* is an act of deference to cultural tradition, there is an obvious problem here. It would be difficult to accept that *Ulysses* mocks the ridiculous cultural aspirations of its characters, only to exercise its own authentic classical parentage. The argument I want to elaborate, however, is that far from deferring to the 'precursors' of Western cultural tradition, and 'advancing beyond them into the literature of the future'[5] in some continuum of cultural excellence, *Ulysses* exposes the

---

[5] Richard Ellmann, *The Consciousness of Joyce* (London: Faber & Faber, 1977), 10-11. According to Ellmann, perhaps the most eminent and influential Joycean of the post-war period, Homeric correspondence in Joyce is substantially a matter of 'deference'. It signals Joyce's intention of moving beyond his own 'personal moment' to invoke 'the collective past as well', by which Ellmann means the literary past. However iconoclastic the Joyce text might be, Homeric

ideological basis of literary value and, to a very significant degree, it does so through a highly subversive practice of 'correspondence'.

The word 'correspondence', apart from its usual epistolary meaning, also refers to congruity or agreement, 'a relation between persons or communities'. It is in this latter sense that 'correspondence' is particularly suggestive of cultural process. The word registers a long history by which Homeric epic has been constructed as the 'crown of creative achievement in the history of European literature from the days of ancient Greeks to modern times'.[6] There is perhaps no other text, with the exception of the Bible, which better illustrates the politics of literary culture, the nationalistic and hegemonic basis of conceptions of literary value. Ironically, establishing 'correspondence' with Homeric epic, far from being characteristically Joycean or even modernist, has been a deeply conservative cultural practice probably since the earliest transference of oral culture into the printed word. The first attempt at collecting and recording the tales which comprise the *Odyssey* is usually regarded by classicists as the work of 'a declining ruling class looking not to the future but back over the years to a more glorious past'. In obvious correspondence to the makers of Ireland's own cultural revival, these Athenians of the eighth century B.C. have been understood as displaced 'émigrés', looking back through the story where the motif of 'return' is so fundamental to 'the greatest exploits of the days when their adventurous Achean ancestors were united and masters of the world'.[7] According to an influential literary historiography, literature starts with the writing down of the Homeric epic, in which case literature starts with correspondence. The first

---

correspondence, for Ellmann, signifies continuity with the literary canon of Western civilization. The weight of classical Greece also produces 'archetypal significance'.

[6] C. Gillie, *Longman Companion to English Literature* (London: Longman Group, 1972), 567.

[7] H. C. Baldry, *Greek Literature for the Modern Reader* (Cambridge: Cambridge University Press, 1951), 67. Baldry's discussion on this subject is perhaps suggestive of Ireland's history. He writes, for example, of: 'the disintegration of aristocracy and the rise in Ionia of tyrants dependent on support from the East'. This was, 'unlikely to favour anything so national and pan-Hellenic as a heroic story of the Trojan War' and brought about 'the decline of epic in the region where it was born' (91).

written version of the *Odyssey* is itself hegemonic, and revivalist — an assertion of cultural relatedness to a much earlier culture.[8]

The Roman variety of Homeric epic also reformulates its prototype in directly political ways. The *Aeneid* both appropriates and transforms Homeric epic. Virgil's poetic imitation of the *Iliad* and the *Odyssey* adapts the aesthetic power of the Homeric prototype to 'fuel the ambitions of imperial power'. In this decisive intervention, epic becomes 'committed to imitating and attempting to "overgo" its early versions'. It becomes 'overtly political'.[9] According to David Quint:

> Virgil's epic is tied to a specific national history, to the idea of world domination, to a monarchical system, even to a particular dynasty .... Epics of the Latin West subsequently took political issues as central subjects, whether they perpetuated the imperial politics of the *Aeneid*, or, as in the case of *Pharsalia*, sought to attack or resist empire.[10]

In an interesting essay entitled 'The Dynastic Epic', Andrew Fichtian, also sees the dynastic theme, 'the rise of the imperium, the noble house, race or nation to which the poet professes allegiance', as central to the development of epic, and argues that this produces a centrally defining characteristic:

> The dynastic theme ... brings into focus what must be considered one of the most basic elements of epic from Virgil onward, its consciousness of history. The narrative strategy of the dynastic poem reflects the assumption of a historically orientated mind that the present may be regarded as the culmination of a course of events set in motion in the past .... The dynastic poet is an analyst of historical experience.[11]

---

[8] See William G. Thalmann, *The Odyssey: an Epic of Return* (New York: Twayne Publishers, 1992), 6, where he describes the eighth-century interest in Homeric epic precisely as cultural revivalism.

[9] David Quint, *Epic and Empire: Politics and Generic Form from Virgil to Milton* (New Jersey: Princeton University Press, 1993), 44.

[10] Ibid., 45.

[11] Andrew Fichter, 'The Dynastic Epic' in R. P. Draper, ed., *The Epic: Developments in Criticism* (London: Macmillan, 1990), 165.

The connection between 'correspondence' and cultural politics has been transmitted in every assimilation of Homeric epic since Virgil. Pope's neo-classical translations, for instance, and translation is a very direct form of correspondence, display a standard of correctness in style which owes much more to a declining English aristocracy clinging nostalgically to redundant aristocratic traditions than it does to the Greek prototype. The contention here is that the centrality of Homeric correspondence in Joyce's schema is the emphatic signal of his consciousness of these cultural dynamics. The identification between *Ulysses* and Homer is not, as some critics have suggested, a subscription to the premier culture of civilized Europe, but rather the exact opposite: a hilarious subversion of the tortuous academic and creative practices by which both the English and the Irish establishments attempted to 'correspond' with a culture that, for Gilbert Murray embodied 'the progress of the human race'.[12]

In order to establish this argument, it is necessary to examine the Homeric incarnations which most influenced Joyce. I am referring here not to the 'fringe' contributions to Homeric study, like Bérard's *Les Phéniciens et l'Odyssée* (1902-03) and Samuel Butler's, *The Authoress of the Odyssey* (1897). These were important to Joyce because they decentred the cultural orientation of the *Odyssey,* Bérard by a racial shifting which linked Homer with an orientalist Middle east as opposed to the 'civilizing' West, and Butler because *The Authoress of the Odyssey* feminizes authorship. However, it was Joyce's sense of the orthodox correspondence which confirmed the importance of the likes of Bérard and Butler, and Joyce was exposed to this orthodoxy, in my opinion, in three main cultural contexts: firstly, the nineteenth-century English academic investment in classical studies, represented here largely by Gilbert Murray's Harvard lectures (1907); secondly, through Matthew Arnold's important cultural realignments in *Culture and Anarchy* (1869) and in *The Study of Celtic Literature* (1867); and thirdly, the context of the Irish Literary Revival itself, which was nothing short of obsessive in its own insistence on correspondence with the Greeks. This version of relatedness to classical Greek culture, so highly profiled in Joyce's immediate cultural environment, was undoubtedly the single most important influence on him. That it owed

---

[12] Gilbert Murray, *The Rise of the Greek Epic* (Oxford: Oxford University Press, 1934, 4th edn), 3.

so much to Oxford academics is an irony ruthlessly exploited in Joyce's own appropriation of correspondence.

Education in nineteenth and early twentieth-century England is usually represented as modernizing, firstly under the demands of England's own industrial development and later in response to the pressure of economic competition from Japan, Germany and America. This is the age of technical and scientific 'instruction', particularly in higher education, and it was accompanied by a concerted attack on liberal education and the classics.[13] There was, however, a strong resistance to these developments throughout the nineteenth and early twentieth centuries, a staunch defence of liberal ideals of education. The classics departments at Oxford and Cambridge were formidable centres of this resistance. As late as 1900 the number of 'pass men' at Cambridge still amounted to half the entire undergraduate population of England and the prestige degrees remained classics degrees from Oxford and Cambridge and pure mathematics from Cambridge alone.

The defenders of this traditional curriculum, who included such luminaries as Edward Copleston, Matthew Arnold and John Henry Newman, constructed Western 'progress' as a continuum of liberal humanist culture which had its origins and its most potent models in classical Greece and Rome. Gilbert Murray, who became Regius professor of Greek at Oxford in 1908, is a late exemplar of this tradition. His *The Rise of the Greek Epic*, which developed from a course of lectures given at Harvard in 1907 and which reached its fourth edition by 1934, begins with the assertion that the Greek epic embodies 'the spirit of progress'. Murray defines this latter as a question of 'both feeling the value and wonder of life and being desirous to make it a better thing'.[14] The origins of 'progress' — the 'seeds of Western culture' — are mostly 'to be found in Greece and not elsewhere'.[15] This status is demonstrated most potently in Murray's

---

[13] This confrontation between modernism and antiquity was probably initiated, as early as 1809, by R. L. Edgeworth's *Essays on Professional Education* with its assertion that the value of knowledge was to be measured by its utility. See Michael Sanderson, ed., *The Universities in the Nineteenth Century* (London: Routledge & Kegan Paul, 1975), 26-61.

[14] Murray, *The Rise of the Greek Epic*, 26.

[15] Ibid., 3.

account of the value of classical Greek poetry, although the impact of the prototype culture is felt everywhere: in medical science (through Galen and Hippocrates), philosophy, ethics, and in physical culture. But Murray's rigorous research, which is presented as a 'scientific' demonstration of absolute cultural value, produces deeply ideological readings. His complete refutation of the notion that 'Hellenism' was pagan, to take the most obvious illustration, is profoundly racist and Eurocentric:

> Anthropologists have shown us what this Pagan man really is. From the West Coast of Africa to the Pacific Isles in many varying shapes he meets us, still with the old gaiety, the old crowns of flowers, the night-long dances, the phallus-bearing processions, and untroubled vices. We feel, no doubt, a charm in his simple and instinctive life, in the quick laughter and equally quick tears, the directness of action, the unhesitating response of sympathy. We must all of us have wished from time to time that our friends were more like Polynesians; especially those of us that live in University towns. And I think, in a certain limited sense, the Greeks probably were so. But in the main, as all classical literature shows, the Greeks and the Pagan were direct opposites.[16]

This linkage between the modern West and archaic Greece is illustrative of a correspondence which echoes throughout Murray's work. Studying Greek poetry erases the distance and difference between Cambridge classics students and Homer because 'the differences lie largely in the accident of our own remoteness'.[17] There is, according to Murray, a liberal affinity between democratizing England and classical Greece. The Greeks did keep slaves, but they were 'characteristically the first human beings who felt a doubt or scruple about slavery'; 'gentleness to the slave population' was part of their 'democratic ideal'. Homer, writes Murray, 'always speaks of slaves with a half puzzled tenderness'.[18] Similarly, 'the Greeks were not characteristically subjectors of women'.[19] But perhaps the most

---

[16] Ibid., 9.

[17] Ibid., 10.

[18] Ibid., 17.

[19] Ibid., 19.

significant correspondence is derived from a different kind of political extrapolation. The study of the classics was generally fundamental to the élitism of university education at this time. It was taken for granted that Latin and Greek were necessary for admission into university, which meant that only the products of a small number of schools were eligible for admission. The content of the classics — Plato's famous defence of government by élites, for instance — reinforced what was fundamental to the educational system. For Murray, Plato, like Aristotle, is 'somewhat anti-democratic', but this becomes a product of 'commonsense' and pragmatism, for 'some men are born to obey, others to rule. Put down a dozen Greeks in a barbarous country: in a few months you will find the Greeks giving orders and the natives obeying them'.[20]

Correspondences constructed to underwrite an ideology of western 'progress' and centrally connected to issues of class and power were embedded in academic work on the classics at this time. The translation of the *Odyssey* that Joyce himself used, by Butcher and Lang (1879), which had the wonderful title *The Odyssey of Homer — Done Into English Prose*, was produced by a collaboration between an Anglo-Irish academic, one-time fellow of Trinity College and later Professor of Greek in the University of Edinburgh and an Hon. LL.D from St Andrews. It too makes heavy investment in correspondence, asserting, with no basis whatsoever, that 'the epics are stories about the adventures of men living in most respects like the men of our own race', and producing connections which bring together the two key texts of Western culture through a totally spurious linguistic parallel:

> Greek epic dialect, like the English of our Bible, was a thing of slow growth and composite nature .... it was never a spoken language, nor, except for certain poetical purposes, a written language. Thus the Biblical English seems as nearly analogous to the Epic Greek, as anything that our tongue has to offer.[21]

It is sometimes remarked that there are correspondences in the Joyce schema which are wilfully obscure, like the identification of Sargent

---

[20] Ibid., 17.

[21] S. H. Butcher and Andrew Lang, *The Odyssey of Homer — Done Into English Prose,* (London: Macmillan, 1893), ix.

with Pisistratus, the cocklepickers with Megapenthus, Cunningham with Sisyphus, or Menton with Ajax. But these and similar obscurities could well be read as wickedly comic appropriations of a customary process, correspondent to the extraordinarily obtuse connections made between modern England, and, as we shall see, Ireland, and ancient Greece as standard practice in the classical studies of the time.

Matthew Arnold's Hellenizing agenda, the second of the contexts under discussion, was well known to Joyce and it is evident from *Ulysses* that he attached particular significance to Arnold. The specific association between Arnold, Oxford and Mulligan's élitist Hellenizing proposal in 'Telemachus' very clearly establishes correspondence, in the opening pages of *Ulysses*, as a hegemonic cultural practice. Moreover, the whole Jew/Greek pattern in *Ulysses* is itself in exploitative correspondence with Arnold's treatment of class, race and culture in *Culture and Anarchy*. Something of the character of the subversion can be seen in 'Circe', the episode where Arnold's face features as a ghostly presence in a brothel and where his elegant homily to 'Hebraism' and 'Hellenism', the two most powerful constituents of culture and civilization in Arnold's account, is reduced to the crass formulation 'jewgreek meets greekjew' (15.2097). All this indicates that Arnold held importance for Joyce, an importance determined partly by Arnold's prominence in the liberal tradition outlined above, but also by the significant divergences from the mainstream orthodoxy in Arnold's thinking. These divergences are clearly illustrated in Arnold's controversial evaluation of ancient Irish culture. Like Murray, Arnold recreates classical Greece as the prototype culture of civilization. 'The best art and poetry of the Greeks, in which religion and poetry are one, in which the idea of beauty and of human nature perfect on all sides adds to itself a religious and devout energy' produces the 'surpassing interest and instructiveness'[22] of the classics. However, for Arnold, materialist, Victorian England has come adrift from congruency with this ideal. England *is* the supreme exemplar of 'progress': 'no people in the world have done more and struggled more to attain ... moral perfection than our English race has.'[23] But it has achieved this elevated state under the influence of Puritanism and Protestant Nonconformity,

---

[22] Matthew Arnold, *Culture and Anarchy* (Cambridge: Cambridge University Press, 1961 edn), 54.

[23] Ibid., 55.

cultural forces which Arnold claims are correspondent with another ancient prestige culture: Hebraic culture. The English 'tendency' to 'over-Hebraise' has produced a 'provincial' and 'narrow' religiosity and a culture which Arnold regrets as being 'mechanical' and 'external'.[24] In Arnold's analysis, the new middle-class rulers of England have displaced Hellenic 'spontaneity of conscience' by a Hebraic 'strictness of conscience'.[25] Hellenism's characteristic perception of 'things in their essence and beauty'[26] has been usurped by Hebraism's consciousness of 'sin'. The new imperative is for England to reconnect with 'spontaneity' and 'imagination' and curiously there is the suggestion, in 'The Study of Celtic Literature', that the literary heritage of the Irish Celt has something to teach the materialist middle classes of Victorian England in this respect. Although Arnold identifies the 'Celtic Irish'[27] in traditionally racist terms as 'undisciplinable, anarchical and turbulent by nature', 'ineffectual in politics' and 'poor, slovenly and half barbarous',[28] he also detects an eloquence and delicacy in Gaelic literature an ardent aspiration 'after life, light and emotion, to be expansive, adventurous and gay'[29] which strikes precisely the Hellenic note. This absurd piece of mystification arrives at an astonishing correspondence: 'the Greek has the same perceptive, emotional temperament as the Celt' (Yeats, *Mem*, 169.)

The Literary Revival's obsessive alignment of Gaelic with Greek culture was distinct from Arnold's in certain key respects. Yeats, who connected Arnold with the degradation of 'classical morality' (Yeats, *Mem*, 169). saw parallels of aristocratic action, energy, heroism and valour which are inconsistent with Arnold's identification of a more humble and less dangerous 'lightness' and gaiety. But Arnold did identify Celticism with Hellenism. Moreover, there were compelling

---

[24] Ibid., 49.

[25] Ibid., 132.

[26] Ibid., 135.

[27] Matthew Arnold, *On the Study of Celtic Literature and other Essays* (London: J. M. Dent, 1910), 86.

[28] Ibid., 84.

[29] Ibid., 81.

ideological similarities between the Oxford and Anglo-Irish intellectuals both resisting a modernization that was reshaping the two societies. In both instances, cultural retrospection reestablishes the authority of the élites; in both tradition is privileged over innovation, and continuity over change. The irony of England's most eminent cultural theorist massaging the basic Greek/Irish correspondence, was one further illustration of the essentially Anglicized nature of revivalism in Ireland.

In Ireland as in England, establishing correspondence with classical Greece was routine. In fact, cultural nationalists in all countries, certainly from the French revolution onwards, have made claims for indigenous cultural status on the basis of classical parallels and correspondences. In Napoleonic France and Risorgimento Italy, for example, the prototype culture was classical Rome. In Ireland it was classical Greece, partly because, as the 'authorized' version of history stated so unequivocally, the Roman empire had by-passed Ireland, and this explained everything. According to Hume's *History of England* (1767):

> The Irish from the beginning of time, had been buried in the most profound barbarism and ignorance; and as they were never conquered or even invaded by the Romans, from whom all the Western World derived its civility, they continued still in the most rude state of society.[30]

In Irish cultural nationalism, this historiography was turned on its head. Rome was identified with a vulgar and brutalizing materialism 'correspondent' with empire and England, as it is, in a rare, perhaps unique convergence, throughout Joyce's writing. The culture of the Gael, on the other hand, is wild, exuberant, 'spiritual'. In his crucial 'discovery' of Gaelic historical epic, Standish O'Grady disinterred a rough but passionate core, not just correspondent with but actually surpassing classical Greece:

> I cannot help regarding this age and the great personages moving therein as incomparably higher in intrinsic worth than the *corresponding* ages of Greece. In Homer, Hesiod, and the Attic poets there is polish and artistic form, absent in the existing monuments of Irish heroic thought, but the gold, the ore itself, is here massier and more pure, the sentiment deeper and

---

[30] David Hume, *History of Great Britain* (London: 1767), 454.

more tender, the audacity and freedom more exhilarating, the reach of the imagination more sublime, the depth and the power of the human soul more fully exhibit themselves. [31] [My emphasis.]

In its more extreme moments, O'Grady's articulation of correspondence appeared to exploit the new 'science' of eugenics:

In the times of which Homer sung, the Greek nobles had yellow hair and blue eyes. At the time when the heroic literature of Ireland was composed, the Irish nobles had yellow hair and blue eyes.[32]

From O'Grady onwards, this correspondence between Ireland and ancient Greece became a standard feature of revivalist rhetoric. In populist histories, the ancient Greeks actually discovered Ireland, and deified it. The 'imaginative Greeks', a thousand years before Christ, carried out an expedition to 'the Sacred Isle':

yielding to that clinging belief in some blessedness as yet unattained, which, too easily attracted by earth, droops its wearied head towards any spot that is hallowed by distance, conceived that here were situated the Elysian fields.[33]

Yeats's linkage with an earlier Anglo-Irish incarnation of the Irish heroic age was powered by identification of the latter with Homeric images of 'savage strength', 'tumultuous action' and 'overshadowing doom':

a vanquished world in which 'the soul had only to stretch out its arms and fill them with beauty', that he set against the modern world 'of whirling change and heterogeneous ugliness'.[34]

According to James W. Flannery, the image of 'classical Greece',

---

[31] Standish O'Grady, *History: Critical and Philosophical* (London: Sampson & Low, 1881), 201.

[32] O'Grady, *History of Ireland*, 18.

[33] Conor, *History of the Irish People*, 5.

[34] James W. Flannery, *W. B. Yeats and the Idea of a Theatre: The Early Abbey Theatre in Theory and Practice* (New Haven: Yale University Press, 1989), 16.

where 'civilization rose to its highest mark', 'haunted Yeats's imagination'.[35] The Irish Literary Theatre was designed in emulation of Dionysian and Eleusinian models, as a means of effecting spiritual regeneration 'in the body public of Ireland. With the theatre of ancient Greece in mind, Yeats thought constantly of Homer' and dreamed of 'creating some new Prometheus Unbound, Patrick or Columcille, Oisin or Finn in Prometheus's stead'. The intention was to 'plunge' art 'into social life' and to provide Ireland with 'a vision of race as noble as that of Sophocles and Aeschylus' (Yeats, *Auto,* 66). Long before Joyce drew up his own elaborate design of correspondences, Yeats and MacGregor Mathers were undertaking extensive research into parallels between Celtic and Greek gods.[36] The broad analogy became part of the jargon of contemporary critical approval amongst revivalists, so that Moore applauded *The Countess Cathleen* as 'a play as beautiful as Maeterlinck' containing 'verse equal to the verses of Homer',[37] and the Wilde who thought the Irish 'the greatest talkers since the Greeks' compared Yeats's 'art of story-telling to Homer's' (Yeats, *Auto*, 135). Yeats came away from a performance of an old-fashioned historical melodrama by Alice Milligan with his 'head on fire. I want to hear my own *On Baile's Strand*, to hear Greek tragedy spoken with a Dublin accent' (Yeats, *Auto*, 449). In Ireland, Joyce was surrounded by a cultural practice at the heart of which was correspondence with classical Greece. The very word 'correspondence', now connected explicitly with Joycean design, was at one time a revivalist term indicating something much more potent than simple parallelism. A new Irish Odysseus was on the agenda before Joyce wrote a word. Disputing Mallarmé's argument that modernity would make its medium the lyric, Yeats predicted that the Irish epic, modelled on Homer, would really put Irish culture on the map:

> I think that we will learn again how to describe at great length an old man wandering among an enchanted island, his return home at last, his slowly gathering vengeance, a flitting shape of a goddess, and a flight of arrows, and yet to make all these things so different ... become ... the signature or

---

[35] Ibid., 62.

[36] Ibid., 64.

[37] See George Moore in his introduction to Edward Martyn, *The Heather Field and Maeve* (London: Duckworth, 1909), xx.

symbol of a model of divine imagination.[38]

Edward Martyn, who had studied Greek, includes passages in both *The Heather Field* and *Maeve* which proclaim, just as Arnold did, a 'brotherhood' between the Greek and Celtic races. Maeve in the latter play asserts that the Greeks discovered an 'unreal beauty' which has its only parallel in Celtic culture.[39] In the 1890s, Florence Farr and Yeats tried to link Greek and Irish oral culture by a 'rediscovery' of how verse was spoken to music.[40] Certainly, in its rejection of the modern, of 'progress' and the consequent elevated transformation of what Murray would have called the 'primitive', the Literary Revival shifted the significance of terms of correspondence as they had emerged from Victorian England. In revivalist historiography, Homer is the poet not, as in Murray, of civic duty, but of the simple people; 'Homer's Phaeacians', the 'poor of heart' as AE puts it (9.109-10). But the Revival played essentially the same game as the Oxford professors. In its aristocratic defence of feudalism, its conceptions of nobility and service, and its attack on modernity, the Revival exposed its élitist and hegemonic roots. The ridiculous claims to be transforming modern Ireland into ancient Athens, like the English varieties of correspondence, were ideological and fundamentally conservative.

The Hellenist obsession of revivalist Ireland is reflected throughout *Ulysses* as a specific revivalist practice so that, for instance, 'the revival of ancient Gaelic sports' for 'the development of the race' is modelled on 'physical culture as it is understood in ancient Greece' (12.899-903). Hellenism also has its impact on someone as ordinary as Bloom. In the Circean vision of a rejuvenated Ireland, where Bloom develops a scheme for a programme of civic beautification that will edify the citizenry, revivalist Ireland is reproduced in cartoon-like terms:

> *The keeper of the Kildare museum appears, dragging a lorry on which are the shaking statues of several naked goddesses, Venus Callipyge, Venus Pandemos, Venus Metempsychosis, and plaster figures, also naked, representing the new nine muses, Commerce, Operatic Music, Amor, Publicity, Manufacture, Liberty of Speech, Plural Voting, Gastronomy,*

---

[38] Quoted in Ellmann, *Consciousness of Joyce*, 10-11.

[39] Martyn, *The Heather Field and Maeve*, 105-06.

[40] See Flannery, *Yeats and the Idea of a Theatre*, 196.

Private Hygiene, Seaside Concert Entertainments, Painless Obstetrics and Astronomy for the People.
(15.1703-10)

The comedy here works partly through the ironic counterpoint of Bloom's earnest desire for civic improvement and his equally earnest interest in representations of naked women. But this ironic contradiction is more than a simple joke at Bloom's expense. Bloom's attraction to statues of Greek goddesses caricatures the high status which Yeats and his allies gave to the culture of ancient Greece. Hellenization, here, is ruinously combined with a decidedly voyeuristic fascination, and, even more outrageously, it is disastrously conflated with the culture of middle-class modernity that Yeats so despised. In *Ulysses*, however, correspondence with the Greeks is much more than a matter of periodic allusiveness. It is famously constituted in the elaborate architectonic which the schema represent diagramatically. Hellenism is activated in a hugely exaggerated form, becoming a hilarious literalisation of revivalist attempts to synchronize with the first culture of Europe. It skips the Celts entirely, which is the first and most fundamental subversion. When classical epic is translated on the Joycean scale against modern culture as opposed to an idealized past, parallels necessarily become hopelessly strained. The result is that Hellenization suffers a wholesale ideological collapse through chronic over-exposure. *Ulysses* is an absolutely studied delivery of what the Revival claimed was the immanent reality of Irish culture. *Ulysses* announces itself as a thoroughly Hellenized Irish epic where everything corresponds. But the outcome is a farcical entanglement which is characteristically obscurantist, and distorted. Analogies are not just occasionally crooked. They are invariably so. The 'fit' between classical Greece and *Ulysses* has very little to do with deference, homage to the tradition or mythopoeia. In fact, in *Ulysses*, there is an absolute refusal to produce 'correspondence' in any way that is recognisably consistent with the ideology of English and Anglo-Irish traditions. There is almost an enmity between *Ulysses* and the prototype text(s). It is not just at the edges of Joyce's structure, where the Nurses in the hospital stand in so obscurely for 'Lampetie and Phaethusa' or Corley translates as 'Melanthius', that the issue of correspondence somehow becomes compromised. It is compromised from the very beginning, in the title of a book which is itself Romanized, and which establishes correspondence not in terms of consensual tradition, but in terms of cultural appropriation. In the very title of his great novel, Joyce repudiates the very idea of the cultural thoroughbred, and does so from the outset.

Stephen's discourse on the politics of culture, then, is hardly self-contained. It spreads into the architectonics of *Ulysses* and continues in the ridiculously appropriative Bloom/Odysseus parallel. Bloom is neither a Greek nor an Irish Celt, but an Irish Jew. He is neither aristocratic nor rural, but bourgeois to his boots and utterly urban. He does not heroically resist the temptations of women; on the contrary, he will go to great lengths for a glimpse of underwear. He is no displaced traveller, desperate for return, although he has taken a pleasure cruise round Dublin bay on a boat called 'Erin's King'. His 'Penelope' is simultaneously his Calypso and his home the 'prison' from which he 'escapes' at the start of the day. These and many other 'variants' are not simple instances of artistic license; they are far too embedded in the novel to be so. Distortion and discordance expose the obscurities, contradictions and absurdities that are inherent in conventional correspondence. It may be that Bloom embodies some standard of personal heroism held to by Joyce, but this would not be inconsistent with the point being made here, which is that, in every conceivable respect, Bloom is a deep affront to the aristocratic notions of heroism and heroic action that were fundamental to the Revival's version of correspondence with the Greeks.

Reading Bloom against the Revival's cult of aristocratic heroism, the subject of the next section of this study, is only one way of measuring the effect of literalisation. Reading Molly against the Revival's idealization of women, the subject of a later chapter, is another. The relationship between *Ulysses* and the Homeric event and Homeric geography is similarly incongruous. It, too, illustrates that, in Joyce, the architectonic practice, which Arnold saw as characteristic of 'true art' and 'great works, such as the *Agamemnon*'[41] is comprehensively subversive of conservative correspondent practices. Once again difference and distortion is not a resource drawn on when an otherwise smooth parallel proves to be limiting. It is characteristic. Events which are briefly referred to in the *Odyssey* become whole

---

[41] According to Arnold, 'the Celt has not patience for' this kind of art (Arnold, *On the Study of Celtic Literature*, 83).

episodes, like 'Wandering Rocks', in *Ulysses*. Identities shift, so that in 'Scylla and Charybdis', for instance, it is Stephen and not Bloom who steers a course between the rock and the whirlpool. The latter are completely removed from any geography in this episode, because Homer's Scylla and Charybdis in *Ulysses* are correspondent with Aristotle and Plato. Stephen and Bloom meet much earlier than Telemachus and Odysseus in the Homeric prototype and the former pair are not father and son. The displacement of the one-eyed monster blinded with a stake, by a drunken nationalist who is in proximity to Bloom's cigar is only the most famous example of a pattern of mismatch which is absolutely central in *Ulysses*.

Arnold denied that the Celt had any capacity for architectonic, in a passage which one suspects Joyce must have known. He also suggested that, unable to face 'the facts of human life', the Celtic poet 'runs off into technic' and 'sentimentality'. *Ulysses* is both an emphatic confirmation and a forceful refutation of this statement. It squares up to reality in obvious ways, and refuses sentimentality. But it does indeed deploy 'technics'. Ironically, technic is incorporated precisely into the design of *Ulysses*, into its architectonic. The use of technic is again made part of the practice of subversive correspondence. In 'Aeolus', for instance, the Homeric prototype produces a particularly accumulative linkage: the Aeolian 'bag of winds' translates into a barrage of rhetorical devices and a whole wind lexicon. There are phrases like 'what's in the wind' and 'raise the wind', the vocabulary includes 'breath', 'puff', 'draught', 'zephyrs', 'breeze', 'squalls', 'gale', 'whirlwind', 'hurricane', 'cyclone'; and a range of allusive words and phrases, like 'bladderbags', 'afflatus', 'breath', 'flatulence' and so on. There are similar lexicons in 'Ithaca', where the root is the idea of return, and in 'Sirens' where musical terminology corresponds to the sirens' song, and in 'Proteus' where the idea of change is linked to wordplay. These textual characteristics are 'subtle' only because they work. They are 'readable' as features of a text which is not just a list. As a conception, however, the process seems grotesque. The point is that they are no more grotesque than the importunate corresponding practices which they displace.

Literalization, exaggeration, distortion and over-determination: these, then, are the central characteristics of Joyce's art of correspondence and they are key in the following analysis of how the textuality of *Ulysses* confronts revivalist culture. There is a strong sense of Joyce outdoing his Anglo-Irish contemporaries with his ornate Homeric design, and also a liberating articulation of the absurdity of the practice of correspondence which was so dear to cultural nationalism. Hilarity, however, is the most obvious characteristic of Joyce's 'Celtic revenge', and this is quite distinct from the bitter splenetic of Stephen's 'voice of Esau'.

That this hostile interference with the cultural élitism of Anglo-Ireland constitutes a class position is clear from one further defining feature of the schema, which is its Aristotelian insistence on structure. Architectonics is about structure and form. Again, according to Arnold, the 'failure' of 'the Celtic race' to produce great painters or sculptors is an indication of how far the ill-disciplined Celtic mind is incapable of structuring.[42] Yeats turned this argument upside down by privileging a mystique of art where the Irish artist is an unconscious mediator between the divine and the earthly. Spontaneity and 'ill-discipline' have great status in the Yeatsian aesthetic. Joyce, however, takes up Arnold's challenge and produces obsessive structure, insistent order, the catalogue and the list. All these are signatures of a Catholic intellectual tradition which has its greatest philosophical exposition in 'The Angelic Doctor', who proved the existence of God in five ways, and who took as his own classical authority, ironically enough, Aristotle. The 'supersaturation' of the Joycean aesthetic in *these* cultural traditions constitutes correspondence of a different kind and with a very different cultural tradition.

Mr Leopold Bloom

As a character in a novel, Bloom has no great interest in the Anglo-Irish or in revivalism. Cultural dispossession, which drives Stephen, has little meaning for Bloom. He does think that revivalists are cranks and, in 'Lestrygonians', his mild curiosity about George Russell (AE) and Lizzie Twigg produces some delicious humour:

> A.E.: what does that mean? Initials perhaps. Albert Edward, Arthur Edmund, Alphonsus Eb Ed El Esquire. What was he saying? The ends of the world with a Scotch accent. Tentacles: octopus. Something occult: symbolism. Holding forth. She's taking it all in. Not saying a word. To aid gentleman in literary work.

---

[42] See Arnold, *On the Study of Celtic Literature*, 94-96.

His eyes followed the high figure in homespun, beard and bicycle, a listening woman at his side. Coming from the vegetarian. Only weggebobbles and fruit. Don't eat a beefsteak. If you do eyes of that cow will pursue you through eternity. They say its healthier. Windandwatery though. Tried it. Keep you on the run all day ....
Her stockings are loose over her ankles. I detest that: so tasteless. Those literary etherial people they are all. Dreamy, cloudy symbolistic. Esthetes they are. I wouldn't be surprised if it was that kind of food you see produces the like waves of the brain the poetical. For example one of those policeman sweating Irish stew into their shirts you couldn't squeeze a line of poetry out of him.

(8.528-547)

But, comic as this is, it is hardly amounts to cogent cultural criticism. This is revivalist mysticism and vegetarianism coming up against Bloom's bourgeois cultural values and his attempts at scientific rationalism. Elsewhere in 'Lestrygonians', Bloom's world does seem very much an Anglo-Irish construction. Anglo-Irish culture is highly profiled in this episode, with Bloom passing the *Irish Times* building ('best paper by long chalks for a small ad' — 8.334), the building which once housed Grattan's parliament and 'Trinity's surly front' (8.476). He recalls a political scuffle which featured Trinity students and quotes from Samuel Ferguson's poem 'The Burial of King Cormac'. There are many references to Anglo-Irish luminaries from various areas of social and professional life. Bloom passes the memorial to Sir Phillip Crampton, who was surgeon-general to the Armed Forces, and the statue of Sir Thomas Deane, the designer of the National Library and the National Museum who reconstituted 'the Greek architecture' (8.1181). He thinks admiringly of Sir Robert Ball and Professor Joly, both eminent astronomers. He passes the house of the Provost, the reverend Dr Salmon. Bloom wonders about and coincidentally sees Parnell's brother. He reads a placard publicising the Lord Lieutenant's opening of the Mirus bazaar, and he spots Sir Frederick Falkiner, who was the Dublin Recorder and the chairman of the board of the élite King's Hospital School. This concentration, unique in Bloom's perambulations, constructs a world in which the Anglo-Irish have extremely high status, but it elicits no serious political or social response from Bloom. The sayings and doings of the aristocracy as recorded in the 'toady' *Irish Field* does produce sarcasm, but Bloom's more engaged interest is in the horsey society ladies who ride 'astride', 'like a man' (8.343). For the most part, Bloom is deferential to this culture. He thinks Robert Ball's book 'fascinating' and would dearly like an 'introduction to professor Joly' (8.573). Even Falkiner, a notorious anti-Semite, is accepted by Bloom as a 'wellmeaning old man' (8.1156).[43]

Bloom is not consciously involved in the politics of culture, but he is entirely at the disposal of the textual praxis which delivers Joyce's 'Celtic revenge'. Commandeered into a collaboration with the subverting architectonic of *Ulysses*, Bloom is Joyce's ludicrous response to the historical distortions that produced such key texts as O'Grady's hugely influential histories of the Red Branch Cycle; Yeats's Cuchulain plays and Lady Gregory's *Gods and Fighting Men* and *Cuchulain of Muirthemne*. These characteristic revivalist texts operate in a hazy borderland between history, mythology and folk-lore, 'inflaming' the national imagination through the 'contemplation of ... mighty beings'[44] with no regard to historical accuracy. This reconstituted culture of heroism, created in heroic forms and thriving on gigantism and exaggeration, carries the 'ore' which O'Grady thought outclassed classical Greece. Its retrieval into contemporaneity was precisely the primary revivalist goal, and Bloom is the decisive intervention, striking, however unknowingly, at the very heart of the romanticism that produced Anglo-Ireland's cultural 'gigantism'. He is the 'hero' constructed in ironic correspondence to a culture of genuine hero-worship. The supreme 'bad fit', Bloom/Ulysses, the 'hero' of the new Irish epic, is the overdone embodiment of everything the Revival despised about a modernity which was understood as inimical to the national culture.

As I have suggested above, whereas English Hellenization reconstructed classical Greece as the birthplace of modern civilization, the Literary Revival identified with the imaginative vitality of the prototype epic. For revivalism, modernity had its origins, not in Athens, but in the English renaissance, and the process of modernization accelerated wildly in the late eighteenth century. In Yeatsian

---

[43] In June 1904, Falkiner used such 'unrestrained language' in the trial of a Jew, Henry Kahn, who had smashed a window, that questions were asked in the House of Commons.

[44] O'Grady, *History of Ireland*, iv.

historiography, the political revolution in France and the industrial explosion in England were decisive in the making of the modern age. These marked the true ascendancy of science, rationalism and materialism over spirituality, nobility and the imagination. The breach between poetry and modern life, which for Yeats became absolute,[45] was perfectly exemplified in historicist terms by the exercise of English imperialism over native Irish culture. From this standpoint, the defence of what was construed as Ireland's cultural authenticity took on all the dimensions of an evangelical crusade. In Yeats's extravagant, mystical terms, cultural nationalism became a battle for the spirit over matter, for light over dark. The issue of Ireland's political independence which had previously been articulated primarily in rationalist-legal terms was now being articulated in a new discourse of pseudo-mysticism, a discourse which was to surface over a vast range of literary productions of the period, from serious history writing to articles on dairy farming. Fundamental to this discourse was a familiar and virtually all-inclusive antithesis: science stood against art; knowledge against wisdom; materialism against spirituality; the middle class against the peasantry; vulgarity against nobility; capitalism against communitarianism; urban against rural; greed against generosity; innovation against tradition; reason against instinct. These oppositional formulations characterized revivalist writing. The complex relations between England and Ireland became reduced to an easy formula: the conflict between the degenerative new and the vitally creative old was nothing less than the eternal conflict between good and evil.

So reactionary in its defence of tradition and promotion of 'aristocratic' paternalism,[46] the Literary Revival was unyielding in its attacks on what it saw as the lifeless conformity of English middle-class urbanism. 'Education, newspapers, a thousand impersonalities' had 'filled the world with the imitation of what once was gold' (Yeats, *Mem*, 180). According to Yeats, 'the move of thought which has made

---

[45] See John Eglinton, *Anglo-Irish Essays* (Dublin: The Talbot Press, 1917), 42.

[46] See, for instance, Yeat's comment on Lady Gregory: 'She knew Ireland always in its permanent relationships, associations — violence but a brief interruption —, never lost her sense of feudal responsibility, not of duty as the word is generally understood, but of burdens laid upon her by her station and character, a choice constantly renewed in solitude' (Yeats, *Auto*, 395).

the good citizen, or has been made by him, has surrounded us with comfort and safety, and with vulgarity and insincerity'.[47] England and the empire, 'praised in contemporary English literature', was 'the masterwork and dream of the middle class'.[48] Even more than literature, science was presented as the critical supporting ideology of bourgeois cultural imperialism. For Yeats the 'man of science' had 'exchanged his soul for a formula' (Yeats, *UP1*, 174).

Bloom has been famously constructed in Joyce criticism as the outsider, the deracinated Jew on the margins of Dublin society. But in many respects he is entirely representative, the epitome of a modern world which had swamped the heroic Gael of revivalism. His interest in science, particularly applied science, is indicative of how far he embodies the revivalist nightmare. He is curious about the natural world: about why mice never squeal when attacked by cats; about cat vision; about the functions of cats' whiskers; about how chloroform works; whether it is true that emissions from the gasworks cure whooping cough. He does his best to deploy scientific explanations of the world: 'Black conducts, reflects (refracts is it?) the heat' (4.79-80). His struggle to remember scientific laws like the gravitational 'law of falling bodies', is fairly typical of his flawed understanding, which is largely a product of coffee-table science and encyclopaedia knowledge. He uses science constantly in his everyday reading of the world, pondering the horticultural virtues of an application of 'a coat of liver sulphur' to his garden (4.477); wondering whether moisture in the air produces 'long sight' (5.112); asserting at stool that a 'too big' turd is likely to bring on piles again' (4.509-10); estimating the rate at which a cut corpse would bleed; thinking about what causes luminosity and why 'salt water fish are not salty' (8.86); and wondering whether the blind can somehow sense volume. He ponders scientific solutions to everyday questions, how one could automatize tramcars, for example. In most respects, he is a determined materialist, asserting, for instance, that the heart, so-called 'seat of the affections', is just 'a pump, 'pumping thousands of gallons of blood every day' (6.674). He deploys the language of science, as in these thoughts about x-rays, although the 'technical' is invariably mixed up with metaphor, analogy and homely idiom:

---

[47] W. B. Yeats in Gregory, ed., *Ideals in Ireland*, 98.

[48] Ibid., 90.

They could: and watch it all the way down, swallow a pin sometimes come out of the ribs years after, tour round the body, changing biliary duct spleen squirting liver gastric juice coils of intestines like pipes.

(8.1045-48)

These are just a few examples of one of Bloom's centrally defining characteristics of Bloom. The sheer weight of associations between Bloom and science are matched probably only by the volume of observations concerning sex and what could loosely be called 'economics'. Both, of course, are central in establishing his subversive function in relation to romantic revivalism. His interest in all things commercial likewise places him within that network of forces that make up the revivalist anti-world. He admires his father-in-law's hard bargaining, and the latter's foresight in establishing 'that corner in stamps' (4.64-65). He judges businesses according to the commercial value of the location of their premises, contemplates the effect of new tramlines on land values, and knows all about rateable value. He speculates on how much fiddling goes on in the drinks trade and marvels at 'the money to be made out of porter' (5.305-06). He has a suitably professional interest in advertisements, and is always inventing advertising ploys, like the scheme for publicising a stationer's: 'a transparent showcart with two smart girls sitting inside writing letters, copybooks, envelopes, blottingpaper' (8.133-35). He thinks in advertising slogans and asserts that Catholic priests are 'not straight men of business' (5.384). He considers the effect of new technology on employment patterns and has a plan for a new corporation tramway from the 'parkgate to the quays' (6.401). He knows the virtue of insurance and is always saddened at economic waste. Coffins, for instance, are 'a waste of wood' (6.816). Evangelism can be 'a paying game' (8.17), particularly with its spin-offs, like luminous crucifixes. He has schemes for social justice and economic regeneration: 'They could easily have big establishments whole thing quite painless out of all taxes give every child born five quid at compound interest up to twentyone five percent is a hundred shillings' (8.382-88). Bloom is a commentator on the international trading scene, too, remarking, for example, on the undercutting practices of the Germans. In 'Nausicaa', sex and economics converge, as Bloom wonders if Boylan pays Molly for sex: 'Why not? All a prejudice. She's worth ten, fifteen, more a pound. What? I think so. All that for nothing' (13.842-43).

Social eugenics was endemic to Literary Revivalism, where Synge argued that the Irish peasantry seem 'to approach more nearly to the finer types of our aristocracy — who are bred artificially to a national ideal — than to the labourer or citizen, as the wild horse resembles the thoroughbred rather than the hack or the carthorse'.[49] The Irish middle class — 'the half-cultured classes' — were regarded as plastic hybrids, characterized by their 'rampant, double-chinned vulgarity'.[50] For Yeats, the progress of the bourgeoisie was wrecking the virility and nobility of Irish culture:

> In spite of myself my mind dwells more and more on ideas of class. Ireland has grown sterile, because power has passed to men who lack the training which requires a certain amount of wealth to ensure continuity from generation to generation, and to free the mind in part from other tasks. A gentleman is for one thing a man whose principal ideas are not connected with his personal needs and personal successes.
>
> (Yeats, *Mem*, 116)

Joyce's Hellenized/Hebraised hero, who is forever concerned with his 'personal needs and successes', is precisely of this class: definitively commercial, incorrigibly materialistic, and thoroughly respectable.

Joyce does not challenge this classist and conservative view of modernity with any unequivocal elevation of the middle class through Bloom. Bloom is no more or better than he appears to be. Some critics have attempted to dignify him as the confused embodiment of political radicalism,[51] or of humanistic moral vision,[52] but he is notoriously resistant to any imposition of such gravitas. He might occasionally toy with diluted, popular versions of Marxist or anarchist ideas, but this interest, like the interest in science, is no more than a sign of his exposure to modern culture. More importantly, there is in Bloom an

---

[49] Synge, *Collected Works,* II, 66. See below chapter 7, for a further discussion of eugenics and revivalism.

[50] Ibid., 283.

[51] See, for instance, Colin McCabe, *James Joyce and the Revolution of the Word.*

[52] See Peake, *Citizen and the Artist,* for an elegant and informed version of this approach.

intelligent 'heterodoxy'. This is most obvious in the early Bloom episodes, in his penetration of the 'cruelty' behind reality in 'Calypso',[53] in his understanding of the ideological hold which the rituals of Catholicism exercise in 'Lotus-Eaters', and in his refusal to countenance a maudlin sentimentalization of death in 'Hades'. Bloom clearly is established as an unorthodox burgher. As such, he embodies a direct challenge to the revivalist stereotype of the middle class, but it is impossible to identify anything approaching a consistent politics in Bloom, or any real evidence of political commitment. In 1888, it is true, he climbed a tree 'in support of his political convictions' (17.1651-52) to get a good view of the visiting liberals, John Morley and the Marquess of Ripon. Besides following his 'convictions', Bloom might have had a special interest in the Marquess, who, before his conversion to Catholicism in 1874, had been the Grand Master of the Freemasons of England. In 1890, not long before Parnell's death, Bloom was involved with the Parnellites who smashed up the typecases of *United Ireland*, and enjoyed the distinction of handing Parnell his hat back when it was knocked off. At one time, too, when he was inadvertently caught up in a protest against the award of a degree to Joseph Chamberlain and had a narrow escape from a mounted policeman. There is an unlikely rumour that Bloom gave Arthur Griffith the idea for basing Ireland's 'resurrection' on the Hungarian model, and a more likely one that he dispensed with his political principles sufficiently to earn a few shillings selling coupons for 'the royal and privileged Hungarian lottery'. But if political commitment is measured by action, then Bloom's credentials are, to put it mildly, not very convincing.

The long tradition of associating Bloom with a liberal humanist outlook is likewise difficult to sustain in a text which itself laughs at the flimsiness of Bloom's status, in this respect, mocking his 'kindness to animals', for instance. Bloom's responses to women are sometimes taken as an indication of his essential good nature. But for all his sensitivity to Mina Purefoy's birthpangs, Bloom is actually decidedly

---

[53] There is an extreme bloodiness behind the respectable middle-class world of 'Calypso', primarily associated with eating and cooking. Note, for instance, the violent relish of Bloom for his breakfast: 'he shore away the burnt flesh and flung it to the cat. Then he put a forkful into his mouth, chewing with discernment the toothsome pliant meat' (4.389-92). Bloom participates in this world, but is sensitized to its ugliness — thus the significance of his comment, 'Cruelty behind it all' (4.349).

illiberal in his attitudes to the opposite sex. He persuades himself that women enjoy his exhibitionism, for example, and are themselves full participants in his 'attentions':

> Women enjoy it. Never tell you. But we. Excuse, miss, there's a (whh!) just a (whh!) fluff. Or their skirt behind, placket unhooked. Glimpses of the moon. Annoyed if you don't. Why didn't you tell me before.
>
> (5.453-56)

The barmaids in 'Sirens' are vulgarly characterized by Bloom according to what he imagines to be their levels of sexual experience: 'Got up to kill: on eighteenbob a week .... Blank face. Virgin or fingered only. Write something on it: page. If not what becomes of them. Decline, despair. Keeps them young' (11.1076/1086-87). Sex is about all these young women have going for them and they become, for Bloom, quite literally, sex objects: 'Body of white woman, a flute alive. Blow gentle. Loud. Three holes, all women' (11.1006-09). The initial thoughts on Gerty McDowell in 'Nausicaa', when Bloom realizes that she is lame, are even more disturbing:

> Thought something was wrong by the cut of her jib. Jilted beauty. A defect is ten times worse in a woman. But makes them polite. Glad I didn't know it when she was on show. Hot little devil all the same. I wouldn't mind. Curiosity like a nun or a negress or a girl with glasses .... Near her monthlies, I expect, makes them feel ticklish.
>
> (13.774-79)

From the machismo of the nautical image, through the sick joke about 'jilted beauty' to the appalling idea that disablement has the virtue of making women polite, these extraordinary remarks are hardly consistent with the idea that Bloom constitutes some sort of moral yardstick. Here he manages to combine sexism, racism and deep offence to the disabled, virtually all in one breath. Of course, this is not the public Bloom — a Bloom who is, in public, a gentleman to his socks, would never dream of giving offence. But it is Bloom all the same and possibly has greater provenance precisely because it does represent one aspect of his private world.

Indeed in some respects, perhaps most, Joyce's Bloom confirms the Revival's despair at the vulgarity of the bourgeoisie, except for the vital distinction that Joyce's reproduction of bourgeois life is entirely undespairing. Joyce gets intimate with the modern middle class so vilified by cultural nationalists as anti-life, anti-art, and ultimately anti-God. If cultural nationalism was in pious retreat, Joyce is in indecent engagement. He positively revels in his reconstruction of the urban bourgeoisie and the material world. One result of this closeness is that the elevated and precious Revivalist conception of the bourgeoisie as the modern enemy crumbles. For what Yeats and his followers described from a refined distance as a demonic corruption of the spirit is transformed at close quarters into something very much smaller, very much more human and, above all, laughable. The real radicalism of Bloom, then, is not in what he says, or thinks or does, but in the astonishing audacity that places this deeply flawed and essentially comic figure at the centre of the Irish super-epic. He is not simply the antithesis of the 'authentic' Irish hero, but the precise embodiment of the forces which, for the Irish Revival, were destroying Irish culture.

I would stress the point that there is a level of *Ulysses* where Bloom's subversive cultural significance is quite irrelevant. For Bloom himself, the critical encounters are not with revivalist culture, but with the rude Menton; the insensitive Mr Powers; the cuckolding Boylan; the anti-Semitic citizen and of course with Stephen and Molly. However, with the extraordinary textual contortions which develop from 'Sirens' onwards, it is precisely Bloom's self-perception which is undermined. This emphatic eclipse where Bloom's voice is so diminished under the gigantism of 'Cyclops' or the wild theatricality of 'Circe' or the scientism of 'Ithaca', is not a simple matter of challenging or exposing Bloom's limitations, but rather a fundamental shift in terms of the literary strategics of Joyce's book. In the end the centrality of this shift to the experience of reading *Ulysses* is why Bloom-centred readings of the book, which still persist, although now at the edges of Joyce criticism, must fail. The pyrotechnics of 'Oxen' or the 147 pages of 'Circe' cannot seriously be accounted for in terms of 'what happens to Stephen and Bloom'. These later episodes are so important in modern literary culture, not because they somehow, in spite of all the narrative disruption, manage to satisfy an appetite for traditional narrative development and closure, but because they define and displace traditionalist narrative. The contextualisation of this radical aesthetics in the nationalist culture of Ireland is the subject of the chapters that follow.

4 Revivalism in Popular Culture: 'Sirens' and 'Cyclops'

Whilst revisionist historians have tended to marginalize end-of-the-century revivalism as the work of a cranky élite, modern Irish cultural studies have elevated this period of revivalist history to a position of outstanding significance. Declan Kiberd, for instance, understands 'Yeats's generation' as an agency which was somehow fated to transform the idea of nation into a fact of materiality:

> That enterprise achieved nothing less than a renovation of Irish consciousness and a new understanding of politics, economics, philosophy, sport, language and culture in its widest sense. It was the grand destiny of Yeats's generation to make Ireland once again interesting to the Irish, after centuries of enforced provincialism following the collapse of the Gaelic order in 1601. No generation before or since lived with such conscious national intensity or left such an inspiring (and, in some ways, intimidating) legacy. Though they could be fractious, its members set themselves the highest standards of imaginative integrity and personal generosity. Imbued with republican and democratic ideals, they committed themselves in no spirit of chauvinism, but in the conviction that the Irish *risorgimento* might expand the expressive freedoms of all individuals: *that* is the link between thinkers as disparate as Douglas Hyde and James Connolly, Hanna Sheehy-Skeffington and James Joyce.[1]

The argument here is, of course, highly controversial. Whilst it is certain that revivalism had a great impact on 'economics, sport, language and culture', the idea that this amounted to a renovation of 'Irish consciousness', creating a cultural and political watershed, is disputable. For many historians this period is one of political continuities rather than political transformation. The suggestion that the revivalist achievement was to 'make Ireland once again interesting' is arguably self-defeating. At a time when Government estimates conservatively identified over 27,000 Dubliners living in houses unfit for human inhabitation, it might reasonably be asked whether the business of making Ireland 'interesting' constituted a

---

[1] Declan Kiberd, *Inventing Ireland* (London: Jonathan Cape, 1995), 3.

destiny as grand as Kiberd suggests. Above all, however, it is the assertion of a single continuous tradition of revivalism, Kiberd's 'Irish *risorgimento*', that is problematic. Kiberd's list of disparate yet representative thinkers might at least have included the architect of late nineteenth and early twentieth-century revivalism. But, of course, it is not easy to identify Yeats, to say nothing of Lady Gregory and Synge, with the democratic idealism of Connolly. Indeed, this attempt to represent a syncretic culture of nationalism, marred only by a degree of fractiousness amongst an otherwise rosy 'generosity', replicates the conservative ideology of the Literary Revival. The image of a creative outburst of national cultural energy obscures the stark social and cultural divisions which revivalism reproduced and refuses to read the real insecurity of a figure like Standish O'Grady, regarded by Yeats as the father of the Literary Revival, and who in 1881 was signing himself as 'the Late Honorary Secretary of Landlords Meeting in the Rotunda'. For O'Grady, the 1880s were not signalling cultural renovation but a disastrous collapse of the old social order — and the problem was neither Anglicization nor provincialism. 'The political and social horizon today in Ireland', he wrote, 'is, at least for one class, and for the friends and sympathizers of that class, overcast and gloomy in the extreme'. O'Grady sees a storm approaching which will wreck 'the little fleet in which are embarked the persons and fortune of the Irish landlords', and the storm is 'Irish democracy', a storm whipped up by the threats of socialism and 'the two deadly enemies', 'the Land League and the Land Act'.[2]

Kiberd ignores here the Revival's origin in the Protestant hierarchy and the deep conservatism of the social and political agendas embedded in both Protestant and Catholic Celticism. His ingenuous conflation of nationalism, republicanism and democracy suggests that Irish nationalism was specifically defined by libertarianism, whereas the new dynamic of nationalism in Ireland, as in all European countries in this period, was its assimilation by the political right. This identification of nationalism as a changeable, adapting ideology is perhaps the central point of Eric Hobsbawm's compelling account of modern nationalism. Hobsbawm shows how,

---

[2] Standish O'Grady, *The Crisis in Ireland* (Dublin: E. Ponsonby, 1882), 3-5.

in the earlier part of the nineteenth century, nationalism developed as a cornerstone of bourgeois liberalism. Indeed Walter Bagehot, one of the most influential political theorists of nineteenth-century England, regarded the nation state as *the* liberal achievement of the Western bourgeoisie. Nationalism was the eminent example of progress historiography and as such was underwritten by all the authority of Darwinist science. Nation making, in Bagehot's account, was 'the essential content of nineteenth-century evolution'.[3] For Bagehot, the formation of the nineteenth-century liberal nation marked the progress of humanity. During the latter part of the nineteenth century, however, conservatism begins to colonize this powerful ideology in new ways. The period 1870-1914 is characterized by a transmutation of nationalism. The right of national self-determination, formally the mainspring of liberalism, now becomes the foundation of the conservative familial/tribal nation. It is specifically in this late period that 'ethnic-linguistic criteria for defining a nation become dominant',[4] as opposed to the political and legalistic criterion of the earlier period. It is hardly coincidental that this is the era of Social Darwinism, the period when 'race' is established as 'the central social science'.[5] When, in 'Cyclops', the citizen attacks Jews as 'nice things …. coming over to Ireland filling the country with bugs' and contaminating 'our shores' (12.1141-42/1672), the identification is not between Ireland, or nationalism as such,[6] and bigotry, but between bigotry and very precise *forms* of nationalism which are culturally and historically located by Joyce.

Eugenics is perhaps at the margins of the new populist nationalisms in this pre-war period, but broad conservatism is at their centre. Again, according to Hobsbawm, all versions of nationalism in the fifty years before 1914 had in common:

---

[3] E. J. Hobsbawm, *Nations and Nationalism since 1780* (Cambridge: Cambridge University Press, 1990), 23.

[4] Ibid., 102.

[5] Ibid., 108.

[6] A central point of Hobsbawm's study is that there is no nationalism *per se*, but rather varied and competing ideologies which adopt a nationalist identification.

a rejection of the new proletarian socialist movements, not only because they were proletarian but also because they were, consciously or militantly internationalist, or at the very least non-nationalist.[7]

Declan Kiberd, who seems to forget that Connolly's attempt to unify socialist and nationalist ideology actually failed, detaches Ireland from the context in which nationalism is essentially the response of 'traditional' groups threatened by modernity, and would presumably invest the Gaelic League, the Gaelic Athletic Association and the Literary Revival with all the radical values of a very much earlier 'age of revolution'. His position in this respect is an idealistic one. Indeed, the apparently offhand allusion to nineteenth-century Italian nationalism is actually a linkage to a specific romantic historiography. 'Risorgimento' is an ideology which understands the unification of Italy not, as Gramsci would have it, as a complex product of 'contradictory historical development', and of the 'pre-eminent' role of European power politics,[8] but as the spiritual destiny of Italian nationhood. According to Luigi Salvatorelli, a moderate idealist in Italian historiography:

> From Bettinelli to Carducci, from Alfieri to Gioberti, from the Jacobin patriots to Santarosa, from Mazzini to Cavour, all — whether they used the specific term, or expressed the concept in other words — understood by Risorgimento of Italy, a fact, or better a process, of a spiritual character, an intimate and thorough transformation of national life, an affirmation of collective and individual autonomy. Of course, the name had first an exclusively or primarily literary and cultural significance and later assumed also a political and territorial significance. Italy and Risorgimento have both been understood, over the centuries, as before all else facts of consciousness, as spiritual attitudes.[9]

---

[7] Hobsbawm, *Nations and Nationalism*, 123.

[8] A. Gramsci, *Opere*, Vol. 4, *Il Risorgimento* (Turin: Turin Press, 1949), 108, quoted in A. W. Salomone, 'The *Risorgimento* between Ideology and History: the Political Myth of *rivoluzione mancata*', *American Historical Review*, 1962, 47.

[9] L. Salvatorelli, Pensiero e Azione del Risorgimento (Turin: Turin Press, 1943), quoted in Derek Beales, *The Risorgimento and the Unification of Italy* (Harlow: Longman, 1981), 15-16.

One of the central issues glossed here, as in Kiberd's account, is the question of *how* the literary culture produced by an intelligentsia effected something so dramatic as a change in the consciousness of the people, and how *this* produced radical political change. In the case of Ireland, revivalism was produced by an élite. The Literary Revival did belong to a long revivalist tradition and had the backing of powerful academic institutions. It was also publicized with great skill and energy. Anglo-Irish academics and artists in nineteenth-century Ireland had a considerable effect on the cultural process of what Kiberd calls 'inventing Ireland'. But all this taken together does not demonstrate a transformation of the 'national consciousness'. Nor does it illuminate the mysterious mechanisms of conversion which, as the rhetoric of revivalism itself has it, transformed the colonized into a free people. In post-Treaty rhetoric, cultural 'authenticity', the displacement of hybridity by the organic article, was the national destiny, an inexorable and natural expression of the communal will. Kiberd, of course, has a more measured view, but this recent postcolonial account of links between 'high art and popular expression'[10] does seem supported by the notion that the transformation of revivalism into popular culture was somehow inevitable. In this respect, Kiberd continues a long and influential tradition which reads revivalism as a force of nature which just cascaded down to the community.

Joyce's representation of cultural nationalism and the process of cultural transmission is very different. Far from transforming a bastardized modernity into a vital, indigenous and libertarian authenticity, revivalism is itself exposed as Anglicized, élitist and conservative in its agenda. It is also robbed of its transformative power. In the Joyce configuration, cultural nationalism does not suddenly sweep away the alien in an epic thrust of cultural cleansing. On the contrary, Celticism remains at the borders of modern, urban, homogenizing forces. Indeed, it is compelled to merge with modern urban culture. The 'new' cultural nationalism thus has an uneasy and, at times, thoroughly contradictory coexistence with a popular culture which retains strong Anglicized, Victorian, and bourgeois flavours. In this respect, as in so many others, *Ulysses* is a comic demystification

---

[10] Kiberd, *Inventing Ireland*, 3.

of revivalist pieties.

The process of cultural transmission is most famously produced in three contiguous chapters: 'Sirens', 'Cyclops' and 'Nausicaa'.[11] With their respective 'parodic-travestying'[12] of musical culture, political culture and the early twentieth-century equivalent to 'fanzine' culture, these episodes do not, as some recent readings imply, simply reproduce the sound of popular culture. Their exaggerating, ironic and often mocking parodies are analytical. The 'polyphonies' so characteristic of these episodes are interventions that produce thoroughly disharmonic cultural relationships rather than realist reflections. In the case of 'Sirens' and, particularly, 'Cyclops', revivalism is a dominant cultural strand that struggles to accommodate its own internal contradictions and is forced to articulate with the very cultural forces that it was designed to displace.

A 'flood of warm jamjam lickitup secretness': music in 'Sirens'
Cultural nationalism is central to the musicality of 'Sirens'. The first rhythm of the episode is the sound of the 'hoofirons' of the viceregal cavalcade 'steelringing', reproduced as the imperial reverberation 'Imperthnthn thnthnthn'. The last rhythm is derived from Emmet's speech from the dock, famously punctuated by Bloom's fart. In between is a 'rendition' of 'The Croppy Boy'—'our native Doric'— and many allusions to nationalist songs, or to songs which evoke nationalism, like 'The Memory of the Dead', 'Tis the Last Rose of Summer', 'The Boys of Wexford' and so on. This emphatic connection between music and the national culture is hardly surprising. According to Joseph J. Ryan, nationalism has been 'the crucial determinant on the course of music in Ireland in the past two centuries'.[13] Harry White has recently charted how 'the *idea*' of Irish

---

[11] The magazine culture behind 'Nausicaa' is English, rather than revivalist. However, 'Nausicaa' does draw on revivalist symbolism and this is discussed below in chapter 7.

[12] This influential term is Bahktin's. Bahktin's work has been particularly influential on recent readings of these episodes.

[13] Joseph J. Ryan, 'Nationalism and Irish Music', hereafter Ryan, in Gerald Gillen and Harry White, eds, *Irish Musical Studies, Vol. III: Music in Irish Cultural History* (Dublin: Irish Academy Press, 1995), 102.

music became a powerful 'symbol of cultural and then political aspiration'.[14] Davis's famous remark that 'Music is the first faculty of the Irish', invents music as a principal vehicle for national idealism and is derived precisely from a conviction about the power of music to transform the people into a nation:

> The use of this faculty and this power, publicly and constantly, to keep up their spirits, refine their tastes, warm their courage, increase their union and renew their zeal is the first duty of every patriot.'[15]

Like the revival of Irish language and literature, revivalist music had its origins in antiquarianism and was emphatically under the ownership of Ascendancy institutions. George Petrie, who had worked with O'Donovan and Curry on the Ordinance Survey of Ireland, was, along with Edward Bunting and P. W. Joyce, a central figure in the collection and notation of traditional Irish music. In 1851 he founded the Society for the Preservation and Publication of the Melodies of Ireland, which issued his first edition of *The Ancient Music of Ireland* in 1855. This expensive quarto volume, with border designs in gold, was sponsored by a group which included the Marquess of Kildare, the Earl of Dunraven, Eugene O'Curry, Lord Talbot de Malahide, Benjamin Lee Guinness and Ferguson. The idea was nationalist from the beginning: to preserve 'the genius and expression of our Music ... for the admiration of future ages, and the perpetual pride of the Irish race'.[16] Petrie firmly equated Irish music with Gaelic culture, at least rhetorically. But this collection was closely related to English antiquarian work in the same field, a mirror image of William Chappell's collecting of English folk songs, for instance. In fact, there was a direct dynamic between English and Anglo-Irish antiquarians with Chappell disputing the Irish provenance

---

[14] Harry White, 'Music and the Irish Literary Imagination', in Gillen and White, *Irish Musical Studies*, 213.

[15] Thomas Davis, preface to *The Spirit of the Nation* (Dublin: 1845). See also Davis's 'Essay on Irish Songs', in M. J. Barry, ed., *The Songs of Ireland* (Dublin: James Duffy, 1869).

[16] Quoted in Grace J. Calder, *George Petrie and the Ancient Music of Ireland* (Dublin: the Dolmen Press, 1968), 17.

of tunes such as 'The Lodging is on the Cold Ground', 'The Girl I Left Behind Me' and 'The Cruiskeen Lawn', claiming these as English.[17] Like Anglo-Ireland's reproduction of Gaelic literature, Petrie's method of preserving native musical culture involved deeply Anglicized and Anglicizing practices. Improvisation, so fundamental to folk music, was specifically dismissed and replaced by a notation which many have found anodyne. Significantly, Petrie's arrangements were produced, not for traditional instrumentation, but for the instrument of the Victorian parlour, the pianoforte. In these senses, cultural preservation was actually cultural transformation. Above all, the processes of Anglicization and embourgeoisment were embedded in the new texts of nationalism which replaced the lyrics of Irish folk traditions.

The traditional lyrics of Irish folk music were almost universally disparaged by cultural nationalists. These were thought to be 'coarse', 'clannish in opinion', 'bitter and sectarian' in religious terms, and, politically 'Jacobite and concealed by extravagant and tiresome allegory'.[18] One might add that many of these folk songs, and particularly the street ballads that Davis scorned as bombastic, slanderous, coarse and 'united in all cases with false rhythm, false rhyme and conceited imagery'[19] identified not the State but the landlord as the political adversary.[20] Anglo-Ireland, as Seamus Deane explains, colonized 'the old Irish music' and set it to 'new English lyrics', with the assumption that 'the native spirit would hibernicize the English language rather than be Anglicized by it'. Moore's *Irish Melodies* 'provided nationalist sentiment with a degree of

---

[17] See William Chappell, *The Ballad Literature and Popular Music of the Olden Time* with a new introduction by F. W. Sternfield, II (New York: Dover Publications, 1965 edn), II, 529, 708-09, 770.

[18] Thomas Davis in Barry, *Songs of Ireland*, 37-38.

[19] Ibid., 40.

[20] George-Denis Zimmermann, *Irish Political Street Ballads and Rebel Songs 1780-1900* (Geneva: Imprimerie la Sirine, 1966), 60. Zimmerman points out that 'apart from the names of a few heroes, there is hardly any reference to ancient Irish myths and legends in the broadside ballads of the peasantry' (33). This also helps to distinguish between traditional culture and the Anglo-Irish reworking.

respectability that was guaranteed by the possession of a drawing room and a pianoforte' and *The Nation's* poets 'used many old Irish airs and some of their own making to further the militant tradition of rebellion against the English'.[21] These two traditions are often seen as distinct, but there was, in fact, considerable overlapping. M. J. Barry's *The Songs of Ireland* (1869), which has an introduction by Davis, is a clear example of how the martial tone of Young Ireland could be reconciled in popular culture with the sentiment of Moore between the covers of a single book. The authorship of the lyrics in *The Songs of Ireland* is also suggestive of the essentially Anglo-Irish nature of the two traditions. The contributors to Barry's collection include Moore, of course, but also Davis himself and John Philpot Curran, Gerald Griffin, Charles Gavan Duffy and Lady Morgan.

In 'Sirens' these Anglo-Irish traditions and processes are clearly alluded to. Tom Kernan's description of 'The Croppy Boy' as 'our native Doric', for instance, is highly problematic.[22] The lyric, which was not written until 1845, is hardly native or Doric. In fact, the provenance of the tune is obscure. Shakespeare uses the melody, called '*Calino casturame*', in *Henry V*, and although P. W. Joyce included the tune in his *Songs of Irish Rebellion*, so did William Chappell in *Old English Popular Music*'. 'The Last Rose of Summer', a song which echoes through 'Sirens', is similarly representative of cultural hybridity and Anglicizing processes. This melody, which Thornton identifies as 'Moore's song',[23] was actually traditional. The earliest recorded form is from the seventeenth century, when the song

---

[21] Seamus Deane, Introduction to 'Poetry and Song 1800-1890', *The Field day Anthology of Irish Writing* (Derry: Field Day, 1991), II, 4-5.

[22] Tom Kernan is famously Protestant. His eager identification of 'Our native Doric' is arguably an example of how far symbols of national heritage function to conceal rather than expose underlying ideological divisions. Joseph Ryan is useful in this respect: 'A percipient observer might conclude that the republicans' enduring celebration of Theobald Wolfe Tone, a Northern Presbyterian and leader of the United Irishman whose agitation provoked the Act of Union, is as much inspired by the necessity to conceal the underlying divisions within the island's community as it is a parading of a convenient totem to a united nationalist ideal' (Ryan, in Gillen and White, *Irish Musical Studies*, 114).

[23] Thornton, *Allusions in Ulysses*, 240.

was called 'Eamonn an Chnuic' (Edmund of the Hill). In his *Irish Melodies*, Moore used two modifications of this tune to produce 'As a beam o'er of the waters may glow' and 'The Last Rose of Summer'. The latter was incorporated by von Flotow into his opera *Martha*, which, according to Hector Berlioz, had the effect of 'disinfecting the whole work'.[24] This last importation suggests another distortion of the integrity of music's status as a symbol of renascent culture: the integration of 'national' music into popular light operas, like Balfe's *The Bohemian Girl* (1843), Benedict's *The Lily of Killarney* (1862) and Wallace's *Maritana* (1845). These operas formed the staple of bourgeois Dublin's musical diet.

Whilst Davis called for national songs which would 'bring home Love, Courage and Patriotism to every heart'[25] (and the statement is suggestive of the three main songs sung in the Ormond Hotel, 'M'appari', 'Love and War' and 'The Croppy Boy'), Joyce reconstructs a much less indigenous musical culture in 'Sirens'. Ben Dollard may transmute into a thoroughbred patriot as 'Dollard the croppy' (11.1074), but the style of singing in 'Sirens', the instrumentation, and the eclectic assimilation produces a musical environment which is not too far removed 'from what one would find in any English provincial town'.[26] Far from providing the resource which Hyde cherished as 'our most valuable and most characteristic expression',[27] the symbol *par excellence* of the national culture, music in 'Sirens' is deeply hybridized and much more characteristically Edwardian than Celtic-Irish.

The real engagement of 'Sirens', however, is not derived from musical classification but from the revivalist conception of the metaphorical properties of music. Certainly Joyce does challenge the authenticity of the revivalist transformation of an ethnic folk music.

---

[24] Further details about these and other songs referred to in *Ulysses* 11 can be found in Bauerle, *The James Joyce Songbook*, 352-415.

[25] Thomas Davis in Barry, *The Songs of Ireland*, 47.

[26] Ryan in Gillen and White, *Irish Musical Studies*, 107. Ryan is not writing here of the representation of music in 'Sirens', but about Irish musical culture generally.

[27] Douglas Hyde quoted and discussed by White in Gillen and White, *Irish Musical Studies*, 219.

He also lays bare a process of acculturation that assimilates the 'native' repertory into popular parlour ballad and light opera. But the more pervasive subversion is of the idea that music is a vehicle for cultural and political aspirations. In part this subversion is produced by Bloom's cold, materialist insistence that music is just sound, 'vibrations' and mathematics, or 'musemathematics' as he puts it. However enraptured Bloom becomes by performance, he always returns to the basic and the physical. His remembrance of an orchestral evening includes the memory of the 'other brass chap unscrewing, emptying spittle' (11.577). More fundamental and much more wicked is the displacement of the idea that song is a repository of the national soul by the emphatic association made between music and sexuality everywhere in this chapter. It is perhaps not usually recognized as such, but 'Sirens', the most musical chapter of *Ulysses*, has a reasonable claim to being the novel's most erotic chapter. This is the sensuous episode of revealed garters, exposed thighs, wet lips and wet underwear. The episode is full of innuendo (is Molly Irish? 'Buccinator muscle is ....What?' — 11.512). It is the chapter in which Boylan's erection is a recurring leitmotif:

> One rapped on a door, one tapped with a knock, did he knock Paul de Kock with a loud proud knocker with a cock carracarracarra cock. Cockcock.
>
> (11.986-88)

The narrative continually slips and slides into a sexual prose, so that the welling 'tenderness' of Simon Dedalus's voice becomes: 'slow, swelling, full it throbbed. That's the chat. Ha, give! Take! Throb, a throb, a pulsing proud erect .... Flood of warm jamjam lickitup secretness flowed to flow in music out, in desire, dark to lick flow invading' (11.705-09). Bloom's unwitting insult which closes this chapter, his fart over Emmet's last words from the dock, is a minor transgression against the national gods compared to the text's audacious violation of another national treasure, 'The Croppy Boy'. It is the emotional aftershocks of a rendition of this song which produces that most remarkable style of pulling a pint:

> On the smooth jutting beerpull laid Lydia hand, lightly, plumply, leave it to my hands. All lost in pity for croppy. Fro, to: to, fro: over the polished knob (she knows his eyes, my eyes, her eyes) her thumb and finger passed in pity: passed, reposed and, gently touching, then slid so smoothly, slowly down, a cool firm white enamel baton protruding through their sliding ring.
>
> (11.1112-16)

These are just a few examples of that 'essence of vulgarity' (11.418) which is the dominant note of 'Sirens'. Even a seemingly innocent whistle becomes crudely suggestive as Richie Goulding 'cocked his lips apout' (11.630). Music in Joyce does indeed produce a communality where individuality merges. Something is certainly rasied by the musicality of 'Sirens', but not, as Davis would have it, the national spirit. Bloom's prim and fairly trite observations about music as escapism and fantasy pall into insignificance against the wrecking of romantic cultural nationalism produced by the lewdness of the narrative interventions. Music, the 'trove of cultural remembrance, a vital resource in the propagation of the nationalist ideal',[28] becomes in 'Sirens' a hilarious vindication of Archbishop McCabe's warning about music's capacity to 'most effectually degrade man to the lowest depths of voluptuous sensuality'.[29] In the chapter where 'Tenors get women by the score' (11.686), music is above all else libidinous, and this particular charm catches Bloom just as it does everyone else.

The further subversion of revivalist constructions of musical culture lies in the technicality of the narrative, the extraordinary attempt to make text like music, which according to Stuart Gilbert involves the imitation of such devices as *trillando, staccato, fermata, appoggiatura, martellato, sordamente, portamento* or *glissando, rondo, affrettando, stretto,* suspension and resolution, hollow fifth, polyphony, augmentation and final cadence.[30] On the one hand this is a comic literalization of the traditional association made between text

---

[28] Ibid., 216.

[29] Quoted in Patrick O'Donoghue, 'Music and Religion in Ireland', in Gillen and White, *Irish Musical Studies*, 128.

[30] Gilbert, *James Joyce's 'Ulysses'*, 249-51.

and music in late nineteenth-century literary culture generally, but in revivalist culture most specifically. For Yeats's generation of revivalists in particular, the act of cultural recovery was engaged by the sound of lament. Yeats himself sees the poet as a lyricist and the poem as essentially a song, a form of 'lyric redress'. 'Song', 'minstrelsy', the 'Celtic note', the 'bardic' — these are metaphors not just for poetry but for an entire cultural discourse. This very firmly asserted connection between music and text carried over into performance, with Yeats speaking his own verse as a rhythmical chant and believing 'that this chant, or tune, had a relatively specific melodic line'.[31] Synge, who first trained as a musician, took the associations between music and text even further, producing a dramatic language which is conventionally described as musical, and a dramatic form which, a number of critics have argued, can be analysed in musical terms.[32] In 'Sirens', these analogies and associations are dramatically literalised and exaggerated. The attempt to transform text into music produces no Celtic note or 'music of the spheres', but rather a series of inane and discordant repetitions. What Budgen calls 'the more banal tiddleypom aspects of music'[33] are reproduced in monstrosities like the following:

> Bald Pat who is bothered mitred the napkins. Pat is a waiter hard of his hearing. Pat is a waiter who waits while you wait. Hee hee hee hee. He waits while you wait. Hee hee. A waiter is he. Hee hee hee hee. He waits while you wait. While you wait if you wait he will wait while you wait. Hee hee hee hee, Hoh. Wait while you wait.
>
> (11.915-20)

This is not so much a serious attempt to make text musical as ironical play with another romantic revivalist obsession. It is a joke version of what happens when the text is taken literally as music.

On the other hand, there is a more serious, professional investment in identifying with the real mechanics of music in 'Sirens', as

---

[31] See Flannery, *Yeats and the Idea of a Theatre*, 196-97.

[32] See White in Gillen and White, *Irish Musical Studies*, 220-21 and Ann Saddlemyer, 'Synge's Landscape', *Irish University Review*, XXII/1, 1992, 55-68.

[33] Frank Budgen, *James Joyce and the Making of 'Ulysses' and Other Writings* (London: Oxford University Press, 1972 edn), 141.

opposed to a mystification that is the product of metaphor. The Sirens-text, for all its comedy, is a startling demonstration of musical erudition and there are times, especially perhaps in the section dealing with Simon Dedalus's delivery of *M'appari*, when the grip on comic play is loosened to produce textual effects which really do seem musical, or, at least, which display a deep technical knowledge of music. This musical literacy is certainly a product of Joyce's own expertise, but I would suggest that the closeness to musical theory and practice also operates as a response to both the Revival's reverence for song as 'natural' instinct and its intemperate refusal to recognize music as a distinct art form. Music was the text of nationhood. Thus in 'Cyclops' melody is dispensed with altogether as songs titles are incorporated into speech acts as a matter of course:

> — The memory of the dead, says the citizen taking up his pintglass and glaring at Bloom.
> — Ay, ay, says Joe.
> —You don't grasp my point, says Bloom. What I mean is ....
> — *Sinn Fein*! says the citizen. *Sinn Fein amhain*! The friends we love are by our side and the foes we hate before us!
>
> (12.520-26)

In revivalist terms, music was cultivated specifically to energize a climate of political commitment. For Davis, musicality was quite secondary to music's power to effect social and political change. 'It is not needful', he claimed, 'for a writer of our songs to be a musician'.[34] Moreover, the imperative to define and restore native musical traditions produced a strong resistance to the European aesthetic in modern music. 'Cultural separatism', certainly as it was preached by Young Ireland and later by Douglas Hyde, 'reached its apotheosis in music'.[35] It is for these reasons that recent cultural historians have argued that cultural nationalism may have had a negative effect on the development of music in Ireland.[36]

---

[34] Thomas Davis, *Essays Literary and Historical by Thomas Davis* (Dundalk: W. Tempest, 1914), 274-75.

[35] White in Gillen and White, *Irish Musical Studies*, 216.

[36] See Ryan and White in Gillen and White, *Irish Musical Studies*, 101-15 and 212-27.

The elevation of music in cultural nationalism could then be perceived as an anti-musical puritanism, a puritanism which is challenged in 'Sirens' firstly by the value-free eclecticism which encompasses music-hall songs, folk music, street-ballads and light-opera, as well as the music of 'Sea, wind, leaves, thunder, waters, cows lowing, the cattlemarket, cocks, hens don't crow, snakes hissss' (11.963-64). The sheer range of musical allusion in 'Sirens' and in *Ulysses* generally is not simply a matter of Joyce's musical interest combining with his so-called obsessive desire for inclusiveness. The narrow exclusivity of revivalist identification of *the* music is countered by a liberal, if not anarchic, allowance and the 'technic' of 'Sirens' supports this challenge, incorporating a barrage of musical devices which define the European tradition, and which ironically serve only to demonstrate the essential difference between music and text. For the most part, the more musical the text of 'Sirens' attempts to become, the more we laugh at what is obvious fakery. The fact is that words are not music and this finally may be the most fundamental subversion of the Celtic note enacted in 'Sirens'.

Kratos and *ethnos*: political culture in 'Cyclops'

'Cyclops' is the first episode of *Ulysses* to dispense completely with the appearance of authorial intervention in the narrative. The chapter which has been frequently read as the one didactic site in *Ulysses* actually looks entirely mimetic in its intent, reproducing, on the one hand, a written culture authenticated by publication, and, on the other, an oral, demotic culture. This double narrative of 'Cyclops' images culture as a process. It presents an articulation, or more usually a 'disarticulation', of high with low cultures, literary and non-literary discourses, and the intelligentsia and the people. The juxtaposition of discourses in this episode insists not so much on cultural traffic as on a collision of cultures. The satire of 'Cyclops' then derives in part from the inherent characteristics of the parodic-travesties themselves, but it is also a product of the grotesque dissonances of this bi-narrative.

A second characteristic of 'Cyclops' is its obvious engagement with revivalism. This is one of the few places in *Ulysses* which has long been recognized as a place where revivalism is attacked by

Joyce's literary strategics.[37] Or, to be more precise, the Literary Revival has been identified as just one of a whole range of targets. For most critics have understood 'Cyclops' as a heterogeneous satire which assaults legalese, varieties of journalese, literary genres such as epic, romance, gothic and so on, *as well as* the characteristic styles of the Literary Revival. Revivalism thus becomes simply one of many contexts for 'Cyclops'. This tendency, as we shall see, badly understates the significance of revivalism in 'Cyclops'. There is a further common difficulty which derives from the usual understanding of revivalism as unproblematic national culture. Thus the Joycean parody or pastiche[38] is, of course, of Yeats and Lady Gregory, but the mockery is deemed equally of Mangan's translation of 'Prince Alfrid's Itinerary through Ireland', or of Geoffrey Keating's *The History of Ireland*.[39] The parodies of revivalism are read then not as a Catholic assault on a Protestant culture, but as a modern, cosmopolitan rejection of a provincial and, at its extremity, bigoted

---

[37] See, for instance, Hugh Kenner, *Dublin's Joyce* (London: Chatto and Windus, 1955), 191, 255.

[38] Some commentators prefer the term 'pastiche' to describe the interpolations in 'Cyclops'. However, Frederic Jameson's reading of pastiche in postmodernism raises some doubts about this application. For Jameson, 'Pastiche is, like parody, the imitation of a peculiar mask, speech in a dead language; but it is neutral practice of such mimicry, without any of parody's ulterior motives, amputated of the satiric impulse, devoid of laughter and of any conviction that alongside the abnormal tongue you have momentarily borrowed, some healthy linguistic normality still exists' ('Postmodernism, or the Cultural Logic of Late Capitalism', *New Left Review*, July/August 1984, 146). Pastiche defined thus is miles away from the interpolations of 'Cyclops'.

[39] Keating (1570-?1644?) was a Catholic priest who wrote his four volume history in Gaelic, attacking the historiographies of the English historians, like Stanihurst, who 'hated the Irish' and wrote 'at the instigation of a party who were hostile to the Irish.' See Geoffrey Keating, *The History of Ireland*, edited and with a translation by David Comyn, (London: published for the Irish texts society by David Nutt, 1902), I, 33. There were a number of incomplete translations of Keating's work in the nineteenth and early twentieth centuries, and Joyce certainly knew of Keating — indeed Keating is referred to in the working notes for 'Cyclops'. There is no evidence, however, to suggest that Joyce shared the view of Catholic revivalists who saw in Keating an authentic alternative to the histories of Protestant academe.

nationalist culture.

In fact, revivalism is *the* target of 'Cyclops'. It is clearly identified here as an Anglo-Irish culture, an Anglicized, Victorianized version of the Celtic prototype. Of the thirty-one interpolations, thirteen are obviously parodic of the Literary Revival, reproducing and often outdoing the key characteristics of revivalist literary and historiographical practice. Thus entire passages of 'Cyclops' are comprised of 'a composite mock-bardic set of styles and devices'.[40] The exaggerations of size; the double epithets; the lists or 'runs'; the *dindsenchas* — all directly exploit Anglo-Irish versions of the bardic tales:

> A pleasant land it is sooth of murmuring waters, fishful streams where sport the gurnard, the plaice, the roach, the halibut, the gibbed haddock, the grilse, the dab, the brill, the flounder, the pollock, the mixed coarse fish generally, and other denizens of the aqueous kingdom too numerous to be enumerated.
>
> (12.70-75)

This passage is typical of revivalist parody in 'Cyclops', firstly in the exaggerated Celticism of the fish-run. As some commentators have noted, Joyce's parodies have a tendency to restore some of the stylistics of Celtic literature which nineteenth-century translators edited out as outlandish or vulgar. The long lists of 'Cyclops' could thus be read as a reclamation of the Celtic run in its full inflation, although the restoration is hardly purist.[41] Secondly, the fish-run is characteristic of 'Cyclops' in its over-exposure of Anglicization which echoes in anti-heroic Englishisms like 'denizens of the aqueous kingdom', 'too numerous to be mentioned' and in the poeticism 'in sooth'. As well as this series of interpolations which are so distinctly parodic of revivalism, there are others which parody important

---

[40] Andrew Gibson, ' "History, All That": Revival Historiography and Literary Strategy in the Cyclops' Episode in *Ulysses*' (61), *Essays and Studies*, 1991, 53-70. This essay is the first detailed analysis of revivalism in 'Cyclops'. Gibson reads the chapter as 'a sustained assault on revivalist historiographies and constructions of Irish history, and the aesthetics and politics implicit in them' (54).

[41] The list of 'Irish' heroes in the fourth interpolation includes 'the Last of the Mohicans', 'Dick Turpin' and 'Ludwig Beethoven'. See 12.168-205.

offshoots of revivalist culture. The theosophical fad that gripped Yeats's generation of revivalists is ridiculed in the eighth interpolation, for instance, where Paddy Dignam's spirit exhorts those living 'who were still at the wrong side of Maja to acknowledge the true path for it was reported in devanic circles that Mars and Jupiter were out for mischief on the eastern angle where the ram has power' (12.357-60). Most of the parodies of revivalism occur in the first part of 'Cyclops'. They are continuous from the second to the tenth interpolation. Joyce clearly wanted to establish revivalism as central to the episode. Thereafter, the periodic returns to the romance literature of revivalism (see, for instance, the nineteenth, twenty-first and twenty-fourth interpolations) are interspersed with parodies of contemporary journalese (sports reportage, travel journalism, gossip pages and so on).

But these latter interpolations are also substantially implicated in revivalist culture. Sports reportage, for instance, is concerned with the 'resuscitation of the ancient Gaelic sports and pastimes, practised morning and evening by Finn MacCool' (12.909-10). One of two interpolations which parody legal discourse involves 'sir Frederick the Falconer' administering 'the law of the brehon':

> And there sat with him the high sinhedrim of the twelve tribes of Iar, for every tribe one man, of the tribe of Patrick and of the tribe of Hugh and of the tribe of Owen and of the tribe of Conn and of the tribe of Oscar and of the tribe of Fergus and of the tribe of Finn and of the tribe of Dermot and of the tribe of Cormac and of the tribe of Kevin and of the tribe of Caolte and of the tribe of Ossian, there being in all twelve good men and true.
>
> (12.1124-30)

There are, in my estimation, only six interpolations which are not in some way connected with revivalist culture. The initial concentration of revivalist parodies, and the later filtration of romance styles and revivalist concerns into press and magazine culture implies a process of revivalism spreading its influence into more populist cultural forms. Thus the thirteenth interpolation (12.712-47), which reports the verse-speaking achievement of the Citizen's dog, is an absurd amalgam of sensationalist press and language revival linguistics. The cultural process implied here is a long way from the revivalist mission. Far from exorcizing the otherness of Anglicization, this process is a joke aggregation, an ironic assemblage which mixes elements, but never blends them, so that the components are obviously, even blatantly, on display.

This design feature alone demonstrates the central importance of revivalism to this episode, but there are further and equally fundamental interactions with revivalist culture. Both the 'technic' of gigantism and the device of interpolation are themselves imported from revivalist historiographical practices, drawing particularly on the enterprising narratives of the most influential popular historian of the late nineteenth century, Standish O'Grady.[42] O'Grady's two volumes of the *History of Ireland: the Heroic Period* (1878-1880) were ostensibly written to 'express the whole nature of a race or nation'.[43] His broad enterprise — to 'recover' from a mythic past, 'the gigantic conceptions of heroism and strength with which the forefront of Irish history is thronged' and which 'prove the great future of this race and land' —[44] was entirely consistent with revivalist traditions and was to prove, as we have seen, a major influence on the revivalists of Yeats's circle. His literary strategies, however, were quite at odds with the disciplined methods employed by the antiquarians of the Royal Irish Academy in their research. The painstaking scholarship of these early historians produced the first wave of new Irish historiography in the early nineteenth century and O'Grady acknowledged their importance. But he himself was a proselytizer with little patience for detail and accuracy. In his 'gigantic' version of bardic history-telling, historical 'fact' was despised as having the 'vulgarity of actual things',[45] a vulgarity which conveniently allowed O'Grady to dismiss virtually the whole of Irish history from St Patrick onwards as discontinuous with Ireland's heroic destiny. Just as revivalist music identified itself as being anti-musical, so revivalist historiography became unashamedly ahistorical in a development which served a clear and obvious Anglo-Irish agenda. Medieval and scholastic

---

[42] Gibson's essay on 'Cyclops' clearly demonstrates the great importance of O'Grady to this episode.

[43] O'Grady, *History, Critical and Philosophical*, 5.

[44] Ibid., 58.

[45] Ibid., 7.

Ireland was dismissed as being responsible for a 'rationalism and logic' which all but destroyed the 'vividness of perception' and 'grandeur of thought'[46] allegedly typical of ancient Irish epic. The Catholic contribution to Irish culture was thus substantially underplayed, the development of the plantation economy was ignored, and modern society, which had so marginalized the landlords, was execrated. This historical invention, so indifferent to historical analysis and argument, was passionate about 'the gigantic treatment' of Fenian heroes who 'historical or not' 'are real'.[47]

'Giganticism', the art of 'Cyclops', is directly appropriated from revivalist historiography, and so are the time shifts that Joyce exploits in his interpolations. O'Grady's history making and indeed revivalist culture generally, insisted on the immanence of the past. 'Entrelacement' whereby 'the reader moves from the present to a more ancient past and back again' typifies the revivalist historical imagination. In O'Grady's *Histories* and in the versions of the Red Branch or Ulster Cycle which he wrote for children

> ... a sequence of events, the present, is set off with its own day-to-day consciousness, then suddenly it intersects with another sequence of events, the past, with a consciousness that understands it even though the present had no knowledge of the other's existence.[48]

This reasonably describes Joyce's own version of 'entrelacement'; except, of course, that in Joyce's interpolations past and present are hardly continuous. On the contrary, in 'Cyclops' the mythic past collides with contemporaneity to produce comic incongruity, contradiction and radical discord. The relationship between the life at 'the back of the courthouse' and in 'the land of holy Michan' is a ridiculous one, as is the relationship between Bloom and 'O'Bloom, the son of Rory', 'the prudent soul' who is 'impervious to fear' (12.215-17). The inflation of 'Little Alf Bergan ... squeezed up with the laughing' into the grandiose 'O'Bergan' 'godlike messenger ... radiant as the eye of heaven' (12.249-50/244-45) is patently absurd, as

---

[46] Ibid., 47.

[47] Ibid., 355.

[48] W. I. Thompson, *The Imagination of an Insurrection: Dublin, Easter 1916* (Oxford: Oxford University Press, 1966), 22-23.

is the gigantic transformation of 'that bloody old pantaloon Denis Breen' into 'an elder of noble gait and countenance, bearing the sacred scrolls of law' (12.253/246-47); or the transformation of Paddy Dignam, the Dublin burgher who in death becomes a national myth:

> O'Dignam, sun of our morning. Fleet was his foot on the bracken: Patrick of the beamy brow. Wail, Banba, with your wind: and wail O ocean, with your whirlwind.
>
> (12.374-76)

Just as 'Sirens' mocks and effectively sabotages the Revival's precious elevation of musical culture through its withering exposure of revivalist romanticism to the life and culture of the street, so with 'Cyclops'. The angle at which 'gigantic' interpolation meets realist I-narrative produces a range of effects, but the most obvious result of, for instance, the transformation of the citizen's handkerchief into 'the muchtreasured and intricately embroidered ancient Irish facecloth attributed to Solomon of Droma and Manus Tomaltach og MacDonogh' (12.1438-40) is a hilarious disposal of revivalist romantics. Certainly, revivalism is presented as a hugely prolific culture which has influenced fashion writing, travel writing, sports reportage and so on, but the comic distance between the two narratives of 'Cyclops' insists on the irrelevancy of epic Celticism to modern Ireland.

Some readers have put forward a different argument: that the two narratives, linked by something like colourful exaggeration, belong to an organicist unity. Any such view, however, must inevitably struggle with the glaring incongruity between the discourses of interpolation and the demotic speech of the I-narrator. There is an obvious gulf between these two narratives. It is most obvious in the incompatibility of the respective stories that they tell, but evidenced also, for example, in terms of 'style'. One narrative is stylized and composed, the other is casual and spontaneous; one elevates, the other is vulgar; one seems public and often declamatory, the other is private and gossipy, and so on. At a different level, the consciousness behind the interpolations is ostensibly deeply patriotic in a very end-of-century manner. The I-narrator, on the other hand, is completely indifferent to Ireland's cultural regeneration. He is scornful of the citizen, who he describes as a 'bloody clown' (12. 1794) and presents the language revival as itself a culture which is alien to the masculine and boozy bar-room life he knows (see 12.679). It is true that as the men in Kiernan's bar drink more and the atmosphere becomes more heated, there is a sense in which all the assembled company become more self-consciously national, but, this 'patriotism' is deeply compromised and hardly expressed in terms that could seriously articulate with the formalities of cultural nationalism, which is not to deny that it is strongly and even powerfully expressed. Here Joe Hynes objects splendidly not to monarchy, nor even to English monarchical rule of Ireland, but to the corruption that produces German-English monarchs:

> — And as for those Prooshians and the Hanoverians, says Joe, haven't we had enough of those sausageeating bastards on the throne from George the elector down to the German lad and the flatulent old bitch that's dead.
>
> (12.1390-92)

The argument that 'Cyclops' relentlessly ridicules cultural nationalism has repeatedly been used in support of the once commonly held view that Joyce is apolitical. But the satire in the chapter does not dismiss Ireland and Irish nationalism, any more than 'Sirens' dismisses music. Nor can it seriously be claimed that a supra-nationalist, Joycean politics is somehow crystallized in Bloom's little slippage, when he offends against the macho culture of the bar with his inappropriate and naïve plea for love in a world of hatred. All these views, which were once common in 'Cyclops' criticism, now seem quaint refusals to read the detail and sophistication of the political engagement of this episode. 'Cyclops' is precise and analytical about nationalist formulations, nationalist ideologies and the transmission of nationalism in popular political culture. Page after page of this episode assaults, not the legitimacy of Ireland's right to self-determination, but conservative forms of nationalism which were ascendant in the late nineteenth and early twentieth centuries. These cultural nationalisms, cultivated by both the Church and the old Ascendancy and often operating to conflicting agendas, claimed a pedigree from radical traditions of Irish dissent. But they were in fact quite distinct from, for example, both revolutionary nationalism, which in the late eighteenth century defined the nation state in legalistic as opposed to ethnic terms, and from the constitutional nationalism of Parnell.

This reading of 'Cyclops' would understand the citizen not as a reproduction of the stereotypical ogre-republican of the English *Daily Express* at the turn of the century, but as an old nationalist who has overdosed on several generations of nationalist ideologies. He is in many ways a pathetic product of the failure to bring the Irish State to reality. Unwilling or unable to read the social and political agendas underlying different nationalist movements, for the citizen, there is just one continuous, noble and unfaltering tradition of Irish nationalism: a tradition of manly, belligerent dissent. Stuffed to overflowing with the songs and poems of nation, he is the undiscriminating repository of just about every nationalist text since the United Irishmen. As such, he delivers some wonderfully venomous attacks on a Britain which has 'the only hereditary chamber on the face of God's earth and their land in the hands of a dozen gamehogs and cottonball barons. That's the great empire they boast about of drudges and whipped serfs' (12.1346-50). At the same time, the citizen is very much a product of the cultural nationalism which dominated turn-of-the-century Ireland. Quite apart from his personal involvement in the GAA and his unqualified support of the Gaelic League, he has thoroughly assimilated Protestant Celticism as a politics. Thus the émigrés to 'the land of the free' 'will come again and with a vengeance, no cravens, the sons of Granuaile, the champions of Kathleen ni Houlihan', to attack England on Ireland's behalf (12.1373-75). The citizen's 'new Ireland' is actually deeply retrospective, a restoration, with some technological help, of an old mythological Ireland. The Irish trade of antiquity will apparently return:

> — when the first Irish battleship is seen breasting the waves with our flag to the fore, none of your Henry Tudor harps, no, the oldest flag afloat, the flag of the province of Desmond and Thomond, three crowns on a blue field, the three sons of Milesius.
>
> (12.1306-10)

Ironically, the citizen takes his nickname from the tradition of revolutionary and republican France which defined *la patrie* in terms of commitment to a nation created by the political choice of its members. But his nationalism, which owes a great deal to revivalism, is quite distinct from this revolutionary tradition. It is firmly based on loyalty to a pre-existing existential culture and to ethnicity. The cornerstone of the citizen's nation is exclusion. 'We want no more strangers in our house'[49] (12.1150-51), says the citizen, echoing Yeats. The notorious anti-Semitism which despises Bloom as contaminative, a bug, an un-man and 'a white-eyed kaffir' (12.1552) is a product of ethnic nationalism, of a politics of exclusivity. The citizen's espousing of such views is an indication not of Joyce's rejection of nationalism, but of what nationalism had become, in his view, under Ireland's cultural renaissance.

The citizen's brand of nationalism is itself gigantic and freakish and in this shows its exposure to the Anglicized historiographies popularized by O'Grady, Lady Gregory, Yeats, Douglas Hyde, Ferguson and Curry. It deals in a romanticized past and a wildly improbable future which re-runs the Heroic Age. His consciousness is not representative, but distinctly at the edge of the Dublin community presented in 'Cyclops'. His rhetoric is treated largely as a joke to be exploited, as at the beginning of the episode, when Joe Hynes is egging him on, or an embarrassment, as when Cunningham is trying to extricate Bloom from the bar at the end of episode. Indeed, there is actually very little in the communality here to confirm the revivalist specification of the national culture, which is the point of the narrative juxtapositions. There is, however, one issue which does bind the community together, an issue which is of much more interest to the drinkers in Kiernan's bar than stories of Cuchulain or Deirdre, and that is the issue of law and the legal process — or, to be more precise, the issue of English law and English legal process. In fact, the importance of law to this episode can hardly be underestimated. It is not too much to say that Joyce produces an image of a popular culture which is essentially defined by an engagement with the law and its dispensation.

This aspect of 'Cyclops' is important to our concerns here because it is so intimately connected to Joyce's specifically *political* objections to cultural nationalism. But before these connections are

---

[49] In Cathleen ni Houlihan, Bridget Gillane asks The Poor Old Woman, 'What was it put you wandering?'. The Old Woman replies 'Too many strangers in the house' (Yeats, *CPL*, 81). Of course, the identification of the enemy as the 'stranger' is common within Irish cultural nationalism.

elaborated, it is necessary to illustrate something of the extent to which law and legal process pervades 'Cyclops'.[50] The setting of the episode in Barney Kiernan's bar in Little Britain Street makes an important announcement. Quite apart from the immediate colonial and Anglicizing geography, the bar is located just behind the Green Street Court. Some of the drinkers are connected with the courthouse, and come directly from there, which may explain something of the ubiquity of law stories in the episode. But the law does not simply provide a 'background' of barroom talk. On the contrary, in this chapter of politics and nationalism, the foregrounding of law has a special significance because law is the very process by which colonial rule in Ireland is both coerced and legitimized. The Court which backs on to Kiernan's bar had a particular significance in this respect. Green Street Court was notorious for its trials of nationalists. Young Irelanders, Fenians, Invincibles, members of the IRA, Robert Emmet, the Sheares Brothers — all were tried in this Court. 'Cyclops', then, is located in an environment where a principal mechanism of colonial rule is conspicuous and greatly emphasized. The law is a very obvious presence from the beginning of this chapter of courts, legal cases and crime. An agent of the law, a DMP man, features in the very first line. One might expect the first interpolation to initialize the pattern of the subsequent eleven by parodying revivalism, but it does not. This first interpolation is a deployment of legalese. Law figures in further interpolations. Parliamentary process is reproduced at line 860, for instance, and the longest interpolation, the twelfth, performs a special ceremony of state, the execution of the Irish 'hero-boy' who 'went to his death with a song on his lips as if he were going to a hurling match in Clonturk Park' (12. 645-46). In the twentieth interpolation, 'poor old sir Frederick' [Falkiner] dispenses the law of Celtic Ireland.

Involvement with law and the legal process is just as much a characteristic of the I-narrative. Insurance law is discussed around line 770. Specific cases of the day are debated, including the trail of 'James Wrought alias Saphiro alias Spark and Spiro' for fraud, as are the performances of individual judges and magistrates. 'Decree *nisi*' is referred to at line 1159 and corporal punishment at 1334. Mob law is deplored at 1324, and Bloom and the citizen are said to be 'arguing about law and history' (12.1234). 'Packed juries' are mentioned at

---

[50] There has been little critical discussion of this aspect of the episode.

line 1575 and the process of changing one's name by deedpoll at 1640.

These examples illustrate a fundamental characteristic of 'Cyclops'. Crime and punishment, law and legality are an essential part of the fabric of this episode. To some extent, the law is recognized by the men in Kiernan's bar as sustaining English rule, perhaps particularly by the citizen, in his attack on English naval law (12.1330-40) and in his identification of Rumbold, the English executioner, as a 'bloody barbarian' (12.431). But this particular engagement with the State is considerably deflated by the story of Garryowen's attack on the 'constabulary man' who once visited the citizen 'with a blue paper about a license' (12.156). The challenging of English law, even on trivial grounds and in trivial ways, is not at all typical of Joyce's characters in 'Cyclops'. On the contrary, characters in this text are concerned with knowledge of the law and usage of legal process. They assimilate the language of the law, presumably because it is a high status discourse. There is very little sense of the law's significance in maintaining colonial power, but a very strong sense of English law penetrating the Dublin community. It does so not as a perceived ideology but as an authentic system of justice. Thus within ten lines of the chapter's opening, the I-narrator tells us he is 'on two minds' about using the law against a sweep who is 'obstructing the thoroughfare'. Usage of the language of law is quite common amongst characters in the episode. Sometimes the usage is comic:

> — Was it you did it, Alf? says Joe. The truth, the whole truth and nothing but the truth, so help you Jimmy Johnson.
> (12.1038-39)

but elsewhere the debating of due process is a more serious business:

> — the truth of a libel is no defence to an indictment for publishing it in the eyes of the law.
> (12.1048-49)

There are further illustrations of characters using English law in defence of their individual rights. Geraghty, the plumber, threatens to have Moses Herzog *'summonsed up before the court ... for trading without a license'* (12.28-29). 'Bearing the sacred scrolls of the law', Denis Breen is repeatedly referred to in 'Cyclops' as in search of legal redress. Elsewhere, engagement with the law can be by-passed by insider contacts and deals. Paddy Leonard avoids being 'lagged' at line 801, only because 'he knew the bobby, 14A'. The I-narrator believes that J. J. O'Molloy, 'his majesty's counsel who is learned in the law', and who is himself 'half-smothered in writs and garnishee orders', is using influence to get Ned Lambert off the jury list (12.1009/1022/1025).

There is a sense in which these characters work the law and articulate some degree of ownership of the legal process, even though the whole legal system is clearly fundamental to the exercise of colonial power. There is, of course, a clear contradiction here. It is difficult to take the nationalist climate of 'Cyclops' seriously when its characters are so deeply implicated in endorsing the legal system. This contradiction, however, is not presented in moral terms in 'Cyclops'. The 'Cyclops' text is not outraged by this playing of the game. On the contrary, this narrative understands the law as both a brutal and a subtle ideological force. Law is not simply a matter of coercion. It also the means by which justice is constructed as a universal, objective reality, to be dispensed with due ceremony. Gramsci suggests that 'law plays an important role in sustaining the domination of the ruling class because it operates both as a form of coercive domination and of ideological domination.'[51] The law, which supports and legitimizes the power of the State, sells itself as a glamorous protector of the individual.[52] It is this ideology which in part lies behind the eager engagement with the legal process in 'Cyclops' and behind the morbid interest taken in the pathology of execution and the clamour for the sensationalism of *The Police Gazette*.

---

[51] *Selections from the Prison Notebooks*, edited and translated by Q. Hoare and G. Nowell-Smith (London: Lawrence & Wishart, 1971), 12.

[52] See Alan Hurst in *Explorations in Law and Society* who argues that 'one particularly interesting feature of bourgeois legal ideology in the context of English law is the way in which it holds itself out as the protector of the individual against the incursions of the state' (London & New York: Routledge, 1993).

'Cyclops' is a deeply comic episode and much of the comedy is derived from its ridiculing of cultural nationalism. As so often in *Ulysses*, but with special force in this episode, the dignity of the Revival is shattered by being forced into a wickedly funny conjunction with Joyce's version of social and cultural reality. The technic of this episode is entirely designed around this purpose. But there is perhaps a more serious constituency to 'Cyclops', for cultural revivalism is being presented, not just as an Anglicized, romantic redundancy, but as a conservative substitute for the democratic political and social transformation of Ireland. This may be the real point of Joyce's treatment of law here and it is, incidentally, consistent with Hobsbawm's historical understanding of nationalism at this time as 'a mild substitute for socialism' amongst the allies of the First World War, which 'in the defeated countries ... reemerged as fascism'.[53] Certainly, part of Joyce's concern in 'Cyclops', as elsewhere, is to expose what is so studiedly obscured by the heroics of revivalism. He presents a really sophisticated version of the mechanics of colonial power and its impact on those who live under it. But the further articulation is that cultural nationalism, with its obsessions with language, literature, games, clothes, food, flags and so on is actually a diversion, of no real threat to the state precisely because it makes no impact on the power of the state. And, of course, the most obvious expression of that power is the law.

'Cyclops' *is* the most overtly and radically political episode in *Ulysses*, and it carries a radical and explicit politics. It says, everywhere, that cultural nationalism is conservative and élitist, an irrelevancy to the politics of a modern Ireland; it understands the cultural nationalism of revivalism as a surrogate for political independence and social change; and always behind the 'gigantic' grotesquerie, the fake-nationalism, there is the absolutely clear commitment to a specifically Joycean conception of Irish independence.

Elsewhere in the later episodes of *Ulysses,* the engagement with revivalist culture is not so obvious, nor so circumscribed by what can be read as relatively formal political positions. In 'Circe', for instance, Joyce targets the Irish National Theatre, operating on just about every

---

[53] Hobsbawm, *Nations and Nationalism*, 130.

aesthetic precept deployed by Yeats in his theorizing and delivery of a national stage. This dismantling, even more than the strategics of 'Cyclops', is too wild, too enthusiastic and too wicked to be appropriately described in terms of 'political position'. Joyce's engagement with revivalism triggers something more raw, more fundamental, as 'Circe' demonstrates so clearly.

5 'Circe' and the Irish Literary Theatre

'Circe' purports to be a play, and theatre was the medium through which revivalism expressed itself most forcefully, most radically, and most controversially. During the first decade of the twentieth century, according to the Anglo-Irish directors of Ireland's cultural rebirth, the success of revivalism was crucially dependent on the creation of a theatrical space in which the ceremony of Irish nationhood could be performed. Yeats argued that the purpose of drama was to provide Ireland with 'a vision of race'; he conceived of the nation itself as being 'like an audience in some great theatre'.[1] 'Circe' proclaims its own theatricality and, given what was invested in the creation of an Irish Literary Theatre, it is hardly surprising that in writing his play of plays Joyce should draw so heavily on revivalist-type materials. Hallucinations, dreams, masking, fantasy are common to Joyce's massive extravaganza and to the Revivalist texts which he dubbed 'dwarf dramas'. So is the Circean motif. *The Shadowy Waters* opens with Forgael locked 'in some crazy dream' (Yeats, *CPL*, 148) and contains the story of souls emerging from the dead to be transformed into man-headed birds. In Yeats's *Deirdre* the wife of Lugaidh Redstripe has 'a seamew's body half the year' (Yeats, *CPL*, 179); *The Green Helmet* contains talk of cat-headed people, and has a talking decapitated head. Revivalist plays are also alive with ghosts. There is an obvious likeness between all this and, say, Paddy Dignam's emergence from the body of a beagle at 15.1208 '*half of one ear, all the nose and both thumbs*' being '*ghouleaten*', except, of course, that Joyce takes none of it seriously and the revivalists under Yeats's leadership did. Revivalist plays and Joyce's text are both concerned with hero cultism, messianic traditions and apocalyptic visions. Magical transformations, usually associated with pantomime traditions in 'Circe' criticism, are commonplace in revivalist theatre. The climax of *Cathleen ni Hoolihan*, for instance, where an old crone is transformed into a young girl who has 'the walk of a queen' (Yeats, *CPL*, 88) is reminiscent of, say, Stephen's famous transformation into

---

[1] From a commentary on 'Three Songs to the Same Tune', quoted in Flannery, *Yeats and the Idea of a Theatre*, 66.

Rudy at the end of 'Circe'. These broad 'parallels' further can be taken further. The conspicuous use of song is present in both 'Circe' and revivalist theatre (granted, though, the difference between Yeats's misty-eyed evocations of the Celtic twilight and Joyce's raucous street ballads), and so is ritualistic dance (allowing once more for some startling differences between Yeats's delicate and evocative dance patterns and Stephen's rampaging hoofing to the tune of 'My Girl's a Yorkshire Girl'). If Joyce's play is technically impossible, revivalist theatre was at least notorious for its technical demands. Producing angels and fairies, and having butterflies emerging from characters' mouths, indeed, staging the so-called Heroic Age generally, could not have been easy, and occasionally one comes across a stage direction in a revivalist play that would be quite at home in Joyce's text. Here, for instance, Edward Martyn transforms a nineteenth-century bedroom into a timeless Tir-na-Nog in not much more than a blink of an eyelid:

> *There is soft music of harps, while the aurora borealis arises and glows in the sky. Soon a ghostly procession is seen to emerge like vapour from the neighbourhood of the cairn. Presently as it advances it grows more distinct and then is discovered to consist of QUEEN MAEVE, tall pale-faced and fair haired, in a golden crown and gold embroidered robes; of BOY PAGES in garlanded tunics and wearing wreaths of roses upon their heads; of ancient Irish harpers with their harps; of chieftains and warriors in conical caps; of people, etc.*[2]

This common stock of materials is an encouragement towards reading 'Circe' as a kind of high-jacking of revivalist theatre. The first 220 lines of 'Circe' echo revivalist theatre to such an extent that they constitute something approaching an incitement to such a reading. This is, after all, the beginning of Joyce's play; the orientation towards the Literary Theatre is thus immediate and decisive. The opening of 'Circe' may not allude to any specific revivalist text, but it is a transposing of a mode of beginning that was virtually traditional in revivalist theatre. Revivalist plays, particularly Yeats's, invariably began with techniques of defamiliarization. Sometimes this was done by scenery and lighting, as in the opening stage directions of *The Land of Heart's Desire*:

---

[2] Martyn, *The Heather Field and Maeve*, 119.

Through the door one can see the forest. It is night, but the moon or late sunset glimmers through the trees and carries the eye far off into a vague, mysterious world.

(Yeats, *CPL*, 53)

But more usually defamiliarization involved swirling mists and fogs as in Martyn's *Maeve*, or in Yeats's *On Baile's Strand* which begins with '*misty light as of sea-mist*' or *The Green Helmet* which has '*a misty moon-lit sea*'. Openings were also often initiated by strange alienating figures, like the masked players at the beginning of *The Hawk's Well*; the Red Man and the Black Man at the beginning of *The Green Helmet*; '*A Fool and Blind Man, both ragged, and their features made grotesque and extravagant by masks*' (Yeats, *CPL*, 247) in *On Baile's Strand* and so on. It is this kind of mystification, along with some heavily signalled Freudian symbolism,[3] that Joyce uses and inflates for the opening of 'Circe' with its '*will of the wisps*' (15.3), '*Snakes of river fog*' (15.158), and its transformation of urban people and urban objects into strange and unfamiliar figures from a romance twilight. An ice cream trolley becomes a '*gondola*', floating under a lighthouse (15.5), a totter bending over rubbish becomes a '*gnome*' (15.28); there is an '*idiot*', a '*virago*', a '*pygmy woman*' and a '*crone*' (15.14,51,25,32). A street cleaning cart becomes '*a dragon sandstrewer*' (15.184-85). There are further connections between the opening of *Ulysses* 15 and revivalist theatre. There are, for instance, many references to light in this opening: the children's question 'Where's the great light?' at line 22; Stephen's distortion of the street light which shatters '*light all over the world*' (15.100); his comment about 'a light of love' (15.112), and so on. This ceremonial illumination seems ironically related to the inaugural play of the Irish Literary Theatre which was prefaced with a prologue written by Lionel Johnson called 'The Lord of Light'.[4] In imitation of the religious

---

[3] See, for instance, the Freudian dream imagery of '*Rows of grimy houses with gaping doors*' (15.3-4).

[4] Extracts from Lionel Johnson's prologue were published in the first issue of *Beltaine*, the literary organ of the Irish Literary Theatre. These are reproduced in Flannery, *Yeats and the Idea of a Theatre*, 82 as a footnote. The prologue begins, 'the May fire once on every burning hill/All the fair land with burning bloom would fill;/All the fair land, at visionary night,/Gave loving glory to the Lord of Light./Come, then, and keep us with an Irish feast,/Wherein the Lord of Light and

observances which preceded performances in Greek theatre, Johnson's poem proclaimed a new religious rite based on a unity of Celtic, Christian and mystic doctrines.[5] But, for the most part, it is this exotic defamiliarization which links the opening of 'Circe' with revivalist theatre most firmly — except that 'links' becomes a thoroughly inappropriate word given the wildly displaced context in which Joyce employs this material. The city slum, and the red-light district, were places that simply did not exist in the topography of an Irish revivalism which had somehow managed to exorcise sin from the Irish national consciousness and, indeed, regarded the city as responsible for producing an anti-theatrical theatre, the 'theatre of commerce' as Yeats called it (Yeats, *E & I*, 169). There is surely the beginnings of some violent subversion in these images of urban squalor, disease and the mess of human sexual desire and fantasy which are so oddly in conjunction with the romantic mystification of the Irish revival.

If 'Circe' is allowed the status of an Irish play, then the fact that the play is set in Nighttown becomes an announcement of Joyce's intention to confront a national theatre which dramatized love as something at the centre of the Irish spirit and proclaimed sex to be an English contamination. The centrality of this intention to the whole Circean show is firmly underwritten by the fact that Joyce works not just with the fabric of revivalist theatre, but with the whole neo-Platonic paraphernalia that served as revivalist underpinning. The collective unconscious imaged through ritual, with magic serving as a metaphor for a kind of id/ego interface are the essentials of 'Circe' and they owe everything to revivalist theatre because ceremony, ritual and magic were precisely the ingredients out of which, as Yeats put it so tellingly, 'The Protestant Ascendancy' was to make 'its parting gift' to 'the New Catholic Ireland'.[6] The unrestrained aristocratic *hauteur* in

---

Song is priest'.

[5] There are numerous further references to light in the opening of 'Circe'. At one point, for instance, Bloom sees a glow and thinks it might be a 'flasher' or a 'searchlight' and then realizes he is watching a fire (15.165-72). In almost all cases the 'light' is either an invoked absence (as in the question 'Where's the great light?') or of obscure origin. This may further reinforce the idea of an ironic reference to Johnson's prologue which itself presents revivalist theatre as a beacon bringing light to the nation.

[6] W. B. Yeats, *The Irish National Theatre* (Roma: Accademia D'Italia, 1935), 8.

this remark makes it perfectly clear that the makers of revivalism were claiming to convey in their work not just 'personal ideas', but nothing less than the characteristics and elements of a nation. They purported to be in the process of somehow dramatizing a national collective unconscious, 'that national soul which has been slowly incarnating in our race from its cloudy dawn'.[7] In the process of delivering this outrageously ambitious enterprise, revivalist theatre, consistent with other forms of revivalist writing, indulged itself with historical fabrication, replacing a history of oppression and subjugation with a myth of cultural syncretism, and remaking the past around a myth of aristocratic heroism. It attempted to divert the process of Ireland's modernization (the process which had so reduced the economic and political status of the Anglo-Irish) by conflating the modern with the Anglicized and by idealizing rural life. But above all, as far as Joyce was concerned, revivalist theatre had the audacity to speak for Ireland and, more than this, claimed to represent its very soul. Revivalist theatre was to be a celebration of the collective Irish unconscious. Again we are referred back to 'Circe' in most direct ways and again it is in the very early part of the episode that Joyce advertises his intention of writing his own theatre of the collective mind. 'Circe' begins with the redcoats prowling Nighttown and insulting Stephen. A communal historicism is evoked which suggests that Joyce's text is plugging into some kind of collective psychology. Before Bloom can enter Mabbot Street he must negotiate the sinister 'figure' who asks for a 'Password. *Straid Mabbot*' (15.218). Bloom takes this figure to be a Gaelic League spy, which would make him an appropriate guardian of the Irish species of the Anima Mundi. More generally, the opening of 'Circe' uses landscape just as Yeats used it, as a natural symbol for the collective unconscious,[8] but with that vital distinction that Joyce's

---

This was Yeats writing with grand aristocratic largesse, though some 25 years after the critical events actually occurred. At the time that the Irish National Theatre was created there was considerably more to play for and the Abbey must have seemed more like a battleground than an almshouse, judging by the responses of the early audiences and the assertive Protestant ideologies explicit in the plays.

[7] George Russell, 'Nationalism and Imperialism', in Eglinton et al., *Literary Ideals*, 18.

[8] This idea is developed in Yeats's essay, 'A Note on National Drama', where he

landscape is an urban red-light district as opposed to an Irish wilderness and the psychological states it evokes are concerned with shame, guilt and survivalism, as opposed to Yeats's romance of dispossession. All this, and the fact that characters in 'Circe' are frequently in possession of information and language registers that they either cannot or do not possess establishes 'Circe' as Joyce's comic version of the collective unconscious.

It is clear from Russell's comment about the 'cloudy dawn' of the 'national soul' that although revivalist theatre was centrally concerned with the national collective unconscious, the psychological direction of revivalist theory was reactionary and emphatically anti-modern. Notions about a collective mind might be generally suggestive of Jung, but Freudian psychology was considered by Yeats to be symptomatic of diseased modern fragmentation. For Yeats — who was *the* theorist of revivalist theatre — the major influence on both the theory and practice of drama, was, in fact, neither Freud nor Jung but Wagner.[9] The romantic historicizing, the emphasis on myth as a carrier of eternal truth, the supreme value attached to Greek theatre, the rejection of reason in favour of the emotions and the spirit, the search for a form that would combine music, language, gesture and dance to create a 'total art', the appeal to a 'folk' audience, all these were freely adapted by Yeats from Wagnerian opera to meet the Irish context. To a large extent this Irish version of a Germanic theatre was conceptualized by Yeats in terms of his obsession with magic. According to his essay 'Magic' (1901), there were three fundamental doctrines underlying magical practices, and all three had vital theatrical implications as far as Yeats was concerned:

> (1) That the borders of our mind are ever shifting, and that many minds can flow into one another, as it were, and create a single mind, a single energy.

---

writes that the 'Irish Romantic Movement' should 'make Ireland, as Ireland and all other lands were in ancient times, a holy land to her people'. See Eglinton et al., *Literary Ideals*, 19.

[9] Wagner had a very great influence on Yeats's thinking about the theatre. For a descriptive account of this influence see Flannery, *Yeats and the Idea of a Theatre*, 102-09. There is a considerable irony here — it could be argued that the Irish Literary Theatre was more strongly influenced by European traditions than is 'Circe'.

(2) That the borders of our memories are as shifting, and that our memories are a part of one great memory, the memory of Nature itself.
(3) That this great mind and great memory can be evoked by symbols.
(Yeats, *E & I*, 28)

These doctrines shaped and determined Yeats's conception of a theatre which would ignore what he saw as 'the arbitrary surface peculiarities of life' to focus on the archetypes of the unconscious where 'no mind's contents [were] necessarily shut off from one another'.[10] They also coloured his conception of a tragic drama which enacted a communal historicism. The same doctrines also shaped his conception of the dramatist as priest, not in control of the mysterious creative powers he exercised and determined his conception of a ritualistic theatre which tuned in to 'pure life' through the mediation of symbolism.

If we imagine all this thinking transmuted through Joyce's rationalist comedy, then we find ourselves yet again precisely in the landscape of 'Circe'. It becomes quite clear that 'Circe' is a satirical deployment of revivalist theatrical theory, which involves literalising aspects of the theory, and letting the new formulation run amok. This is certainly what happens to the magic which is so important to Yeats's drama, and which becomes subjected to a hilariously deflating exploitation as the 'art' of 'Circe'. There is Bloom's absurd talisman 'Potato Preservative against Plague and Pestilence'[11] (15.1952) and all the allusions to tricks and sleight of hand and the paranormal, like Zoe's dabbling in palmistry, Bloom drawing coloured silk handkerchiefs from his mouth, the thrown cushion which becomes a bird, the ventriloquism of Lynch's cap which appears to speak and the cigarette which to a drunken Stephen appears to float out of nowhere. The language and gesture of the magician's act is built into 'Circe'. Bloom '*disappears*' into '*Olhausen's, the porkbutcher's*' (15.155),

---

[10] Unpublished note of 1919, quoted A. Norman Jeffares, *W. B. Yeats, Man and Poet* (London: Routledge and Kegan Paul, 1962), 210.

[11] For Yeats the talisman was of great importance, a metaphor, in fact, for art itself: 'All art that is not mere story-telling, or mere portraiture, is symbolic and has the purpose of those symbolic talismans which medieval magicians made with complex colours and forms, and bade their patients ponder over daily and guard with holy secrecy' (*E & I*, 148-49). There is also the suggestion here of the artist as physician, healing the sicknesses of society, which is possibly subject to some interesting variations in 'Circe'.

Tommy and Jacky Caffrey *'vanish, there, there'* (15.241-42), Bloom *'produces'* a flower from his pocket (15.738), Canon O'Hanlon *'elevates and exposes a marble timepiece'* (15.1128-29), Lynch wields a poker which becomes a 'wand' (15.2071), Svengali Bloom makes a swift hypnotic pass *'with impelling fingers'* (15.2723), and so on. The point about this material is that it is all at the level of parlour magic, and like the 'transformations' which constitute the dynamic of the episode and which could be metaphorically described as 'magic', they are part of the self-conscious and deliberate mechanism of the text. The method is a thorough refutation of Yeats's conception of the divinely inspired artist, and the effect is to ridicule Yeats's neo-Platonic universe. Such ridicule is completely consistent with Joyce's general opinion of the Dublin mystics who, he felt, had left their Church only to become saints: 'As such they do not compare either for consistency, holiness or charity with a fifth-rate saint of the Catholic Church.'[12]

Perhaps the most obvious and compelling structural linkage between Joyce's play and revivalist theatre is the fundamental importance that ritual has to both. Given the centrality of magic to Yeats's thinking, it is hardly surprising that he understood the theatre to be a temple, the actor a priest ('a reverent reciter of majestic words' — Yeats *UP1*, 325) and the play a ritual which celebrated the 'sacred' history and culture of Ireland, often through enactment of ritualistic death and rebirth, a cycle, incidentally, which lies behind many of the key 'transformations' in 'Circe'. For many observers of the early Abbey productions it was precisely this ritualistic quality that gave the company a distinctive style: 'With an art of gesture admirably disciplined and a strange delicacy of enunciation they perform the best dramas of our time in the method of lovely ritual.'[13] It cannot be coincidental that 'Circe' is also structured around ritual, to the extent that one critic has read the chapter itself as constituting a Mass.[14] As one would expect, there are wild divergences between Joyce's use of

---

[12] Stanislaus Joyce, *The Dublin Diary*, ed. George Harris Healey (London: Faber & Faber, 1962), 106-07.

[13] A review of the opening performance of the Abbey Theatre, quoted in Flannery, *Yeats and the Idea of a Theatre*, 244.

[14] See Peake, *Citizen and the Artist*, 277-78. My illustrations of Joyce's parodies of Catholic ritual are taken from Peake's much more detailed enumeration.

ritual and the delicate, if portentous ceremonials of revivalist theatre. As with Joyce's treatment of magic, his strategy here is partly to ridicule by overkill. There are rites of birth, death, marriage and baptism; rituals of confession, atonement and resurrection; Masonic rituals, Jewish rituals, Hindu rituals. All are put to service in a chapter where any object can become cultist, any gesture can become sacramental, and language is frequently litanic and catechistic in profane contexts:

> BELLO
> ... Hound of dishonour!
> BLOOM
> *(infatuated)* Empress
> BELLO
> *(his heavy cheekchops sagging)* Adorer of the adulterous rump!
> BLOOM
> *(plaintively)* Hugeness!
>
> (15. 2836-41)

Although Joyce uses rituals from all kinds of contexts and cultures those most frequently commandeered are the rituals of the Catholic Church. This represents a particularly significant divergence from revivalism, because for all its sense of itself as a ceremony of Irish culture, ironically enough, revivalist theatre almost entirely ignored Catholicism as ritual. Yeats did propagandize the notion of a theatre which would effect an integration of Catholicism and Celtic mysticism (a piece of grafting which, in the modern age, could seriously be entertained only by the very naïve or the very non-Catholic), but the plays themselves reserved very little space for Catholicism in their actual enactment of the collective unconscious. Catholicism was invariably presented on the stage as a 'foreign' phenomenon which corrupted the Celtic spirit and was usually associated with materialism and conformity. The priest was visualized as suppressing, or even oppressing, the Celtic spirit. His function was to protect the hero from the dangerous wildness of the Celtic imagination. Thus, in *The Land of Heart's Desire*, Father Hart warns Mary Bruin of the dangers of reading about 'Princess Edain/A daughter of a King of Ireland', tries to convert 'a faery child', and concludes the play with this comment on Mary Bruin's ceremonial exit into the Celtic mists :

> Thus do the spirits of evil snatch their prey
> Almost out of the very heart of God;
> And day by day their power is more and more.
>
> (Yeats, *CPL*, 72)

In 'Circe' on the other hand, the rituals of Catholicism have a central position in the psychological landscape, and with their conspicuous presence, Joyce's engagement with Anglo-Irish theatre takes a different turn. This is not mockery through literalization, but rather implies a new formulation of the Irish mind which radically takes issue with the revivalist conception. Indeed it is the structural usage of the rituals of Catholicism which above all establishes a sense of Joyce anatomizing the contours of a collective unconscious. Amongst the many references to Church ritual are Stephen's first appearance as a priest presiding over a Mass chanting *'with joy the* introit *for paschal time'* (15.73-74). There is a mock litany for Bloom and the chapters of the book he has survived, which is followed by *'a choir of six hundred voices, conducted by Vincent O' Brien'* (15.1953). A mock blessing is delivered by *'His Eminence, Simon Stephen Cardinal Dedalus ... round his neck a rosary of corks ending on his breast in a corkscrew cross'* (15.2654-56). The whores enact a mock confession; a Black Mass is celebrated on the belly of Mina Purefoy. That these examples without exception parody the Mass does not at all diminish the sense of Joyce restoring to his version of the Irish psychodrama the Catholicism which had been erased in revivalist theatre. The images of defilement are completely consistent with the sense of guilt which is embedded in the minds of characters in the chapter. Or, to put it differently, such images frequently represent the liberated unconscious expressing itself against the dominant religious culture. Thus the 'Pig God' Christ who is a bastard of the 'pope' (15.2572-73); Mary, the whore who has been polluted by the 'genitories' of a Roman centurion (15.2600); the priest in the brothel who represents the fall of man, these are examples of a kind of language thorough which an unrestrained unconscious wickedly exercises itself. Elsewhere Joyce's theatre of ritual uses not rituals of religion but rituals of state and empire: of trials, executions, coronations, the opening of the British parliament, foxhunting and so on. These litter the pages of Joyce's text, and their conspicuous presence again challenges the revivalist conception of what made-up the collective unconscious, undermining the representation of an authentic Irish-Celtic spirit which had remained pure and impervious to the invading 'stranger' and his alien culture. Anglicization, in Joyce's account, is not 'exterior', but forms the very stuff out of which his joco-serious representation of the collective mind expresses itself.[15]

There are many further ways in which Joyce challenges revivalist theatre, deriding its practices, and mocking the mysticism and esoterism of the revivalist milieu. The thoroughness of Joyce's dissection is wonderfully impressive. There is no characteristic of revivalism that is not victimized somewhere in 'Circe', in ways which sometimes seem blatantly opportunistic. The apocalypse business in 'Circe', for instance, is initiated by nothing more than Florry Talbot's defensive response to Zoe's comment at line 2126 about Stephen's intellectual superiority: 'God help your head, he knows more than you have forgotten.' At which point Florry reveals a piece of inside information which is presumably intended to show that she is not all that daft: 'They say the last day is coming this summer' (15.2129). What follows is a sequence that suggests the patterns of traditional Jewish and early Christian apocalypse.[16] The coming of the Antichrist, represented by Reuben J. and his grotesque son, prefigures 'the end of the world'. 'The consummation of all things' (15.2175) is followed by eternity bookings taken by an Americanized Elijah,[17] which in turn initiates the second coming, represented in 'Circe' by Mananaun Maclir. The tradition itself is ancient, of course, but in 'Circe' it is specifically located in turn of the century revivalism. 'The end of the world' dressed in 'tartan filibegs' (15.2178) suggests MacGregor Mathers, the occultist who for a while led the London Golden Dawn organization and was announcing 'the imminence of great wars' in the mid-1890s (Yeats, *Auto*, 336). He was passionate about Highland dress, although Yeats doubted whether he had ever seen the Highlands.

---

[15] For a fascinating discussion of this aspect of 'Circe' see Andrew Gibson's ' "Strangers in my house, bad manners to them!": England in "Circe" ', in Andrew Gibson, ed., *Reading Joyce's 'Circe'* (Amsterdam-Atlanta: Rodopi Press, 1994), 179-221.

[16] An excellent account of this tradition is given in the opening chapter of Norman Cohn's *The Pursuit of the Millennium* (London: Secker & Warburg, 1957).

[17] In the old testament tradition it is Elijah, as opposed to John the Baptist, who is the precursor of the Messiah.

The collection of Anglo-Irish intellectuals, Russell, Best and Eglinton, are resurrected from 'Scylla and Charybdis' in this sequence, with Russell appearing as Mananaun Maclir (one of the Celtic Gods whom he predicted would return to Ireland), complete with the *'bicycle pump'* which in historical reality would have presumably accompanied Russell as he toured Ireland by bicycle to propagandize Horace Plunkett's co-operative movement. Russell's play, *Deirdre,* is also suggested in this section (15.2261-78), because in Act 3 of that play, Cathyah, the king's druid calls upon Mananaun Maclir to wreck Niasi's ship. The conditions of this play's first production (1902) are also alluded to. Apparently Russell's opening night job was to wail offstage in imitation of the sea (see 15.2274 where Mananaun Maclir 'wails with the vehemence of the ocean').

An obsession with the apocalyptic can be seen in all aspects of the revivalist enterprise. Hyde's propagandizing of the language revival, for instance, presented Anglicization as a great black cloud that could only be dispelled by the Sword of Light wielded by the new age Fenians. The plays of the revival are similarly full of apocalyptic imagery. *The Countess Cathleen*, for example, opens with foreboding of imminent destruction. The 'graves are walking' and there are encounters with men without eyes, ears and mouths and with owls that have human faces.[18] In *The Unicorn From the Stars* Martin Hearne dreams of unicorns on the rampage:

> Martin: They were breaking the world. I am to destroy; destruction was the word the messenger spoke.
> Father John: To destroy?
> Martin: To bring again the old disturbed exalted life, the old splendour.
>
> (Yeats, *CPL*, 349)

This prevalence of apocalyptic thinking and pseudo-revolutionary eschatology amongst the Anglo-Irish intelligentsia was not simply some kind of *fin-de-siècle* malaise. According to Norman Cohn, apocalyptic and millenarianist traditions in medieval Europe had their origins in impoverished social and economic contexts and political repression, and were invariably linked to conditions of great social and

---

[18] See the beginning of *The Countess Cathleen* in Yeats, *CPL,* 3-4.

economic change.[19] The Anglo-Irish saw themselves as impoverished and betrayed by a Britain which was effecting a slow compromise with Catholic emancipation. The landlord class could hardly fail to be acutely conscious of its nineteenth-century decline in terms of political and social status. It was almost certainly this sense of decline that produced the essentially nostalgic tone of revivalist culture and it is in this context that revivalist eschatology, which attempted to represent the modernization of Ireland as a dark force of destruction, takes on a distinctive and reactionary political resonance. As well as ridiculing what he undoubtedly regarded as romantic posturing and sheer crankiness, Joyce's version of revivalist apocalyptic is sensitive to this reactionary context. Thus he conflates the rhetoric of revivalist eschatology with the marketing jargon of the American evangelist, and has the eight beatitudes, the inheritors of the new eternal kingdom, representing not Celtic spirituality, but a collection of quintessentially British vices: 'Beer beef battledog buybull businum barnum buggerum bishop' (15.2241-43). The suggestion here, and it is a savagely ironic one, is that in the revivalist eternity the redeemed Protestants will be returned to the culture of their original fatherland.

It should be clear by now that 'Circe' does not simply allude to revivalist theatre, or parody revivalist styles. Certainly 'Circe' satirizes revivalism, but it is also, as it were, formulated by revivalism. The strange concoction of magic, ritual, heroes, hobgoblins, messiahs, peasants and passion belonged to Yeats before Joyce got his hands on it. Even Stephen's famous coincidence of contraries, which for some critics gives a hermeneutic centre to Joyce's whirling episode, becomes related to Joyce's cultural intervention because it is a secularized variation on the dialectics of Yeats's *A Vision*, in particular, a variation on his theory of the Self and Anti-Self. In the original Irish form these ingredients were synthesized to form a theatre of icons for a lost people, a theatre which contained 'the spiritual seed and kernel of ... national poetic and national moral culture'.[20] In Joyce's reconstruction the same ingredients are never fully reconstituted. Their incongruity is left vulgarly and hilariously on display. The icons get joyfully smashed. The slogans become ridiculously out-sloganed in this

---

[19] See Cohn, *Pursuit of the Millennium*, Chapter 3.

[20] W. B. Yeats, ed., *The Arrow*, 1 (October 20 1906), quoted in Flannery, *Yeats and the Idea of a Theatre*, 105.

satirical version of 'the Paradisiacal Era' *(*15.1632). But the most basic antithesis between Joyce's play and revivalist theatre is probably this. The 'tragic' struggle between 'reality' and 'nobility'[21] which lies at the very centre of Yeats's dramatic conception becomes, in Joyce's version, no tragedy at all but a hugely comic farce, a pseudo-struggle inflicted on Bloom to a great extent, not for the audience's spiritual salvation but for its voyeuristic fascination.

Just as the aesthetics of *Ulysses* are precisely antithetical to the aesthetics of revivalism, so the inflation of Joyce's hero in 'Circe' is an exact negation of those markers of the heroic that were so heavily prescribed in revivalist culture. He is Jewish, urban, bourgeois, thoroughly Anglicized, and modern; when he should be Irish, rural, aristocratic, Celtic and displaced in a mythological past. Ironically, his frantically shifting status in the phantasmagoria of 'Circe' means that at various times he seems to represent just about the whole cast-list of revivalist drama. He is the evicted peasant, the playboy, the demagogue, Ireland's High King, a mystic, a madman, a passionate lover, an ascetic, a social reformer — as various in his 'masks', in fact, as Yeats was himself. It is undeniably tempting to see Yeats's personality obsession fantastically accelerated in Bloom's crazy role shifts, but the real point I want to make is that it is in this episode that Bloom's standing is most explicitly contextualized against the hero-worship of revivalism. The result is not some kind of moral victory for the liberal consensus over the radical heroics of revivalism. Nor does Bloom carry, as some have suggested, a political alternative to nationalism. The image of Bloom struggling with the role of a Jewish Cuchulain who wants to redeem his country through the provision of 'saloon motor hearses' does not constitute any kind of serious alternative agenda and there is no reason why it should. It is simply a hilarious contamination of romanticism by the commonplace, the human. The essential function of this contamination is again to refute the relevancy of revivalism. Far from staging the rebirth of the Irish soul, revivalist theatre becomes a redundancy which is completely out of touch with the realities of life. Bloom's incarnation as 'a man like Ireland wants' (15.1540), an appropriation of the epic that was most sacred to the Revival, works precisely in this way. Revivalist theatre was fundamentally a theatre of hero-worship; thus Synge's joking

---

[21] Cf. Jeffares, *Yeats, Man and Poet*, 318.

reference to the 'Cuchulanoid National Theatre'.[22] Plays like *The Countess Cathleen, Cathleen-ni-Hoolihan*, Lady Gregory's *The White Cockade* and *The Deliverer*, the plays in the Cuchulain cycle and many others celebrated a pantheon of Irish hero-messiahs struggling to lead an ignorant and fickle people to salvation. This cult of the hero was partly a matter of aesthetics insofar as Yeats was attempting to create a tragic theatre in opposition to what he saw as vulgar commercial superficiality. Hero worship was also a matter of cultural nationalism. Its ostensible purpose was to allow an audience to experience 'the sacred drama of its own history, every spectator finding self and neighbour'.[23] Apparently Yeats was fond of quoting Hugo's dictum: 'In the theatre the mob becomes a people.'[24] For at least some of the revivalist intelligentsia, messianism was also a faith. Both Yeats and AE had visions of the 'avatar' (the word for 'messiah' in theosophy), and a newer generation, Pearse's generation, whose own literary and political writings are full of messianic images, inherited that faith.[25] Bloom's magnificent rise to 'emperor-president and king-chairman ... Leopold the First!' (15.1471-72) and his subsequent fall to a dispossessed peasant *'leading a bogoak pig by a sagaun'* (15.1961) is Joyce's subversion of revivalist millenarianism.

The broad terms of this subversion are obvious enough. Joyce takes the detached, aristocratic, 'spiritual' and invariably Anglo-Irish[26] hero

---

[22] Synge's remark was adapted from a phrase coined by Stephen Mackenna. See David H. Greene and Edward M. Stephens, *J. M. Synge* (New York: Collier Books, 1961), 161-63.

[23] From Yeats commentary on 'Three Songs to the Same Tune', in *King of the Great Clock Tower*, 36-38.

[24] See Flannery, *Yeats and the Idea of a Theatre*, 66.

[25] See, for instance, Pearse's farewell speech to his students at St Edna's: 'As it took the blood of the son of God to redeem the world, so it would take the blood of Irishmen to redeem Ireland' (Padraic Pearse, *Collected Works: Political Writings and Speeches* [Dublin: Maunsel and Roberts, 1924], 121).

[26] This identification of heroism with Protestant Ireland is often crudely obvious, as in *The Countess Cathleen*, Martyn's *The Heather Field*, and Lady Gregory's *The White Cockade*. The latter contrasts James II's 'cowardly' betrayal of Ireland with the patriotic heroism of Patrick Sarsfield, Earl of Lucan.

of revivalism and humanizes him through the engaged, eminently practical and Jewish figure of Bloom, both using and demolishing the freewheeling sensualist of the so-called Heroic Age with a new hero who advocates both free love and electric dishscrubbers for all. The motives of the hero-messiah, always self-evident in revivalism (the hero is heroic because he is noble and ... heroic), become ruinously psychologized during the course of Bloom's apotheosis, where the desire to be loved, fear of rejection, the desire to exercise power, sexual and otherwise all lie somewhere behind the creation of the new Bloomusalem. The hero's mission to unify Ireland around an apparently syncretic culture of Gaelicism which would transcend the 'superficial' social and political divisions which separated Protestant and Catholic Ireland[27] is ludicrously outdone in the alliance of Catholic and Protestant and Jew, Presbyterian, Baptist, Anabaptist, Methodist and Moravian, Unionist and Nationalist and *'plumbing contractors'*, *'undertakers'* and *'gentlemen of the bedchamber'* (15.1420-37) who all rally around the call for 'Union of all, jew, moslem and gentile' (15.1686), in this 'promised land of our common ancestors' (15.1517-18). Although there is some evidence to link Lady Gregory's messianic play *The Deliverer* with this section of 'Circe',[28] it is the messianic tradition rather than a particular text that Joyce is satirizing here. Similarly Joyce is not attacking any particular Irish hero, but rather both the romantic aesthetics of the new Irish tragedy and the naïve and reactionary politics which looked for salvation in the leadership of the great man. Absurdly endorsed by his 'classic face' and notable 'forehead' (15.1468), by the unfathomable wisdom which makes him an authority on everything from gardening to diseases of the bladder, Bloom's 'greatness' does not just parody the heroics of revivalism, it laughs at hero-worship. And, in its jokey fashion, it carries a warning as well. The hero becomes an emperor and the emperor, even if he is the famously mild-mannered Bloom, is above the common herd of humanity and cannot tolerate dissent. Thus Bloom accepts the death of paupers constructing the new Bloomusalem as a worthy sacrifice and when the man in the mackintosh challenges the credentials of the new

---

[27] This is Yeats's famous 'Unity of Culture' which was to be based on 'an inherited subject matter known to the whole people' and which would unite 'religious, aesthetic and practical life'. See Yeats, *Auto*, 190-91.

[28] See the appendix below, 243-45.

messiah, he is summarily executed. The desire to serve becomes infected by the impulse to control.

As if he were strapped to Yeats's great whirling antithetical 'gyres', Bloom the saviour marches inexorably towards martyrdom. At the end of the apotheosis section, after being stoned and sacrificially burned, Bloom suffers the final humiliating degradation. He becomes an emigrant Irish peasant, *'in caubeen with clay pipe stuck in the band, dusty brogues'* (15.1960-61). This is one of the few places in 'Circe' where a specific allusion to revivalist theatre has been recognized. It is usually held that this alludes to a Synge play, although, oddly enough, there is nothing to link the passage specifically to any Synge play, other than the fact that here we have a peasant talking in brogue. But then it is quite difficult to think of a revivalist play that did not involve a peasant talking in brogue. Again Joyce concerns himself with a characteristic of revivalism, rather than with a particular text, or writer. Revivalist culture was a culture of peasant worship. The Irish peasant was seen as the repository of an authentic Irish culture and 'a traditional knowledge learned in leisure and contemplation'.[29] This was another of the Revival's most cherished idealizations. It is wrecked in 'Circe', partly because Joyce throws respect for the folk into soppy sentimentality and partly because he inverts the revivalist order of things. In revivalist hierarchy the peasant might be poor, but possessed of nobility, culture and wisdom, he represents the nation's lifeblood. In 'Circe', virtually the lowest state to which man can fall is that of the peasant. In fact, the only option left to Bloom after this decline is self-destruction: 'I am ruined. A few pastilles of aconite .... A letter. Then lie back to rest' (15.1966-67).

This hilarity tells us little that is not already known about Bloom from preceding episodes. Certainly as a character in a novel, Bloom has no great interest in revivalism, and never seriously identifies himself in conflict with revivalism. Bloom is an affront to just about everything the revival represented, but, it is not he who ridicules the revival and its theatre in *Ulysses* 15. He is simply commandeered into a collaboration with the mechanics of an episode which formulates itself against revivalism in fundamental ways.

Stephen, on the other hand, is far from indifferent to the politics of culture. From the first pages of *Ulysses* he has seen himself as a

---

[29] W. B. Yeats, *Plays and Controversies* (London: Macmillan, 1923), 208.

servant, a dispossessed son. This self-image is very specifically defined in terms of race. The 'voice of Esau' is not an articulation of deracinated romantic individualism. It is a product of colonial history. The usurper in *Ulysses* is not Mulligan or Haines, it is the Anglicized culture that they partially represent, and the most contradictory, and hypocritical form of Anglicized culture is revivalism, because it emphatically claims authenticity. Revivalism is also contemporaneous with Stephen. He resents the poets and playwrights of Ireland's renaissance and dismisses much of their work, but he is also predetermined to compete with them, just as was the young James Joyce. Joyce was a voracious consumer of revivalist literature, and a nervous one. In these early responses to revivalist texts, there is always the sense of Joyce dreading what revivalism might throw up in the way of Irish epics. Thus his enthusiastic 'riddling' of Synge's *Riders of the Sea* 'till it has not a sound spot in it .... Thanks be to God Synge isn't an Aristotelian' (*Letters II*, 35). There is a further complexity to Stephen's response to revivalist Ireland. It is one of the dominant cultural contexts which have formed him. Revivalist productions are frequently in his head. Behind the one piece of literature he produces in *Ulysses*, his vampire poem, is the translation of a revivalist, Hyde. Stephen's Shakespeare theory defines itself against revivalist aesthetics and cannot be understood without reference to revivalist aesthetics. Perhaps most suggestively, at the end of '*Circe*' the words that drift out from the half-conscious mind of a knocked down Stephen are from Yeats's 'Who Goes With Fergus'. None of this changes Stephen's engagement with the politics of culture, nor does the end of 'Circe' suggest anything as trite as recognition, despite everything, of Yeats's poetic greatness. Yeats's prominence at this climatic point of 'Circe' is a startling penetration into the extent of Anglo-Ireland's cultural usurpation. It energizes the fact that Stephen himself has no authentic culture to draw on. There is only revivalism. At his weakest moment, when his mind is full of monsters, the 'Black panther' and the 'Vampire' (15.4930), when he has been overcome by the representatives of the State, when he is imaged as an embryo outside the womb, it is, ironically, a revivalist poem which sounds out his disempowerment. It is not so much that Yeats's poem is a perfect expression of his dispossession, but rather that it represents the only 'Irish' culture at Stephen's disposal. In the end, Stephen singing his Irishness thorough a Yeats's song *is* poignant, in the same way that the transformation of Stephen into Bloom's dead son is poignant. And both are also deeply ironic. The same kind of irony is operating in those scenes where Stephen asserts his refusal to serve, but is condemned to act out his rebellion through classic scenes from the revivalist repertoire. However much his re-enactments challenge the revivalist consensus, and they do, the fact remains that when Stephen refuses the call to serve his country, for instance,[30] the terms of his dissent respond to revivalist agendas, and the forms of their expression evoke revivalist forms.

Many revivalist plays dramatize the situation in which a young Irishman is called upon to reject home comforts and conformity and sacrifice himself to the cause of Ireland.[31] The most well-known example is in *Cathleen ni Hoolihan* where, on his wedding day, Michael Gillane is invited into the 'hard service' of 'The Poor Old Woman', but there are many other plays where this scenario is played out. The policeman in Lady Gregory's *The Rising of the Moon*, Owen in *The White Cockade*, Martin Hearne in *The Unicorn From the Stars* are just a few representatives of those enlisted into Ireland's cause. In 'Circe', the sequence where Stephen encounters Privates Carr and Compton and ends up embroiled in high emotion is an ironic treatment of the same scene. There are two allusions to specific revivalist plays here. The first is at line 4578, where Old Gummy Granny *'thrusts a dagger towards Stephen's hand'* demanding that he 'remove' the English privates and free Ireland. This is an obvious parody of Yeats's dramatization of the Poor Old Woman in *Cathleen ni Hoolihan*. The second is at line 4436-37 where Stephen *'taps his brow'* and says, 'But in here it is I must kill priest and king'. This might loosely suggest Blake, but is much more closely linked to *The Unicorn From the Stars* (a Yeats and Lady Gregory collaboration), where Martin Hearne realizes that he was wrong to interpret his apocalyptic dream as a direct

---

[30] It could be argued that Stephen's vision of his mother is an ironic version of the 'visions' which seemed compulsory in revivalist drama. In the revivalist versions, the visions made immanent a glorious, and noble cultural past. The startling contrast between this and Stephen's vision of his mother's rotting corpse, urging him to submit to the Church, is highly suggestive.

[31] Rarely was an Irishwoman asked to make a similar sacrifice. One partial exception is in Yeats's *The Land of Heart's Desire* where Mary Bruin is called not to political action but to an eternal frolic in a Celtic spirit world.

call to political action: 'I was mistaken when I set out to destroy Church and Law. The battle we have to fight is fought out in our own mind' (Yeats, *CPL*, 378).[32] Stephen's line is close to this, which might suggest some sort of concurrence between the young Catholic artist and the Protestant Yeats. However, the lines from *The Unicorn From the Stars* are not deferential quotation. They are a reformulation, and there are some suggestive slippages from the original. In *The Unicorn From the Stars*, Martin Hearne, who, interestingly, is something of an exception in revivalist drama because he is a Catholic hero,[33] rules out direct political violence against the state as a 'mistake'. This is not the case in 'Circe' where Stephen asserts that 'struggle for life is the law of existence' and despises the 'arbitration' that he says was invented by 'the tsar and the King of England' (15.4434-35). In the revivalist play, Martin Hearne's 'we' gives his line the status of a manifesto; Stephen's 'I' identifies his line as a personal statement. Most significant is Stephen's more focused 'priest and king' which replaces Hearne's ambiguous 'Church and Law'. 'Church' is a clumsy attempt at sidestepping the religious controversy, and 'Law' represents a curious de-politicizing of Hearne's revolt. This means that the difference between 'priest and king' and 'Church and Law' refers us to the very

---

[32] Yeats, *CPL*, 378. Yeats, of course, was even more interested in Blake than Joyce. After four years of study, he produced a book in collaboration with Edwin John Ellis called *The Works of William Blake, Poetic, Symbolic and Critical* (London: Bernard Quaritch, 1893). It is likely that Blake lies somewhere behind Martin Hearne's line.

[33] Perhaps 'hero' is not quite accurate. Hearne's status in the play is qualified in various ways. He is a mystic, on whom Catholic teaching seems to have made remarkably little impact, and a man of action. He dreams of freeing his country from England's life-denying oppression and from the soul-destroying materialism of conventional life. He has apocalyptic visions and interprets these to mean that he should burn the landlords' estates. It turns out that he is wrong in this interpretation, although the nature of his error is never made clear. In the end, Yeats and Lady Gregory deprive their hero of any meaningful course of political action. He is shot for his 'crimes', crimes which are the result of his 'misreading' the visions, and dies with a new vision in his head. But we never find out what this vision is or what it means. The obscurity is typical of a revivalist theatre which displaced the real political world in a mythic non-place where 'the signs' had to be 'read'. My feeling is that this displacement and obscurity reflects the contradictions inherent in the nationalism of landlord nationalists.

different social and political positions from which Yeats and Stephen operate. That difference is more emphatically measured in Stephen's complete dissent from the culture of martyrdom. In Stephen's version of the call to country, heroic choice is replaced by mindless mechanism; heroic acceptance replaced by sensible refusal. Yeats's 'Poor Old Woman' who suffers in quiet nobility becomes a virulent bloodthirsty hag in 'Circe'. Stephen's disassociation from the martyr mentality of revivalist theatre is absolute. He is no fighter. He refuses to bleed for some abstract and obscure notion of nationhood, and knows that he has been moulded and shaped by the corrupting ideologies of Church and State. Some critics have seen Stephen's statements of dissent as a significant and necessary development, although in some senses Stephen in 'Circe' is not too far removed from the Stephen at the end of *Portrait*. He is still declaring his independence and a declaration, after all, even a manifesto, is not the same thing as a revolution. Moreover, Stephen's mind remains obsessive in its historicizing, and in this sense it remains a colonial product. At one level the scene between Stephen and the two English privates has nothing to do with noble resistance. The text insists that we respond to that level, on which two drunken soldiers, taking the opportunity to impress a girl, assault a drunken Irishman and run off when the police arrive. The transformation of this seedy little encounter into an Irish epic is Stephen's. Unlike Bloom, who has little or no access to the 'hallucinations' which are inflicted on him, Stephen's head, which is a landscape of Shan van Vochts, strangers and round towers, makes this scene. That is to say, the scene is close to Stephen's conscious psychological state. That he should use the romantics of revivalism to orchestrate his dissent becomes a classic case of the colonized mind resisting through the constructs of the invading culture. The whole scene is a vivid illustration of the 'nightmare' from which Stephen is still *'trying'* to *'awake'* (my italics).

This view of Stephen's continuing entrapment confirms, if any confirmation were needed, that the real extremism of 'Circe' lies not in the 'development' of characters, but in the mechanics of the episode itself. Joyce's play constitutes the radical intervention in the politics of culture. Revivalism is appropriated, deprived of status, stripped to its ideological bones. The revival's pseudo-religiosity is laughed at. The whole revivalist show becomes a redundancy for modern Ireland, a puritanical culture of a dying aristocracy. In 'Circe', Joyce really wipes the floor with Protestant revivalism. From his spoliation of the collective unconscious, that national treasure of revivalism, to his wicked displacement of revivalist materials, he is merciless and unequivocal. This demolition job is not an act of anarchic vandalism, but an expression of social consciousness. Quite simply, the response to revivalism in 'Circe' is so fundamental, so precise, so unyielding, that it could only have been written by an Irish Catholic. No other class or culture could have had that much invested in the issue of revivalism. The corollary of this is that for all the liberated smashing of icons and flouting of revivalist conventions, there must be some primary sense in which 'Circe' is itself the product of a colonized mind. Of course, there are obvious and fundamental distinctions to be made between Stephen's self-dramatizations and the sheer comic vitality of 'Circe'. But for all that, 'Circe' is hardly 'free'. It is crucially decided by its engagement with Anglo-Irish cultural nationalism. In some sense the episode, like Stephen, is programmed to resist, to refute the cultural authenticity of Anglo-Ireland. The more Joyce attacks, the more he is embroiled in formulations of the very conflicts which, so the story goes, forced him out of Ireland in the first place. Joyce in Trieste or Joyce in Paris apparently made little difference to the fact that Joyce remained the churchless Catholic in contest with the estateless landowners over a culture that no longer existed.

One of the essential characteristics of 'Circe', and *Ulysses* as a whole, is that the text is so self-conscious about these formulations and their contradictions. Whilst revivalism flounders about in obscurity, determinedly mystified by its own origins, *Ulysses* revels in the cultural conditions of its own making. In revivalism the conflicts and the ideologies are strategically hidden; in *Ulysses* the strategy is to have these openly on show. In the Revival, Anglicized culture is, ostensibly, banished and authentic culture is imminent. In *Ulysses* Anglicized culture is flaunted. The authenticity of *Ulysses* as a Irish book *is* articulated thorough the novel's usurping challenge to Anglo-Irish culture. But the same status is also underwritten by the fact that *Ulysses* is blatant in its own cultural contamination. Joyce's book is made out of such fabrics as English Victorian melodrama, Anglicized newspapers, English fashions, English women's magazines, the historical development of English literature, and Shakespeare's life and times. All this produces a literature which needs to be distinguished from what D. P. Moran called that 'mongrel thing', 'Irish literature, in the English language'.[34] Joyce manages to write a real thoroughbred out of this bastardized stuff. From really unpromising material, like clichéd English views of the Irish, Joyce is able to make a unique contribution to Irish cultural history. Thus in *Ulysses* a truncated round tower built by William Pitt becomes a more appropriate symbol of Irish culture than the real McCoy. To interpret this anomaly as a laugh at the expense of the so-Irish Irish would be to badly miss the point. Joyce could hardly build his epic of repossession from old jokes about the Irish emulating the English. Joyce's version of the paradoxical Irish is also quite distinct from Wildean wit and has nothing to do with the cool detached intelligence of the aesthete. That Anglicization becomes an absolute condition of Irish authenticity is far more than just a joke in Joyce's fiction. This assertion is powered by a highly sophisticated historical consciousness and it carries both bite and poignancy. You get some sense of the complexity of the issues involved when you realize that however Anglicized the culture reproduced in *Ulysses* may be, there is never any doubt that the Joycean rewrite is Irish, even when the original craftsman is Yeats. Joyce's counterblast to a culture of religious and political retreatism involves both squaring up to and assimilating the realities of cultural colonialism. I would argue then that the most fundamental irony of *Ulysses* is that it is an authentic Irish epic, partly by virtue of its astonishing activation of cultural hybridity.

---

[34] Moran, *The Philosophy of Irish Ireland*, 33-34.

6 'Our Modern Babylon': Modernity and the National Culture in 'Eumaeus' and 'Ithaca'

The *ricorso* finally arrives after the reader has made five hundred pages of serious investment. Expectancies will presumably be high, particularly if we cling to the idea that the Stephen/Bloom business is driving this massive novel, and there is no doubt that the styles of both episodes wickedly exploit such expectations. The 'Eumaeus' narrator, far from being 'tired',[1] is a bustler, eager to feed narrative. This seems promising for eventuality and resolution. 'Ithaca' looks even more viable as a place of closure and completion, because, it articulates in a high status discourse of rationality, fact and scientific procedure.

The narrators of both 'Eumaeus' and 'Ithaca' are contracted to order and authority, albeit of different kinds. In 'Eumaeus', bourgeois ethics and 'commonsense' have inherited the world, the world which 'Ithaca' purports to theorize in scientific terms. A further linkage between the two episodes is that the essential joke in both turns on the collapse of this authority. In 'Eumaeus', for instance, the imperative to narrate, and to narrate 'correctly', produces a pretentious, pompous, pedantic language which only serves to impede narrative dynamics and clarity. The consequent circumlocution is paralleled by digression in narrative content. At a time of impending closure, 'Eumaeus' does indeed practice story telling. In fact there is an obvious concentration of stories, tales and fables here. We listen in on the stories of the Amiens street railway station incident and of Corny Kelleher's intervention in Nighttown; to the rumour about John Corley's true aristocratic parentage and in turn to Corley's story about Bags Comisky. D. B. Murphy is himself a habitual story-teller and through the smug and bumptious filter of the 'Eumaeus' narrative we hear stories of 'Simon Dedalus's' sharp-shooting exploits, magical Chinese pills, the man killed in Trieste, and the sad demise of Antonio who was 'ate by sharks' (16.691). The episode is full of stories and yarns like

---

[1] In the Linati schema, Joyce himself labelled the style of 'Eumaeus' 'Prosa rilassata', relaxed prose. The usual explanation has been that the 'tired' style echoes the mental state of Stephen and Bloom. For the phrase used in the title of this chapter, 'Our Modern Babylon', see 16.514.

'the case of Callaghan' and the history of old Gumley. It is stuffed with tales of shipwrecks and mistaken identity and it disinters some favourite narratives from recent Irish history: the story of the Invincibles, for example, and of Parnell's fall. But for all this narrative busyness, the story which the reader has most investment in, the Stephen/Bloom story, remains not just unresolved, but virtually untouched. Despite Bloom's energetic attempts at engagement, and partly because of them, Stephen is incapable of achieving vague interest, let alone the atonement that the overblown structuring of *Ulysses* promises.

> Over his untastable apology for a cup of coffee, listening to this synopsis of things in general, Stephen stared at nothing in particular.
> (16.1141- 42)

Bored youth meets boring middle age in 'Eumaeus' and nearly nineteen hundred lines testify to the fact.

'Eumaeus' is modern because it is so remorselessly promotes bourgeois values. The episode begins appropriately with a sense of orderly prioritising, and the idiom of middle-class, Edwardian England — 'preparatory to anything else Mr Bloom brushed off the greater bulk of the shavings' (16.1-2). It proceeds by 'bringing common sense to bear' (16.31) on the immediate issues and continues by promising to sort things out. There is the 'confident anticipation' that, by 'putting a good face on things' (16.32), trusting providence and observing the proprieties, useful outcomes will result, undoubtedly to Stephen and Bloom's mutual benefit. The language of 'Ithaca' is modern in a different way. The idioms and grammatical structures of bourgeois social discourse are displaced by a style which evokes popular science and encyclopaedia culture. Positivism, rationalism and progress historiography energize what appears to be a supremely confident first ending to Joyce's novel. The problem in 'Ithaca' is that this narrative style, far from controlling and resolving, has such a flattening effect that it actually robs us of meaning. We get facts in piles, but no meaningful value-system in which to place them. The potentially significant is buried under the probably redundant. The information that Bloom once had a commission to write 'a topical song ... on the events of the past ... entitled '*If Brian Boru could but come back and see old Dublin now*' (17.417-19), and precisely six reasons for not finishing the project (all detailed), is a case in point. Who needs to know?

The fact of the commission itself is, in all probability, not important at all, but the song-title is another matter. It has a certain resonance, reminding us perhaps of Joyce's sustained interference with cultural nationalism in 'Circe', because one of the heroes of Irish history — heroic, at least, according to the revivalist version of events[2] — is getting rough treatment. The figure of Brian Boru is threatened with double contamination, by an irreverent handling in an Anglicized cultural form, the pantomime. More than this, however, the song title takes us quite precisely to the two essential myths of revivalist national culture. Firstly, the mere notion of Brian Boru's presence in the new postlapsarian nightmare of machines and money-making evokes the myth of epic return, a return which in most revivalist culture joined forces with the residual survival of the old, innocent world in the culture of rural Ireland. Yeats's interest in his own country, for instance, was powered by the 'discovery' that:

> the common people ... [who] have not given themselves up to the improvements and devices of good citizens, which we call civilization, still half understand the sanctity of their hills and valleys.[3]

Secondly, the suggestion that '*Dublin now*' would be shockingly alien to the old hero is a trivializing version of the myth of cultural degeneration, a myth which received its most influential exposition in Yeats and which permeated revivalist culture of his day.[4] The Gaelic

---

[2] In revivalist historiography Brian Boru possessed the essential Gaelic virtues: wisdom, nobility and generosity. He is presented as securing Irish 'life, property and chastity' from both Danish and Norman invaders. See O'Conor, *History of the Irish People*, 42-43. Joyce himself regarded Brian Boru as just another 'usurper'. See *CW*, 159.

[3] W. B. Yeats, 'The Literary Movement in Ireland', in Gregory, ed., *Ideals in Ireland*, 100.

[4] Before that time the Protestant antiquarians of Celtic Ireland were using their 'scientific' and 'rationalist' discoveries of an ancient Irish culture to articulate equality with an England in whose cultural and economic status they fully expected to participate. Thus Ireland was itself presented as a colonizing country which had established settlements in Britain 'inspiring Ireland's sister island on to paths of progress' (Hutchinson, *Cultural Dynamics of Nationalism*, 58).

Athletic Association, the Gaelic League, the Irish National Theatre, the *Dublin University Review,* U.C.D.'s *Lyceum* and *New Ireland Review,* Griffith's *United Irishman,* W. P. Ryan's *Irish Peasant,* Moran's *Leader,* a very large proportion of the cultural life of Joyce's Dublin in fact, all owed something to the Yeatsian articulation of the myth of cultural degeneration. There were, as we have seen, wide variations in the ways in which nationalist movements responded to modernization and notorious ambivalences in both Catholic and Protestant relationships to the new age.[5] These were exposed, for instance, in the controversial and deeply ideological issue of the actual dating of Ireland's cultural decline.[6] But both Catholic and Protestant revivalists were in agreement to the extent that they perceived Ireland's empire of spirit as being virtually wrecked, somewhere along the line, by the dark corrupting forces of materialism.

These two stories about cultural decline, and the returning hero take us close to the centres of 'Eumaeus' and 'Ithaca'. Return is precisely what these episodes are all about. In 'Eumaeus', the fable of homecoming and recognition is related in precisely the 'joyless' and 'pallid' language of urban bourgeois culture that Synge thought inimical to dramatic poetry.[7] In 'Ithaca', Joyce's joke-hero, himself a man of

---

[5] The Literary Revival was contemporary with William Morris's neo-medievalism and Matthew Arnold's 'hellenism'. Thus the Gaelicism of Yeats's movement could be described as part of a British-wide romantic reaction against materialism. This kind of irony partly explains why sectarian divisions were to characterize the crystallization of Irish cultural revivalism in the late nineteenth and early twentieth centuries.

[6] Anglo-Irish revivalists dated cultural degeneration from the conversion to Christianity, a conversion which was seen to repress Celtic vitality. Catholic nationalists would have identified with Joyce's line that 'Ireland ceased to be an intellectual force in Europe' from 'the time of the English invasion' (*CW,* 161).

[7] See Synge's Preface to *Playboy of the Western World,* where Synge acknowledges his artistic debt to the language of the Irish peasantry which is 'rich' and 'copious'. The 'literature of towns', however, has no such linguistic life: 'On the stage one must have reality, and one must have joy; and that is why the intellectual modern drama has failed, and people have grown sick of the false joy of the musical comedy, that has been given them in place of the rich joy found only in what is superb and wild in reality' (J. M. Synge, *Plays, Poems and Prose,* edited by Ernest Rhys, [London: Dent, 1941], 107-08).

'scientific temperament' (see 17.560), returns under the icy, unreflecting gaze of materialist scientism, the very 'move of thought',[8] as Yeats put it, that was considered to be destroying Irish life. Of course, Joyce's text and his characters are consistently exposed to a modern urban environment, but 'Eumaeus' and 'Ithaca' get their discourse status from the very fact that, here, narrative itself is usurped, firstly by the voice of the middle class, and secondly by the process of materialist scientism. These are the episodes where modernity is crudely and blatantly in control of the actual 'story-telling'. The homeland in the *ricorso*, then, is not just a domestic territory, 7 Eccles Street with Molly Bloom as 'Penelope', but an Irish city which is under the obvious authority of the modern, Anglicized, bourgeois world. Which means that Bloom's song that never gets written emerges from the rubble of Ithacan facticity to take on particular significance. The displacement of an ancient Irish hero in modernity images the central dynamic which shaped and determined Irish cultural nationalism,[9] the negotiation of modernization by organicist Gaelicism.[10] Thus the amazed regard of the resurrected Gael confronted by urban modernity replicates the perspective of revivalism attempting to articulate Ireland's cultural uniqueness in the modern world. In this way the title of Bloom's music-hall song conflates the myth of epic return with the central modernist and post-colonial issues which drive *Ulysses* to its closing chapters.

What are the essential characteristics of this modern Ireland produced in 'Eumaeus' and 'Ithaca'? Imagination and poetry have apparently been completely ousted. The revivalist nightmare is made manifest. In 'Eumaeus', romance and individuality, and the Irish reputation for verbal wit and inventiveness in speech, are displaced by

---

[8] Yeats in Gregory, ed., *Ideals in Ireland*, 98.

[9] For the important dynamic between nationalism and modernization, see Hutchinson, *Cultural Dynamics of Nationalism*. In chapter 5, Hutchinson notes Weber's contribution to the understanding of this dynamic and the substantial contribution of A. D. Smith in his *Theories of Nationalism* (1971), *Nationalism in the Twentieth Century* (1979) and *The Ethnic Revival* (1981).

[10] In fact, all nineteenth and twentieth-century nationalist movements which have promoted ethnic historicism have developed in response to the rise of science and the growth of international secular culture. See Hobsbawm, *Nations and Nationalism*, chapters 2 and 4.

locutions reçues which articulate an utterly conventional ethical bias. 'Ithaca', on the other hand, is narrated in a question and answer routine which evokes scientific procedures, partly because it so remorselessly insists that the world is rationally knowable. For each question in 'Ithaca', except perhaps the last one, there *is* an answer, and quite often the answers carry a sense of indubitable correctness, if only by virtue of sheer weight of words. There is a fervid insistence on the authority of the scientific world: discourses of mathematics, mechanics, physics, astronomy, logic, biology and chemistry are all self-consciously and authoritatively deployed. Answers also come in the form of advertising slogans, songs, lists of books, riddles, rhymes, biographical detail, and historical material. But for all this apparent inconsistency, the chapter feels homogenous, partly because there is a consistency in the narrative tone. It is seemingly flat and emotionless. The narrative appears to be supremely confident in its own powers of reasoning. It is this narrative attitude and the procedure of enquiry involved which, even more than the actual responses, locate 'Ithaca' firmly in the modern age of scientism, reason and materialism, the world which for cultural revivalists was absolutely inimical to art.

The worlds of 'Eumaeus' and 'Ithaca' are also deeply indebted to progress historiography. In the former, progress historiography, like everything in this chapter, is subject to a populist reduction. Like the contradictory 'revolution' which 'must come on the due instalments plan' (16.1101), the serious business of Whig teleology is transmuted into the rather more homespun notion that if the proprieties are observed and opportunities taken, things will generally turn out for the best. This is a 'pull yourself together', 'look on the bright side' philosophy. 'Ithaca', however, is powered by a more compelling dynamic of human self-development and social improvement. In this sense, the chapter enacts the essential drama of bourgeois history making in the nineteenth century. The narrator appears to be a splendid exemplar of self-education, a remarkable product of an encyclopaedia culture which was designed to bridge the gap between 'the people' and 'the learned', selling a knowledge which would 'elevate the faculties above low pursuits', 'refine' and 'purify' and 'help our reason to assuage' the 'violence' of human passion; as well as possibly offering 'some positive advantage in the achievement of 'worldly wealth and comfort'.[11] Some sequences of questions are either gradated by difficulty or urge the responding voice to refine and develop, and this too is suggestive of progress historicism. Above all, despite the cold, empiricist surface, this narrator seems almost elevated in his descriptions of science as applied in the name of civic improvement. He is the poet laureate of water supply and gas on tap. Of course, all these characteristics are consistent with Bloom himself, or at least, with that familiar Bloom who regards self-improvement as a moral imperative and who is so stimulated by 'appreciation of the importance of inventions now common but once revolutionary' (17.564-65). The Darwinist Bloom who luxuriates in many schemes for human improvement of his own devising (see 17.571-575/1710-42) is in obvious sympathy with the cultural assumptions of the Ithacan narrator, just as he is almost seamlessly joined to the entire discourse of 'Eumaeus'. These narrators sound like Bloom because they voice the urban, bourgeois, early twentieth-century world: the 'homeland' which is so much Bloom and, in this novel, so much Ireland as well. The range of this signification is perhaps most obvious in the linkage between science, historiography and civic consciousness in 'Ithaca'.

Just as Bloom's 'tendency' is 'towards applied, rather than pure science' (17.561-62), then, so is the tendency of 'Ithaca' generally. Applied science supports a progress historiography which is illustrated most obviously in long descriptions of civic culture. The delivery of 'every modern convenience' is inevitably accompanied by a growth in political bureaucracy, and this too is reflected in 'Ithaca', which becomes littered with allusions to corporate municipal life and, to a lesser extent, to the State. There are references to borough surveyors (see 17.173), taxpayers (see 17.182), 'the South Dublin Guardians' (17.177), 'the waterworks committee' (17.174), 'the municipal fishmarket' (17.430), the 'new lord mayor' (17.444), councillors (see 17.601), alderman (see 17.1344), 'Queen Victoria' (17.429/1816), 'their Royal highnesses the duke and duchess of York' (17.432), 'the new high sheriff' (17.444), 'the new solicitor-general' (17.444), MPs (see 17.1649-50), resident magistrates and justices of the peace (see 17.1610), the Royal Dublin Society (see 17.2135) and so on.

Modern civilization, then, is the precise and unequivocal locus of

---

[11] James Wylde, ed., *Circles of the Sciences* (London: The London Printing and Publishing Co., n.d.), iii-iv.

Modernity and the National Culture 187

both 'Eumaeus' and 'Ithaca', a civilization which thinks of itself as being the product of a 'natural' evolutionary process, but which is emphatically middle-class. This represents another engagement with the revivalist account of Irish culture. 'Eumaeus' is in the hands of the 'fox that crept into the badger's hole', the 'smallkeepers' and 'clerks', the very class which, Yeats insisted, had risen to 'power ... above the traditions of the countryman, without learning those of cultivated life or even educating themselves' (Yeats, *E & I*, 248):

> It was a subject of regret and absurd as well on the face of it and no small blame to our vaunted society that the man in the street, when the system really needed toning up, for the matter of a couple of paltry pounds was debarred from seeing more of the world they lived in instead of being always and ever cooped up since my old stick-in-the-mud took me for a wife. After all, hang it, they had their eleven and more humdrum months of it and merited a radical change of *venue* after the grind of city life in the summertime for choice when dame Nature is at her spectacular best constituting nothing short of a new lease of life.
>
> (16.539-47)

There is nothing in the above which is not cliché. The genius of this 'Eumaeus' is that cliché here *is* the discourse and it is cliché which most fundamentally isolates 'Eumaeus' from the Yeatsian aesthetic. Indeed, in Yeats's terms, 'Eumaeus' is not art at all, but the epitome of anti-art, a complete confirmation of that revivalist historiography which has the middle classes inheriting the world and its entire works.

Despite its apparent 'objectivity', 'Ithaca' is also everywhere characterized by bourgeois attitudes, as in this sequence of 'questions': 'Prove that he [Bloom] loved rectitude from his early youth'; 'How much and how did he propose to pay for his country residence?'; 'What rapid but insecure means to opulence might facilitate immediate purchase?' (17.1634/1657/1672-73). As in the very first response, where we are told that Stephen and Bloom 'crossed both before George's church diametrically, the chord in any circle being less than the arc which it subtends' (17.8-10), the assured tone and the pompous delivery also underpin the bourgeois identity of the narrator. The redundancy of information, which so puzzles readers of this episode, is substantially a product of a bourgeois frame of reference which so badly wants to insist on its status, its own universal authority. Towards the end of the episode, 'civilization' is increasingly characterized and measured in terms of the bourgeois lifestyle and bourgeois aspirations, as they are meticulously detailed in the remarkable passage which describes Bloom's ideal home, right down to the 'halldoor, olive green, with smart carriage finish and neat doorbrasses' (17.1507-08) and the 'bentwood perch fingertame parrot (expurgated language)' (17. 1534).

One final addition to this characterization of the Ithacan world. There is a determined absence of nationalist historical consciousness in the narrative styles of these two episodes. In 'Eumaeus', historical imagination is defeated by both sensationalism and domestication, and the narrator of 'Ithaca' can only list cold facts from the past; he possesses no sense of national destiny. Almost uniquely amongst Irish story-tellers, the narrators of these episodes possess no historical imagination at all. They are rooted in the mechanics of the now. Historical memory, even more than national language, was *the* defining characteristic of 'the national community'.[12] Thus George Russell was converted from being a recluse, and entered national life as a co-operationist after being spiritually elevated by O'Grady's Irish histories:

> It was the memory of race which rose up within me, and I felt exalted as one who learns he is among the children of kings.[13]

The static 'nowness' of the first two chapters of Joyce's 'nostos' is perhaps one of the surest indicators of the extent to which these episodes plummet into a revivalist hell.

'Eumaeus' and 'Ithaca' seem to bring home the worst fears of cultural nationalism. In the gossipy world of 'Eumaeus', Ireland's historical role becomes the subject of lurid voyeurism or worse, reduced to romanticized mediocrity as Parnell's tragedy transmutes into farce and soap-opera:

> the simple fact of the case was it was simply a case of the husband not being up to the scratch, with nothing in common between them beyond the name, and then a real man arriving on the scene, strong to the verge of weakness, falling a victim to her siren charms and forgetting home ties, the

---

[12] Hutchinson, *Cultural Dynamics of Nationalism*, 5.

[13] Quoted in H. A. O'Grady, *Standish O'Grady: The Man and the Writer* (Dublin: The Talbot Press, 1927), 16.

usual sequel, to bask in the loved one's smiles.

(16.1379-84)

In the cold mechanical world of 'Ithaca', talk about 'nation' becomes just one more item in a series of conversational topics, of no more or less significance than talk about 'Paris', 'careers' or 'the influence of gaslight or the light of arc and glowlamps on the growth of adjoining paraheliotropic trees' (17.12-17). Similarly, Ireland's ancient literary heritage becomes just another list, the 'Book of the Dun Cow, Book of Ballmote, Garland of Howth, Books of Kells' (17. 755-56), being flattened and submerged in a host of other lists. In fact, this whole body of literature seems very much *less* significant in cultural terms than, say, an advertising 'prospectus':

> It heals and soothes while you sleep, in case of trouble in breaking wind, assists nature in the most formidable way, insuring instant relief in discharge of gases, keeping parts clean and free natural action, an inital outlay of 7/6 making a new man of you and life worth living. Ladies find Wonderworker especially useful, a pleasant surprise when they note delightful result like a cool drink of fresh spring water on a sultry summer's day. Recommend it to your lady and gentlemen friends, lasts a lifetime. Insert long round end. Wonderworker.

(17.1824-33)

The Book of Kells might remain as an object for academic study (see 17.747-60), but it is dead culture. This advertisement for the English-made Wonderworker, 'the world's greatest device for rectal complaints' is altogether modern. Its advertising clichés ('it heals and soothes while you sleep'), absurd poeticisms ('like a cool drink' on a 'summer's day') and pseudo-scientism ('discharge of gases'), form a perfect expression of the elements which made up the revivalist anti-world. In this modernity the Irish language which was so central to the defining of the national culture is, like the ancient literature, thoroughly silenced by the sound of a pedantic and pretentious, bourgeois English. Even worse, Gaelic is relegated to a scribble on the blank back page of *Sweets of Sin* (17.733-34), one of those vile alien publications that were thought by Hyde to be sapping the Irish spirit. All this is consistent with T. M. Kettle's bitter contemporary assessment of the 'new Philistinism' choking Irish life,[14] with Yeats's despair at middle-class vulgarity,[15] and even with Moran's powerful rhetoric about 'the battle of two civilizations'.[16] Except, of course, that Joyce's articulation of an Irish city under modern siege is not bitter or despairing, nor does it constitute a diatribe. On the contrary, the essential, defining characteristic of both 'Eumaeus' and Ithaca' is that they are hugely funny.

The comedy of these episodes derives partly from the fact that Joyce gets so close to the modernity that cultural nationalists vilified. The Joycean text is deeply engaged with the modern 'other' so despised by revivalism. His Ithacan texts are constructed from the clichés and ponderous grammatical proprieties of middle-class language codes, and are ridiculously corrupted with the 'impure ... curiosities about politics, about science, about history, about religion' which, for Yeats, characterized the modern 'method'. It is as if Joyce is embracing the very contamination of the other which cultural nationalism so feared. One result of this closeness is that the elevated and precious revivalist conception of the modern enemy crumbles in 'Eumaeus' and 'Ithaca', because what Yeats and his followers described from a refined distance as a monolithically powerful ideology is transformed at close quarters into an absurd one, which is

---

[14] Kettle, *Irish Oratory and Orators*, xv.

[15] 'In spite of myself my mind dwells more and more on ideas of class. Ireland has grown sterile, because power has passed to men who lack the training which requires a certain amount of wealth to ensure continuity from generation to generation, and to free the mind in part from other tasks. A gentleman is for one thing a man whose principle ideas are not connected with his personal needs and personal successes' (Yeats, *Mem*, 178).

[16] Some Joyceans argue that Joyce is close to Moran on the cultural nationalism issue. It is true that Moran, 'the ideologue of a liberal-industrial Catholic nation' (Hutchinson, *Cultural Dynamics of Nationalism*, 173), did scorn the Anglo-Irish contribution to modern political development in Ireland and that he mocked the 'Celtic note', which he identified as an Anglicized invention. But in other respects there are significant divergences from Joyce. Moran's promotion of lay Catholic leadership did not prevent the Catholic clergy from identifying with his conception of a 'purist, uncontaminated Catholic society'. Moreover, Moran was reactionary in his denouncement of the Irish Transport and General Workers Union (1908), which he saw as socialist and therefore as one more example of the tide of 'Anglicization' which was flooding Irish life.

Modernity and the National Culture 191

continually struggling for meaning, wrecking itself on its own authority, and falling into the traps of its own sense of propriety and logic. In the following extract from 'Eumaeus', for example, order, clarity, precision and decorum struggle for survival, eventually collapsing as pronouns lose referents and subjects become utterly obscure:

> Briefly, putting two and two together, six sixteen which he pointedly turned a deaf ear to, Antonio and so forth, jockeys and esthetes and the tattoo which was all the go in the seventies or thereabouts even in the house of lords because early in life the occupant of the throne, then heir apparent, the other members of the upper ten and other high personages simply following in the footsteps of the head of the state, he reflected about the errors of notorieties and crowned heads running counter to morality such as the Cornwall case a number of years before under their veneer in a way scarcely intended by nature, a thing good Mrs Grundy, as the law stands, was terribly down on though not for the reason they thought they were probably whatever it was except women chiefly who were always fiddling more or less at one another it being largely a matter of dress and all the rest of it.
>
> (16.1195-07)

Here, in this embarrassed attempt to handle the subject of homosexuality, the narrative is slipping from control as it attempts to maintain an attitude of 'proper' disapprobation and keep a liberal evenness, whilst simultaneously ensuring that nothing whatsoever is given away. In the following extract from 'Ithaca', the narrative disturbance is of quite a different kind:

> What relation existed between their ages?
>
> 16 years before in 1888 when Bloom was of Stephen's present age Stephen was 6. 16 years after in 1920 when Stephen would be of Bloom's present age Bloom would be 54. In 1936 when Bloom would be 70 and Stephen 54 their ages initially in the ratio of 16 to 0 would be as 17½ to 13½, the proportion increasing and the disparity diminishing according as arbitrary future years were added, for if the proportion existing in 1883 had continued immutable, conceiving that to be possible, till then 1904 when Stephen was 22 Bloom would be 374 and in 1920 when Stephen would be 38, as Bloom then was, Bloom would be 646 while in 1952 when Stephen would have attained the maximum postdiluvian age of 70 Bloom, being 1190 years alive having been born in the year 714, would have surpassed

by 221 years the maximum antediluvian age, that of Methusalah, 969 years, while if Stephen would continue to live until he would attain that age in the year 3072 A.D., Bloom would have been obliged to have been alive 83,300 years, having been obliged to have been born in the year 81,396 B.C.

(17. 446-61)

This mathematical wizardry summons up all the certitude of the scientific age, except that calculations on a proportional relation that does not even exist are completely pointless. The passage aims for authority, but ends up in a cycle that could go on forever without getting anywhere. If there is a potentially interesting idea here, that Stephen and Bloom get closer, as it were, as they get older, that idea is swamped by a process of calculation that exists entirely for its own sake. Some critics have found such apparently cold, pointless passages revealing of 'the bleak and terrifying universe in which man seems minute, insignificant and at the mercy of powers beyond his imagination',[17] just as some have found the narrator of 'Eumaeus' a dark 'posturer' who speaks a 'deadly' 'concealing' language.[18] Such views, which Yeats presumably would have shared, surely miss the real point. The minds behind these narratives are obsessive, petty and pretentious, even insecure in their manic obligation to inclusiveness and certainty. More than that, for all the apparent authority, these narrators, far from exerting control over the world, struggle badly to get things right and often fail. In the 'Ithaca' passage quoted above, control goes awry and increasingly so as the passage progresses, so that by the end there is a pile-up of errors. Given the proportion of 17-1, (16-0 cannot, of course, operate as a proportional relationship in the calculations that are set up) Bloom would have had to be born in 762, not 714, to reach the age of 1190 years in 1952; whereas if Stephen had lived to the same age (in 3072 A.D.), Bloom would have 'been obliged to have been born' in 79,324 B.C., not 81,396 B.C., and would have lived for 20,230 years, not 83,300 years. This vulnerability to error is characteristic of the Ithacan discourse, the chapter in which Bloom is credited with a ridiculously small chest (28 inches) and a very large

---

[17] Peake, *Citizen and the Artist*, 287.

[18] Gerald L. Burns, 'Eumaeus', in Hart and Hayman, *James Joyce's 'Ulysses'*, 369.

neck (more than 17 inches). But there are many other kinds of narrative vulnerability too, many further instances where the narrator's authority slips and slides. The respectable bourgeois character of the Ithacan narrator, itself a slippage from rationalist objectivity, is also subject to a recidivist descent. The 'data' on Bloom kissing Molly's behind, is perhaps the most startling illustration of the mask shattering. Here precision and inclusiveness collide with vicarious salaciousness to produce a most unscientific distortion of language:

> He kissed the plump mellow yellow smellow melons of her rump, on each plump melonous hemisphere, in their mellow yellow furrow, with obscure prolonged provocative melonsmellonous osculation.
>
> (17. 2241- 43)

These slippages, which are characteristic of both episodes, are significant markers of Joyce's general dissent from revivalist hysteria. Russell's passionate devotion to a spiritual purity struggling against the vicious onslaught of 'a nation which has become a byword for materialism' becomes utterly deflated, when materialism is neither dark and dangerous nor alien. Joyce's voice of the new age seems far from inhuman or satanic. On the contrary, beneath the discursive surface, these voices are in many respects decidedly familiar: ostentatious, self-important, pompous, controlled to the point of dullness, but by no means incapable of the occasional enthusiasm. Indeed, there are times, even in 'Ithaca', when the voice manages to aspire to a kind of poetry, and often precisely in the place where it retreats most obviously from the poetic. At line 1039 there is that famous fracture in the cold, detached 'Catechism (impersonal)',[19] when Stephen and Bloom make their joint exit from number 7 Eccles Street and are confronted by the night-time spectacle of 'the heaventree of stars hung with humid nightblue fruit'. Some hundred lines later, there is an equally well-known retraction of this poetic outburst, when Bloom, having 'weighed the matter and allowing for possible error' comes to the 'logical conclusion' that what he observes is not 'a heaventree' but, amongst other things, 'a mobility of illusory forms immobilised in space, remobilised in air' (17.1138-43). This shift would be an effective illustration of Yeats's central point that art and

---

[19] Joyce's term for the 'technic' in the Linati schema.

the modern were absolutely antithetical, were it not for the fact that this narrator's revised articulation does accommodate poetic sensitivity. Metaphor and alliteration may have been displaced, but there is something like a poetic resonance in the controlled paradox of immobilized mobility, and in the poeticized rhythm generated by the absent connective.[20]

Even more subversively, in Joyce's formulation of 'civilization', the wave of alien, imperialist modernity is far from exclusively English. Scientific knowledge is not an English monopoly. The naming of 'the independent synchronous discoveries of Galileo, Simon Marius, Piazzi, Le Verrier, Herschel, Galle' and 'the systematisations attempted by Bode and Kepler' (17.1109-11) evokes a European context of scientific activity. Bloom's library, a shrine to self-improvement, does contain items which very clearly operate English ideology, like 'Lockhart's *Life of Napoleon* (cover wanting, marginal annotations, minimising victories, aggrandising defeats of the protagonist)' (17.1381-82). But it also contains Irish volumes, a book written in German, a book on Geometry originally written in French

---

[20] This presence of poetry in the city would not have surprised John Eglinton, who attacked Yeats for his 'abandonment of the ordinary man'. In his essay 'A Note on the National Drama', Eglinton argued that:

> The kinematograph, the bicycle, electric tramcars, labour-saving contrivances, etc, are not susceptible of poetic treatment, but are, in fact, themselves the poetry, not without a kind of suggestiveness, of a scientific age with which the poetry of Greek and Hebrew tradition vainly endeavours to vie.
>
> (Eglinton et al., *Literary Ideals*, 42)

There is further convergence with Joyce's position on cultural nationalism. Apart from disputing that 'city life, commerce and 'middle-class' vulgarity kill out the visionary faculty', Eglinton argued that the connection Yeats made between the middle class and 'history, science, politics' was absurd. He found the cultural identification with 'kindly and credulous country folk, who see fairies and have not lost the use of charms and simples', equally absurd. In fact, the retrospective cultural nationalism of Anglo-Ireland had become so much of an embarrassment to Eglinton, that he attempted to disassociate himself from the term 'Anglo-Irish': 'perhaps a less invidious name for the Anglo-Irishman would now perhaps be the Modern Irishman, the Irishman, namely, who accepts as a good European the connection with great Britain and yet feels himself to be far more distinct from the Anglo-Saxon than he is from the "mere" Irishman' (Eglinton, *Anglo-Irish Essays*, 42-45).

but translated into English, and so on. Exemplars of financial success in the retail world, 'Ephraim Marks and Charles A. James' (17.577) cross cultures. 'International finance' is 'controlled' by 'the Wall street money market' (17.1985). A Dublin Councillor is Italian (17.601); a chemist has a Scandinavian name, 'Francis Froedman' (17.93). Celtic ogham writing is placed in the context of an international linguistic pattern of development (17.770-77). One of the most strongly Anglicized places in 'Ithaca' is the '1st drawer' of Bloom's sideboard, which holds, amongst other things, a photograph of Queen Alexandra; 'a press cutting from an English weekly periodical *Modern Society*, subject corporal chastisement in girls' schools ... rubber preservatives ... purchased by post from Box 32, P. O., Charing Cross, London W. C. ... two erotic postcards' purchased from the same address; and the 'Wonderworker' prospectus. Even this treasure trove of modern culture, mocking, as it does, the piety of a cultural nationalism which proclaimed sex to be an English export, contains some cultural diversification in the shape of 'some assorted Austro-Hungarian coins' (17.1779-1823). Incidentally, Molly Bloom also goes outside Ireland, as it were, for stimulating items of a different sort; her discarded 'drawers' are of Indian mull, and her elegant cigarettes from Turkey (17.2091). More central to the Europeanization of the Joycean homeland is Bloom's status as a European. One of his earliest memories is of listening to his father's stories about the family migrations, which places the 'Blooms' in 'Dublin, London, Florence, Milan, Vienna, Budapest, Szombathely' (17.1907-08). The young Bloom ('aged 6') charts this movement on a map, subverting the political divisions of Europe 'by suggestions for the establishment of affiliated business premises in the various centres mentioned' (17.1913-15). The mature Bloom persists in thinking up schemes to link Ireland with a European world of commerce — thus his plan for a tramline to link the cattle market with 'the quays' which provides links to English railway lines, the docks, 'the transit sheds of Palgrave, Murphy and Company, steamship owners, agents for steamers from Mediterranean, Spain, Portugal, France, Belgium and Holland' (17. 1738-40).

'Eumaeus' and 'Ithaca', then, set to work on the myth of cultural degeneration. In these episodes, narrative makes manifest the modernity which is anathematized and unreproduceable in the revivalist gospel. The 'technics' involve establishing a kind of satirical convergence with revivalist despair at the modern empire of materialism. The resultant hilarity, of course, hardly makes Joyce's ricorso an enthusiastic advocate for modernity. On the contrary, Joyce's Irish homeland is an obvious product of a 'muddlecrass' (*FW*.152) which, as Yeats and his contemporaries said, was deeply conventional, rationalist and materialist. If 'The Wonderworker' really does stand as an emblem of modernity, the assertion as to what you can do with it is self-evident and emphatic. To this extent, 'Eumaeus' and 'Ithaca' confirm at least some elements of the revivalist story. But the easy comic manipulation of narratives so thoroughly contaminated by modern culture simply destroys the seriousness of cultural nationalism. In the end, the comic embrace between literature and materialist modernity decisively robs revivalism of its historic drama. There is no real territory left for the Anglo-Irish makers of cultural nationalism to take a stand on. In this book, Brian Boru is long dead, buried and irrelevant and the modern demons turn out to be no demons at all. This means that the Ithacan text performs its own variety of 'slaying', just as surely as does Bloom, in putting his personal insecurities about usurpation to rest.

There are further, and more substantial, parallels to be made between the adventures of discourse and the adventures of Joyce's characters. The 'meeting' of Stephen and Bloom, for instance, which is a large part of the fictional action of these episodes, seems in obvious parallel to the textual engagement of the episode. The text stakes out modern materialist urbanism, as opposed to archaic rurality, as the controversial and problematic, but rightful domain of an Irish writer. In the 'story', a deracinated Irish would-be writer drinks cocoa with the exemplar of modern urban culture. *Ulysses* makes massive investment in this meeting of Stephen and Bloom. They are apparently counterparts, and one of the major significances of their 'joining' has to do with the fulfilment of Stephen's artistic potential. In some sense, meeting Bloom is a precondition of Stephen's imminent artistic career. Just as the assimilation of modern materialist culture into art constitutes a wild subversion of a central revivalist text, so this scenario of an Irish writer inexorably drawn to the homeland of a middle-class Dubliner, and a Jew at that, constitutes another such subversion.

The story of the Irish artist deracinated, usurped and silenced was a standard item in the revivalist repertoire of fireside entertainment well before Joyce's intervention.[21] It was a story not only endlessly written out in the tale of the mystical encounter between the lost Protestant intellectual and the wise, old peasant, but also apparently lived out by the key makers of the Literary Revival. All these central figures belonged to a class and a culture which had been virtually destroyed by the modernization which they vilified as Anglicization, and many were 'in flight from a corrupt human world', until they 'discovered' ethnic historicism. George Russell was a celibate recluse, until 1898 and the decisive reading of O'Grady. This apparently led to marriage, the co-operatist movement and the publication of poetry. After leaving Trinity, Synge wandered through Europe with the intention of becoming a musician, until the inevitable meeting with Yeats, who advised him to 'give up Paris' and 'go to the Aran Islands. Live there as if you were one of the people themselves; express a life that has never found expression' (Yeats, *E & I*, 299). According to *Autobiographies,* Yeats himself was struggling under the influence of a rationalist father, and producing pale imitations of Spenser, Shelley and Keats, until his revelatory meeting with John O'Leary, whose library of 'authentic' Irish culture completely shifted the direction of Yeats's work. In each case, creativity was preconditioned by a passionate identification with a thoroughly idealized Irish peasantry.

The saga of Stephen and Bloom, which 'climaxes' in 'Eumaeus' and 'Ithaca', is Joyce's version of a standard revivalist text which images the Irish artist connecting with *the* culture, usually in a non-fictional mode, except that Joyce's articulation demolishes tradition. Here the artist is a Catholic urbanite who disputes the very existence of an authentic national culture, and his 'predestined' meeting is with a

---

[21] In fact the artist has been 'a paradigmatic figure of the national community' in nineteenth-century European cultural nationalism generally. 'For, unlike the great religions, the nationalist cosmology sets up no prophets to be imitated or, indeed any authoritative class of interpreters. The source of creativity is located not in a timeless supramundane order but in the continually evolving community itself, of which its heroes, religious or secular, can be but *exemplifications* who have to be *emulated* according to the needs of each era. Every true member of a nation, then, is an artist creator, and the great artists are they who create out of the collective experience of the people, preserved in historical legends, and dramatize these as lessons for the present' (Hutchinson, *Cultural Dynamics of Nationalism*, 15). The importance of all this to Joyce's obsession with the figure of the artist is obvious, although Stephen has rarely been placed in this kind of context by Joyceans.

bourgeois Jew. Far from inspiring Stephen, this encounter struggles famously for any meaningful status.

The narratives themselves are acutely conscious of their responsibility for making something substantial of the Stephen and Bloom affair. In 'Eumaeus' there is a narrative excitement, ill-founded given Stephen's virtually complete lack of interest in Bloom, which has Bloom relishing 'the vicinity of the young man ... educated, *distingué* and impulsive into the bargain' (16.1476-77). This narrative presents the view, against all the evidence, that 'a certain analogy there somehow was as if both their minds were travelling, so to speak, in the one train of thought' (16.1579-80). Both chapters take every opportunity to make parallels, establish differences or similarities, convergence or divergence. As far as it can, 'Ithaca' inflates matters, so that Bloom and Stephen become a 'duumvirate' (17.11), or a more homely, but equally misplaced, 'couple' (17.81). Bloom becomes a symposiarch (see 17.361). The narrator here has Stephen 'obeying' Bloom's 'sign' (17.118). The simple making of a nightcap becomes the preparation of a 'collation' (17.355). This tendency to transpose trivial actions into resonant ritual reaches absurd proportions when Stephen and Bloom go off to urinate:

> In what order of precedence, with what attendant ceremony was the exodus from the house of bondage to the wilderness of inhabitation effected?
>
> Lighted Candle in Stick
> borne by
> BLOOM
> Diaconal Hat on Ashplant
> borne by
> STEPHEN
>
> (17. 1021-28)

Wildly inappropriate biblical allusion, evocative, but misplaced diction, capitalized names, line layout: all this paraphernalia is geared towards investing the business of going outside for a pee with a distinctive resonance. Perhaps the greatest, and most absurd, textual effort to secure significance is in the passage where Bloom becomes 'Stoom' and Stephen becomes 'Blephen'. Some readers have seen this childish transposition as *the* 'union', a linguistic resolution 'of the paternal/filial quest',[22] which means that they have been deceived by a very obvious moment of narrative desperation.

This straining for significance is all very different from the text which relates, say, Synge's encounter with 'old Mourteen', the Aran story-teller who recited 'old Irish poetry with an exquisite purity of intonation that brought tears to my eyes, though I understood but little of the meaning'.[23] Here, by contrast, reality throbs with significance, which the text simply and humbly transcribes. The narrator apparently effaces himself before the purity, simplicity, spirituality and 'beautiful charm' of the common people, although there are occasional gaps and 'silences' which perhaps reveal a certain narrational dishonesty.

> The complete absence of shyness or self-consciousness in most of these people gives them a beautiful charm, and when this young and beautiful woman leaned across my knees to look nearer at some photograph that pleased her, I felt more than ever the strange simplicity of the island life.[24]

It is not the absence of meaning that characterizes this text, but rather the overabundance and richness of meaning. Similarly, in Yeats's encounter with a 'Paddy Flynn', suggestiveness drips off every simple word:

> The first time I saw him he was cooking mushrooms for himself; the next time he was asleep under a hedge, smiling in his sleep. Assuredly some joy not quite of this steadfast earth lightens in those eyes-swift as the eyes of a rabbit — among so many wrinkles, for Paddy Flynn is very old. A melancholy there is in the midst of their cheerfulness — a melancholy that is almost a portion of their joy, the visionary melancholy of purely instinctive natures and of all animals. In the triple solitude of age and eccentricity and partial deafness he goes about much pestered by children.[25]

---

[22] Constance V. Tagopoulos, 'Joyce and Homer', in Cheng and Martin, eds, *Joyce in Context*, 190.

[23] J. M. Synge, *Plays, Poems and Prose*, 252.

[24] Ibid., 274.

[25] From an Introduction by W. B. Yeats to *Fairy and Folk Takes of the Irish Peasantry*, reprinted in W. B. Yeats, *Selected Prose*, edited by Norman Jeffares,

The Ithacan narrators have the much more difficult job of working with material which consistently resists any transfiguration. The encounter which is narrated here is characterized, not by magical recognition but by an emphatic and sustained distinctness between artist and common man. In *Ulysses,* Synge's intense identification with the Aran islanders is displaced by potential and actual embarrassment, by misunderstandings. Revivalist passion for assimilation into rural culture is ousted by Stephen's polite refusal of intimacy. Peasant transparency is displaced by substantial concealment, particularly on Bloom's part. Not only does he suppress many views that he thinks likely to promote indifference or even tension. The second half of 'Ithaca', after Stephen's departure, unlocks drawers of Bloom's life that are certainly not for public scrutiny. Above all, that inspiring moment when the common man offers the all-important gift of cultural identity to the lost artist is laughed at in 'Ithaca'. Like 'old Mourteen', the storyteller whose poetry makes Synge weep, Bloom also intones for his visitor. The potential for weighty meaning is clearly signalled by a surge of narrative inflation. According to the narrator, Stephen is privileged to hear 'in a profound ancient male unfamiliar melody the accumulation of the past' (17.777-78). But what Bloom actually 'chants' is two lines from 'Ha-Tikvah', a song which, quite apart from being Jewish, was actually written in 1878 and was about as profound as 'My Girl's a Yorkshire Lass'. Far from being awe-struck by this rendition, Stephen responds with an anti-Semitic ditty, which is quite insensitive to Bloom's feelings, and then with an obscure reading of this 'Ballad of Harry Hughes' which is completely lost on Bloom.

There is a certain amount of confused 'getting-on' in both 'Eumaeus' and 'Ithaca', but the portentously signalled symbiosis between artist and citizen simply never materializes. This 'failure' is a very clear measure of Joyce's refusal to accept the absurdly romantic stories of dramatic cultural conversion peddled by revivalist writers, and of his rejection of revivalism as a meaningful cultural position in the modern world. The commitment to a retrospective cultural nationalism which crucially defined writing for Yeats and the Revival, did not drop from the sky. It was a political position determined by a long and bitter ideological conflict. It was also characterized by striking contradictions. There is no evidence to suggest any parallel

---

(London: Macmillan, 1962), 162.

conversion of Stephen in 'Ithaca'. There is his 'quasisensation' (17.782) that Bloom is Christ, but this simply repeats an earlier drunken and unfortunate joke. Nor is there much, in more than a hundred pages, to change or develop our view of Bloom. His response to Molly's infidelity, far from reaching new heights of heroism, confirms what is already known about him. He does not really 'return' to modernity to restake his claim. He has never been anything other than an urban man. Despite the cold, empty, materialism that, for the Revival, defines middle-class modernity, this burgher manages to sustain his humanity quite unproblematically and undramatically.

The Stephen of these chapters remains dispossessed and in servitude, for all his stance against Church, state and nation, and Bloom's 'epic' return to 7 Eccles Street is notably unepic. On the other hand, 'Ithaca' *is* the place where Joyce works hardest to sustain the parallel with the Homeric prototype.[26] Comic deflation is part of that paralleling. But there is also the extraordinary embedding of return and recognition in the fabric of the text, as repetition of words and motifs, for instance. This overloading is surely a very wearisome literary joke, if that's all it is. As Tagopoulos points out, 'words like 'enter /reenter', 'reappear', 'return' and 'comeback' endlessly reproduce themselves textually throughout this chapter'. There are 'long chains of returns and entrances'[27] in the movements of Bloom and Stephen. There are also rhetorical returns in grammatical structures. The text is 'returning' in a literal sense, and this perhaps identifies another kind of Ithacan hero, besides Bloom and Brian Boru: the Ithacan text itself, which, after two centuries of an essentially retrospective Irish literary culture, insists so firmly on its modern status.

If we take that text for what it surely is, a decisive intervention by an Irish Catholic writer, then some significant cultural positions are made clear. Firstly, in the intimacy with urban modernity there is the relative ease of a Catholic writer whose class had itself been created by modernizing forces. Joyce has no obvious ideological commitment to modern urbanism, but he approaches it in ways that Yeats simply could not. This means that Joyce's engagement with modernization and Anglicization is very much more complex, intimate and penetrating

---

[26] This is Tagopoulos's contention. See Tagopoulos, 'Joyce and Homer'.

[27] Ibid., 186.

than anything Anglo-Ireland could mount. It is also more ambiguous, with Joyce both ridiculing urban modernity as an ideological construction and revelling in its degeneracy. Secondly, in the sustained attack on Anglo-Irish romanticism, and the staking out of new territory for the Irish artist, there is the mature expression of Catholic dispossession and repossession. The colonial experience, in Joyce's version of epic return, is both widened by insistence on a European, even Western dimension — as well as its simply British one — and shrunk by the highly controlled conversion of the imported culture into an hilarious absurdity. Whilst the romantic text of revivalism avoids, even denies, the facts of modernization and Anglicization, Joyce, in these chapters as elsewhere in *Ulysses,* accumulates these facts, revelling in the complex reciprocity between colonial culture and the colonized. This does not make *Ulysses* a victim of colonial culture. On the contrary, the text itself controls and masters that culture. This is perhaps the essential significance of Joyce's Ithaca, the place where he takes the 'civilization' which he once described as 'a vast fabric, in which the most diverse elements are mingled, in which nordic aggressiveness and Roman law, the new bourgeois conventions and the remnant of a Syriac religion are reconciled', and does with it precisely what cultural nationalism claimed could not be done. He makes art out of the modern stuff that apparently destroyed both art and the nation, to produce an epic demarcation of urban modernity as the Joycean estate.

7 Engendering Nation: Nationalism and Sexuality in 'Nausicaa', 'Oxen of the Sun' and 'Penelope'

The intimate relation between nationalism and sex is at least as old as the French revolution.[1] In popular revolutionary tradition, for example, patriotic fervour is often represented as sexual freedom. Eugene Delacroix's classic of this tradition, *Liberty Leading the People at the Barricades*, has Marianne, a feminized image of the revolutionary spirit, depicted barefoot and half-naked, waving a tattered republican flag as she leads the patriots over a wall of dead reactionaries. In 1848, just after the newly empowered bourgeois government had smashed the Parisian working class, a competition was held to find a modernized allegorical image for the new France. That the nation should continue to be represented by a woman was never in dispute, but Marianne did suffer a sanitizing makeover. She was decently clothed and respectably seated. The powerful image of revolution in action was to be displaced by an enthroned figure. Thereafter the feminized image of Second Empire France was invariably sat down, surrounded by equally frozen images of liberty, equality and fraternity. This new design identified revolution with immutability, protection and prosperity. In short, the fierce, young, freedom fighter became transformed into a sedate and more mature matron. Behind this dramatic shift in the representation of the nation lay fundamental changes in French politics and society — the point being, of course, that there is no such thing as mere representation of the nation.

Perhaps the crucial cultural construction for the nineteenth-century nation state was the manufacture of what Jeffrey Weeks calls the 'sacramental family'.[2] The precise sense in which the family evolved in such intimate relationship with wider society is, of course, a matter of

---

[1] For an account of this relationship, with particular reference to modern Germany, see, George L. Mosse, *Nationalism and Sexuality: Middle-Class Morality and Sexual Norms in Modern Europe* (London and Wisconsin: Wisconsin University Press, 1985).

[2] See Jeffrey Weeks, *Sex, Politics and Society: The Regulation of Sexuality since 1800* (London and New York: Longman, 1989 edn), chapter 3.

sociological and historical controversy. But there is no doubt that a relationship existed between family and nation building. The process of identification was self-conscious, a matter of state legislation, for example, embedded not only in laws regulating marriage but also in property laws, laws controlling advertising, laws against homosexuality and abortion, and so on. Culture — be it legal, religious, educational, medical, or literary culture — insisted on a moral, biological, and spiritual identification of the family with the state. According to George L. Mosse in *Nationalism and Sexuality*:

> the prevailing sentiment was that the family was a cheap and efficient surrogate for the state, controlling the passions at their source. Clearly, the family was the policeman on the beat, an indispensable agent of social control as directed by physicians (more often than not the family doctor), educators, and the nation itself.[3]

Gender, defined by differentiation, itself became a state resource. In the late nineteenth century, a new emphasis on sport and militaristic training in English public schools created a cult of maleness, enshrining, with obvious racial and imperial undertones, 'the separation of boys from the world of women'.[4] Men embodied order, efficiency, 'progress', civilization and culture. Divorced from the busy world of empire building by a perceived physical inferiority which was evidenced on the authority of science, women were defined in terms of refinement, continuity, and belonging to nature. As Lord Roseberry put it for Edwardian England, 'an empire such as ours requires as its first condition an imperial race'.[5]

Lord Roseberry's comment illustrates how the state constituted itself as an ideological presence in private and most intimate spaces. Towards the end of the nineteenth century, when eugenics and sexology became part of common intellectual currency, sexual acts were legitimized, or outlawed, by scientific classification and the so-called laws of Social Darwinism. A new sexual repression, directed against prostitution, homosexuality and masturbation, was manifest in the

---

[3] Mosse, *Nationalism and Sexuality*, 20.

[4] Weeks, *Sex, Politics and Society*, 40.

[5] Lord Roseberry, *Miscellanies. Literary and Historical*, ed. John Buchan (London: Hodder & Stoughton, 1925), II, 250.

widespread social purity campaigns. Masturbation in particular, was demonized. In men, 'the great weakener' produced blindness, general debility and led inexorably to homosexuality. In women, the claim was that masturbation was responsible for ulcerated vaginas and dementia. As late as the 1920s, eminent sexologists like Havelock Ellis and Albert Moll were attempting to check the solitary vice by recommending for children 'little suits of armour fitted over the genitals and attached to locked belts as prophylaxis'.[6] Masturbation, anal sex, oral sex — indeed, any kind of sexual practice that was 'non-productive' or dysgenic — was anathematized as a crime against the race and the nation. The general case for coupling the histories of nationalism and sexuality, then, is well established. In the specific case of Ireland, the full history of colonial and post-colonial relationships between nationalism and sexuality has yet to be written. But it is clear that gendered images have been fundamental to the construction of Ireland's culture, particularly in the modern period. In many ways, the constitution of the new Irish state marked the 'manifest destiny' of a conservative and purist conception of nation first configured in the culture of revivalism. Much to Yeats's later disdain, some elements of an essentially Protestant patriotic culture proved to be highly serviceable for the Catholic nation. Of course, there were many participants in the cultural nationalism which was so essential to nation building at the turn of the century. But the Literary Revival is usually regarded, for good reasons, as a key participant in this process. Once again, Yeats's importance to the gendering of state and nation can hardly be overstated. It was he, for instance, who was primarily responsible for importing pre-Raphaelite medievalism into Irish nationalism, thus producing the courtly, devotional love song to the feminized nation which was to become so characteristic of revivalist Ireland.[7]

---

[6] Weeks, *Sex, Politics and Society*, 51.

[7] Elizabeth Cullingford comments that Yeats's 'inviolate Rose' fuses the 'courtly worship of the sexually unavailable goddess with the representation of Ireland as a beautiful woman. The culture of Irish nationalism offered a publicly and politically acceptable form for a private obsession with male martyrdom' (Elizabeth Butler Cullingford, *Gender and History in Yeats's Love Poetry* [Melbourne & New York: Cambridge University Press, 1993], 54).

The 'Gaelic' contribution to this 'rediscovered' form was extremely limited. The anthropomorphization of the land as woman has prehistoric roots in Irish culture,[8] and Yeats certainly drew on that tradition. He adapted the figure of the *cailleach* (Dedalus's 'wandering crone' — 1.404) and used the traditional *speirbhean*. The latter was the vision-woman of the *aisling*, a genre which enjoyed a 'meteoric rise' in the seventeenth century.[9] According to Elizabeth Butler Cullingford, Yeats also:

> reached back into prehistory to resurrect the tradition of human sacrifice to the goddess, in which sexuality is conflated with violent death as the blood of the young male victim sinks into the receiving earth.[10]

But in other respects, Yeats's poetry is quite divorced from Gaelic traditions, most fundamentally by language itself. His verse forms owe little or nothing to bardic culture or to post-bardic culture of the sixteenth and seventeenth centuries. Indeed, as Joep Leersson has shown, 'bardic poetry', so elevated in revivalism, is a highly problematic concept. The culture it refers to was not bardic, in that the bard only *spoke* the poetry. It was composed by the fili, who was higher in the hierarchy. Nor was this cultural form recognizably poetry, in the modern sense.[11] The Yeats texts which image Ireland as a goddess and the poet/nationalist as a devotee are obviously not problematic in this way. They clearly *are* poems and owe much more to Dante Gabriel Rosetti than to any Irish poet, bardic or otherwise. There are many further illustrations of the very large space separating the poetry of revivalist Ireland from bardic traditions. The Rose as a figure for Ireland, for instance, so important in Yeats's early poetry, was not a refugee from the Celtic mists as Yeats claimed, but a nineteenth-century invention.[12] The 'pale' aristocratic lady, poor but still ennobled and representing the state of Ireland, was another image constructed in

---

[8] See Leersson, *Mere Irish and Fíor-Ghael*, 154.

[9] Leersson, *Mere Irish and Fíor-Ghael*, 216.

[10] Cullingford, *Gender and History*, 57.

[11] See Leersson, *Mere Irish and Fíor-Ghael*, 152.

[12] Cullingford, *Gender and History*, 60.

the nineteenth century, again, largely by Yeats himself.

This romantic culture claimed an authenticity which it could not possess. It also engaged a deep social animus, precisely at the point where nationalism converges with ideologies like eugenics to share territory with the worst excesses of exclusivity and prejudice. Yeats's image of the poet/lover bringing gifts of organic culture to the goddess/nation rests on half-baked racial notions of a 'natural' aristocracy. Indeed, I would suggest that the whole courtly disposition of this poetry is bound up with the social conservatism which led Yeats so enthusiastically to eugenics in the 1930s.

Eugenics was the only science to interest Yeats, because it confirmed what he had always known in his 'soul'. Authentic Ireland, the hard Ireland, was a genetic reality precariously held in the 'germ plasm'[13] of the 'hard-riding gentlemen' and the 'peasantry' of rurality. These were the 'indomitable Irishry', as against the modern, bourgeois 'sort now growing up':

> All out of shape from toe to top,
> Their unremembering hearts
> The products of base beds.
>
> (Yeats, *CPO*, 400)

Such absurd and dangerous ideas have sometimes been dismissed by Yeatsians as the innocent and irrelevant faddism of a bitter old man.[14] It is certainly the case that Yeats 'discovered' eugenics late in life. R. B Cattel's *The Fight for National Intelligence* (1937),[15] converted Yeats,

---

[13] A term used by scientists, before the discovery of cells, to designate the means by which genetic information is transmitted.

[14] See for example, David Bradshaw, 'The Eugenics Movement in the 1930s and the Emergence of *On the Boiler*', in Deirdre Toomey, *Yeats Annual No. 9* (Basingstoke: Macmillan, 1992), 189-215. Bradshaw argues that was nothing 'remarkable ... nor necessarily 'questionable' about Yeats's views on eugenics in the context of the 1930s' (211). For Bradshaw this settles matters. Paul Scott Stanfield gives a rather more penetrative account in *Yeats and Politics in the 1930s* (Basingstoke: Macmillan, 1988), 145-83.

[15] Both Bradshaw and Stanfield give accounts of the influence of this book on Yeats. The book was so extreme that in caused a furore in the Eugenics Society, which tried to distance itself from Cattell's views.

prompting him to conduct a correspondence with the Eugenics Society in London in an attempt to discover whether any research had been done on the Intelligence Quotas among 'people living upon inherited money'. Yeats seriously expected that I.Q. levels among this class would be 'pretty high'.[16] The interest in eugenics is also certainly consistent with Yeats's politics generally in the 1930s — with the terms of his attacks on De Valera; his early conception of how the Irish Senate would provide aristocratic leadership for those 'merely' elected by the 'mob', and his brief excitement at the appearance of Fascist blueshirts in Ireland. But Yeats did not suddenly turn to the political right at the end of his life and in fact the late fascination with eugenics indicates something fundamental and relatively constant about Yeats and his conceptualization of the nation. His deepest instincts were always with the aristocracy, which he had idealized from the beginning. The historiography which he devised in *A Vision*, and which centrally defined the Yeatsian aesthetic, was, to a very large extent, a challenge to Hegelian and Marxist dialectic. Yeats's Ireland, as Paul Scott Stanfeld argues so persuasively in his study of Yeats and politics in the late period, was *always* deeply conservative and because his Ireland was *always* idealized as a purity, uncontaminated by 'foreign' modernity, it always implied the operation of eugenics.

The Literary Revival's essentialist portrayal of the nation as goddess, with worship and devotion as a decadent surrogate for political action was, to understate things, a controversial statement. The central issue was whether such images operated as repressive and divisive stereotypes or as empowering and unifying symbols of cultural identity. With his outsider-hero and his blurring of the distinctions between masculinity and femininity,[17] Joyce would have found little that was liberating in the Revival's idealization of gender difference. The sensational exposure of the body which once made *Ulysses* infamous and which is usually contextualized against Catholic purism in Joyce criticism, also engages with Protestant images of immutable

---

[16] Quoted in Bradshaw, 'The Eugenics Movement', 209.

[17] This blurring was extremely radical in its day. Absolute gender differentiation was thought to be essential for the maintenance of culture. Even Havelock Ellis, sometimes presented as the most tolerant of the sexologists, 'was alarmed to find that the masculine-feminine dualism was in jeopardy' (Gosse, *Nationalism and Sexuality*, 24).

and denatured beauty. Joyce was, of course, highly sensitive to the obvious paternalism and social exclusivity of revivalist image-making. For Joyce, the peasantry simply did not embody the nation. Peasants were not distinguished by their moral purity. They might have married late, but that was hardly out of choice. According to Stephen Daedalus in *Stephen Hero*, behind closed doors they found relief from the rigours of economic necessity in 'doing it by hand' (*SH*, 54). As for Maud Gonne, this important socialist was presented by Yeats as a Great House beauty, who, before she mingled with the masses, perfectly embodied the essence of Irish nationhood. There is, however, no evidence to suggest that Joyce, lover of homologies, could see the basis for that particular analogy at all.

Before the feet of the goddess
For all his dissent, Joyce hardly eschews traditionally feminized images of nation. In 'Nausicaa', Gerty McDowell certainly evokes the traditions discussed above, albeit in complex and often contradictory ways. She is exposed as an overblown image of nation, in some respects conforming to the gender ideology of both the Church and the Nation. She is thus a 'sterling good daughter', a 'ministering angel' and 'a second mother in the house' (13.325-26), as well as a more Yeatsian creature with 'a strange yearning tendency to the beautiful eyes' (13.106).

The first narrative voice of 'Nausicaa' subscribes to the conceit that Gerty personifies the nation. Although she is not a 'gentlewoman of high degree', she could have 'held her own with any lady in the land' given the right opportunities. This suggests the appropriate usurpation motif, particularly with reinforcement from Gerty's 'innate refinement' and from her possession of 'a languid queenly hauteur' (13.97). She is worshipped by 'patrician suitors at her feet' (13.103), one of whom — Reggy Wylie — is a Protestant. This reproduces an obvious motif from revivalist culture. The text insists that Gerty has the correct genetic credentials. Her eyes 'were of the bluest Irish blue' (13.108). She is 'as fair a specimen of winsome Irish girlhood as one could wish to see' (13.81-82); 'God's fair land of Ireland did not hold her equal' (13.122). She has both the purity and the sensuality associated with the goddess of the land:

> The waxen pallor of her face was almost spiritual in its ivorylike purity though her rosebud mouth was a genuine Cupid's bow, Greekly perfect.
>
> (13.87-89)

Above all, Gerty's status as an icon of nation is established through her objectification. Eyes, mirrors and the act of gazing or staring are of special significance in this chapter, and Gerty regards herself as a 'shrine' to be worshipped at (see 13.564). Clearly 'Nausicaa' relates this ritualisation to mariolatry. But Gerty's identity is also built from elements in revivalist culture. In fact, the ironic assimilation of different and sometimes opposing cultures is one of the subversions of this episode. The 'namby-pamby jammy' (*Letters 1*, 135) narrative style owes most to Anglicized ladies' magazines and romance novels, but the ritual of the Catholic Church and the culture of Protestant revivalism are both strongly implicated in the creation of the 'Nausicaa' narrative. This 'filtering down' of cultures privileged as being both 'high' and 'deep', a process despised by the Church and revivalists alike, produces the narrative of 'Nausicaa'. Declensions from the elevated amalgam are frequent, as in this extract from the physical description of Gerty where 'refined tones' collide against a failing grammar, misplaced idiom and, finally, against the unfortunate usage of the word 'discharges':

> Her figure was slight and graceful, inclining even to fragility but those iron jelloids she had been taking of late had done her a world of good much better than the Widow Welch's female pills and she was much better of those discharges she used to get and that tired feeling.
>
> (13.83-87)

The debt to Literary Revivalism may not be immediately apparent in this passage. Indeed, the extract seems to be precisely a product of the commercial Anglicization that all revivalists were united in excoriating. But there are linkages between the Literary Revival and 'Nausicaa' in terms of design, structure, motif and image, as this early Yeats's poem, 'He Gives His Beloved Certain Rhymes', demonstrates:

> Fasten your hair with a golden pin,
> And bind up every wandering tress;
> I bade my heart build these poor rhymes:
> It worked at them, day out, day in,
> Building a sorrowful loveliness

> Out of the battles of old times.
>
> You need but lift a pearl-pale hand,
> And bind up your long hair and sigh;
> And all men's hearts must burn and beat;
> And candle-like foam on the dim sand,
> And stars climbing the dew-dropping sky,
> Live but to your passing feet.
>
> (Yeats, *CPO*, 71)

It is possible that Joyce had this particular poem in mind for 'Nausicaa'. A seaside location links the two texts, as does the symbolism of candle, star and dew. In 'Nausicaa', these romanticized images are inflated to famously colourful and erotic proportions. Similarly, the two texts share a stylized representation of feminine beauty and an obsession with hair. Gerty's 'crowning beauty was her wealth of wonderful hair' (13.116). Significantly, the release of this glory becomes the erotic moment which triggers the dynamic of Bloom's 'tumescence':[18]

> Gerty just took off her hat for a moment to settle her hair and a prettier, a daintier head of nutbrown tresses was never seen on a girl's shoulders — a radiant little vision, in sooth, almost maddening in its sweetness.
>
> (13.509-11)

What really joins the two texts, however, is firstly, the generic status of the two 'women' as national icons — in the case of the Yeats poem, an icon revered by the young nationalist/poet/suitor and honoured with that suggestive love token: a reconstructed past made from 'sorrowful loveliness'. Secondly, the texts are merged by the courtly tradition which is everywhere vulgarized in 'Nausicaa', both in Gerty's

---

[18] The style of 'Nausicaa' is designated as 'tumescence/ detumescence' in the Linati schema. This derives from terminology used by Havelock Ellis to describe the rise and fall of sexual passion. According to Ellis 'tumescence and detumescence' are 'alike fundamental, primitive and essential; in resting the sexual impulse on these necessarily connected processes we are basing ourselves on the solid bed rock of nature'. Interestingly, in 'Nausicaa', there is a reversal of the eminent sexologist's delineation of gender roles in the 'processes of arousal and relief'. For Havelock Ellis, 'tumescence' was achieved 'through much activity and display on the part of the male and long contemplation and consolidation on the part of the female'. See Havelock Ellis, *Studies in the Psychology of Sex* (Philadelphia: F. A. Davis, 1920), I, 15.

construction of herself as possessor of the 'loveliness' that makes men 'gaze' (13.541) and in her construction of Bloom as a 'gentleman' who comes 'gallantly to the rescue' (13.350).

This intertextuality is not an 'allusion'. Or, at least, the idea of allusiveness does not explain the nature of a complex relation where difference is as important as similarity. One essential difference, for example, is that in the poem the female figure, like Marianne in Second Empire France, is passive. It is not simply that she sits, monumentally, whilst the worshipping poet 'works' and 'builds'. She has no consciousness or voice at all. She is composed, in all senses, entirely by the male viewer. Gerty is also physically immobile, although this is contextualized in her physical disability, and compromised by her enlivening backward leaning. However, in direct contrast to the silent figure of the Yeats's poem, Gerty speaks herself, as it were.

The first narrative of 'Nausicaa', is a representation of Gerty's consciousness. The execution is not of itself particularly empowering. It certainly does not produce a radicalized conception of gender because in articulation Gerty is above all else a servant of convention, a product of culture. As we have seen, Gerty fits herself to conventional images of respectability, gender, beauty, sexuality and so on. However, 'Nausicaa' does obviously sign-up to a radicalizing agenda because it reads religious, political and literary culture as part of an ideological constituency. This is the culture that supports patriarchy and attempts to define gender and gender roles. The point here is that both the 'Nausicaa' text, and the character, Gerty, are amply revealed as cultural and social products, with some telling roughened edges where the fit between reality and cultural identity is loose. This marks a fundamental distinction between 'Nausicaa' and the revivalist poem. In the Yeats poem, there is no reflexive consciousness of ideology. The formulation of the silent woman as nation is a real mystery — an essentialist truth which requires no reading.

There is a further usage of a standard revivalist figure in 'Nausicaa', a usage which writes against the Yeatsian prototype in a particularly strong, even dramatic, way. In the nationalist texts which import so much from courtly, medievalist traditions, the feminine nation is frequently worshipped at her feet. The nationalist/poet/lover often abases himself in this way, to the extent that Cullingford identifies a foot fetish in this culture.[19] In Yeats's 'To Ireland in the Coming Times', the poet's heart follows 'After the red-rose-bordered hem' of Ireland. In 'The Rose of the World', the world is made 'to be a grassy road/Before her wandering feet'. The 'queen' in 'The Cap and Bells' has 'the quiet of love in her feet' (Yeats, *CPO*, 58/41/73).[20] 'Nausicaa' takes-up this foot obsession, with the vital difference that Gerty's foot is not naked and timeless in its beauty, but thoroughly dressed-up and very much a sign of the times. It is encased in footwear that is the height of fashion, 'with patent toecaps, and just one smart buckle over her higharched instep' (13.167-68). Her stylishly shod feet are then contemplated and adored — her 'well-turned ankle' is apparently of 'perfect proportions'. But in the end, of course, this praise is to be understood as the embarrassed avoidance of a delicate issue, because Gerty is dramatically exposed as a 'cripple'. That entire sequence of images produces a highly suggestive variant on the idolatry which features so frequently in early Yeats's poems. Interestingly, it is not the first identification that Joyce establishes between Ireland and disablement. In 'Eveline' for instance, the only street-kid with a Gaelicised name, 'little Keogh', is also 'a cripple' (*D*, 29). The faint association here is developed into a full-blown engagement with revivalist representation in 'Nausicaa', where the lovely, pale, aristocratic figure of Ireland is displaced by the crippled young victim who is a construct of contradictory and competing ideologies. Far from embodying a set of authentic Irish values, this young woman is thoroughly Anglicized. She is a long way from being culturally centred. In fact, she struggles to make an identity for herself, not from the certainty of cultural continuity but in the very uncertain, hybrid world of materialist modernity. She has a number of models at her immediate disposal, provided by the Church, for instance, by *the Princess Novelette* and the likes of Maria S. Cummins, all of these being of very dubious value. As for the cultural models of Irish antiquity, these are simply absent and presumably irrelevant.

Equally, 'Nausicaa' supplies a thoroughly subversive variant on the figure of the nationalist worshipper. In the Joyce text, the Irish artist devoted to recovery of a glorious past which honours the feminized,

---

[19] Cullingford, *Gender and History*, 35.

[20] See Cullingford, 35-36, for more examples of Yeats's deployment of this image.

dispossessed nation is displaced by an opportunistic Jewish cuckold who thinks of Gerty as a 'little limping devil' (13.852). He masturbates over her display of underwear and is thankful for the relief. In the context of early twentieth-century attitudes to race and sexuality, this masturbation in a public place and the portrayal of the complicit female, seriously offends. For an imagologist,[21] intent on reading 'Nausicaa' in terms of national iconography, however, there is worse than offence here. This exposé of the nation's underclothes, where the 'spiritual' worship of the nation becomes so rudely transposed in the famous wank, amounts to an outrageous defilement of cultural orthodoxies. This might seem to us, today, to be a light-hearted piece of 'naughty' interference with cultural nationalism. In its day, however, it was surely a peculiarly virulent subversion. 'Nausicaa' may not carry much in the way of progressive gender implications. Although it does puncture the purist denaturing of women which has been so pervasive in Irish culture, one could hardly construct Gerty as a positive image of woman. The wonderful exploitation of nationalist iconography, however, is hilariously comic and a great deal of free space is released by the desecration of conservative pieties. In this sense, far from confirming stereotypes, the Nausicaa tableau is one of the most recreant and irreverent images in *Ulysses*.

'Let me parturiate!': art and the race in 'Oxen of the Sun'

There is a more 'literary' desecration of patriotic culture in the Swiftian story of 'an Irish bull in an English Chinashop' at lines 581-646 of 'Oxen of the Sun'. In this 'apologue', traditional gender images are again utilized, but only to the very limited degree that Ireland is feminized, and the 'stranger' made masculine. The Catholic Church, which the Literary Revival was wisely quietist on, is placed at the centre here, imaged as a parasitical bull feeding off his fiefdom ('and a plumper and portlier bull ... never shit on shamrock', as Vincent puts it). Although the bull was gelded 'before he came over', the women of Ireland are deeply attracted to him and would rather 'get a lick on the nape from his long holy tongue than lie with the finest strapping young ravisher in the four fields of all Ireland'. The bull is worshipped and

---

[21] See Leerssen, for a discussion of this term, which he defines as 'the study of discursive or literary expression of national attitudes' (*Mere Irish and Fíor-Ghael*, 7).

adored by the women of the country, who cater for his every need and desire. His appetites are monstrous and he becomes 'so heavy that he could scarce walk to pasture'. The 'father of the faithful', as the bull becomes known, grows increasingly proprietorial and will allow nothing but 'green grass' to be cultivated. At first this produces 'bad blood' between him and 'lord Harry' (representing the English state that was responsible for the dispatch of the bull from Rome in the first place). Upon discovering, however, that he is 'a lefthanded descendant of the famous champion bull of the Romans', the English monarch begins to emulate the bull (this presumably alluding to the founding of the English Church). English monarch and Roman bull now strike up a new agreement, becoming 'as fast friends as an arse and a shirt' and united in their exploitation of the Irish plantation. At the end of this 'parable', the women being 'all of one mind' in their devotion to the two bulls, the 'men of Ireland' make 'a wherry raft ... and put to sea to recover the main of America' (14.581-646). This radical historiography, where Catholic Church and English State are in collusion, involves a challenging variation on the aisling woman or the *speirbhean*. Here, far from being revered as the violated woman, or the dispossessed mother of tradition, the figure of the feminized Irish nation is the betrayer, one of the 'gratefully oppressed' of 'After the Race' (*D*, 35), and utterly complicit with the advances of her oppressors.

The conventional figure of Mother Ireland is further interfered with in 'Oxen'. The nation is traditionally represented as a mother-figure in Irish literary culture. Sometimes the figure is nurturing, but often she is empty and dry and demands the replenishment of the son's sacrificial blood. In 'Oxen', the former kind of mythopoetics is exploited in the inflated images of maternal fullness and fruition which accompany rainfall and the birth of Mrs Purefoy's ninth child. There is a splendid superfluity of mother-homage as the universe takes on a pregnant aspect. Clouds become 'turgidly distended' and 'heavy with preponderant excess of moisture' (14.1384-85); 'raindew moisture' becomes 'a life essence celestial' which glistens under 'starshiny coelum' (14.1407-08). Elsewhere in 'Oxen', the Mother Ireland tradition is assaulted by Stephen's sense that the nation-mother is a whore who has 'welcomed' the interloper and dispossessed her own flesh and blood. 'Erin' brought 'a stranger' to the 'gates to commit fornication in my sight and to wax fat like Jeshurum' (14.367-410).

This, of course, is the voice of the dispossessed son who has been 'suckled with a bitter milk' (14.377-78) by a Mother Ireland that beds down with England. The more substantial engagement in 'Oxen of the Sun', however, is not with patriotic iconography, but with nativist and eugenic conceptions of culture which involve the idea that artistic creation is somehow analogous to giving birth. The idea itself is an old one and not specific to nationalist culture. In *Ulysses*, Mulligan attempts to discredit Stephen's Shakespeare theory by suggesting that it presents art as gestation. There is nothing revivalist about Stephen's account of Shakespeare:

> — Himself his own father, Sonmulligan told himself. Wait. I am big with child. I have an unborn child in my brain. Pallas Athena! A play! The play's the thing! Let me parturiate!
>
> (9.875-877)

According to Terry Castle, however, this organic, childbirth metaphor did reappear in nineteenth-century romanticism after being discarded by neo-classical poets.[22] It was thus available in a fairly immediate way to the neo-romantics of the Yeats circle, which seems to have been particularly drawn to the analogy. Maud Gonne described Yeats's poetry as the child of their relationship, and identified Yeats as the mother-figure and herself as the father. She also described the Irish Literary Theatre as the child of Yeats and Lady Gregory.[23] In *Memoirs*, Yeats writes that 'Man is a woman to his work, and it begets his thought', (*Mem*, 232) and Cullingford has shown how Yeats's earlier poetry cultivated a feminine aesthetics which Yeats himself was later to find 'unmanly', and unsuited to a revised and more macho nationalist position.[24]

But if Yeats was to discard what he came to see as an over-feminized image of the artist, he never rejected the idea that artistic production was somehow connected to human reproduction. This view

---

[22] 'La'bring Bards: Birth Topoi and English Poetics, 1660-1820', *Journal of English and Germanic Philosophy,* Vol. 78 (1979), 193-208.

[23] See *Always Your Friend: Letters between Maud Gonne and W. B. Yeats, 1893-1938*, eds Anna McBride White and Norman Jeffares (London: Hutchinson, 1992), 302.

[24] Cullingford, *Gender and History*, 11-24.

may have been influenced by the Revival's early projection of itself as a nurturing movement. But the idea of art as sexual reproduction is more strongly related to Yeats's fascination with issues of lineage, racial degeneration and the survival of the race. The celebration of a culture based on heredity remained fundamental to the Yeatsian agenda from the 1890s to the 1930s, and Nietzschean linkages between art and genetics were abundant in this ceremonial. Interestingly, Yeats took what had been a simple analogy drawn between art and human reproduction and articulated a literal relation. Thus, in his view, racial hygiene was the proper business of the artist. According to Yeats, 'the artistic genius of Japan ... continually renewed itself through dynasties of painters' (Yeats, *Auto*, 57).[25] The artist was bound to Havelock Ellis's 'cosmic conservatism',[26] because art determined what 'types' would survive:

> If, as these writers affirm, the family is the unit of social life, and the origin of civilization which exists to preserve it ... it seems more natural than it did before that its ecstatic moment, the sexual choice of man and woman, should be the greater part of all poetry. A single wrong choice may destroy a family, dissipating its tradition or its biological force, and the great sculptors, painters and poets are there that instinct may find a lamp. When a young man imagines the woman of his hope, shaped for all the uses of life, mother and mistress and yet fitted to carry a bow in the wilderness, how little of it all is mere instinct. How much has come from chisel and brush. Educationalists and statesmen, servants of the logical process, do their worst, but they are not the matchmakers who bring together the fathers and mothers of the generations nor shall the type they plan survive.
> (Yeats, *Ex,* 274-75)

In this bizarre privileging of art, the artist operates on the national gene pool, determining through image that the ideal Irish male will construct his ideal mate as the traditional whore and mother. This multi-skilled woman can, in addition, put meat in the pot by virtue of her facility

---

[25] This is an absurd simplification, partly because so-called dynasties of artists often proceeded from apprentices who then simply took on the family name.

[26] This was the biological justification of gender differentiation which, Ellis thought, penetrated 'at the level of the cell', where 'maleness was characterized by the tendency to dissipate energy (katabolic), and femaleness by the capacity to store or build up energy (anabolic)' (Weeks, *Sex, Politics and Society*, 146).

with the bow and arrow. All parts of this view are, and were, outmoded enough. The suggestion that woman might hunt, however, really does suggest a particularly alarming degree of remoteness from the modern world.

Yeats, then, constructs the artist as a curious hybrid of shaman and biochemist. Art becomes linked to race and nation through its operation on natural selection. The practice of art is absolutely central to the very survival of race and nation. Far from being some last, late aberration, these opinions were being expressed by Yeats as early as 1904.[27] In *The King's Threshold*, an old pupil recalls his response at being asked long ago by Seanchan, the bard, why poetry is honoured:

> *Oldest Pupil*: I said the poets hung
> Images of the life that was in Eden
> About the child-bed of the world, that it,
> Looking upon those images, might bear
> Triumphant children. But why must I stand here,
> Repeating an old lesson, why you starve?
>
> *Seanchan*: Tell on, for I begin to know the voice.
> What evil thing will come upon the world
> If the Arts perish?
>
> *Oldest Pupil*: If the Arts should perish,
> The world that lacked them would be like a woman
> That, looking upon the cloven lips of a hare,
> Brings forth a hare-lipped child.
>
> (Yeats, *CPL*, 112)

This is one of several occasions in the play where Seanchan insists that 'poetry physically transforms humanity'.[28] He asks two cripples, for instance, 'What bad poet did your mothers listen to/That you were born so crooked?' (Yeats, *CPL*, 133).

This strange territory is worked on to produce the massively overdone symbolism and technique of 'Oxen of the Sun'. The 'nineparted' (*Letters I*, 138) episode plays havoc with the Yeatsian notion that art somehow facilitates the biological process of

---

[27] See Stanfield, *Yeats and Politics*, 145-83. The argumentation and illustration here is indebted to Stanfield's work on Yeats and eugenics.

[28] Ibid., 150.

reproduction. Characters and locations are comically literalised as organic participants in the reproductive process:

> Bloom is the spermatozoon, the hospital the womb, the nurse is the ovum, Stephen the embryo.
>
> (*Letters I*, 138-39)

Literary history itself becomes a developing foetus, not just in parallel to Mina Purefoy's real labour, but actually undergoing a developmental gestation. Of course, in the Joyce version this is all self-consciously concocted. He ends the famous letter to Budgen which outlines the 'Oxen' scheme with a playful 'How's that for high?'. Joyce knows perfectly well that there is no substance to the absurd analogies and parallels made in 'Oxen'. The fact is that writing is not childbirth; nor is childbirth like the history of English literature. Stephen is not an embryo, and Bloom is not a sperm. Joyceans have been consistently overawed by this chapter precisely because they have tried to fathom it in terms of weighty seriousness. The design and execution of 'Oxen', however, is essentially comic and the comedy certainly works at the expense of Yeats, who spent much serious ink on his aesthetics of race.

'Oxen' commandeers the cultural and scientific environment that was so important to Yeats and was most notably represented by the likes of Havelock Ellis, Sir Francis Galton and C.W. Saleeby. The language and agendas of sexology and eugenics frequently surface in the drunken debates which punctuate the episode. Lynch argues, for instance, that unexplained infant deaths are likely to be 'in the long run beneficial to the race in general in securing thereby the survival of the fittest' (14.1284-85). The climate of eugenics is also evoked in the talk about 'monstrous births' (14.974) and in the debate about whether the mother or baby should be saved when the lives of both are threatened during childbirth (a positive eugenics would require the saving of the mother). There is also the ridiculously dysgenic eugenics, so to speak, proposed by Mulligan. Mulligan, who, taking the standard eugenicist line that there has been a 'fallingoff in the calibre of the race' (14.1250), has a plan for 'a national fertilising arm to be named *Omphalos*'. He himself offers 'his dutiful yeoman services for the fecundation of any female of what grade of life soever' (14.687). The plan has a very aristocratic flavour to it and, indeed, a distinct Anglo-Irish cast. In order to locate his project geographically, Mulligan resolves to:

> purchase in fee simple for ever the freehold of Lambay island from its holder, lord Talbot de Malahide, a Tory gentleman of note much in favour with our ascendancy party.
> (14.681-83)

This joke stud farm,[29] like the mock-lionization of the prolific Purefoys, obviously deflates the eugenics championed as serious science by both Yeats and Synge.[30]

'Oxen of the Sun' makes further comic connections between human reproduction and the national culture. Medicine in general and childbirth in particular become a matter of 'Celtic' pride as the 'Oxen' narrative expresses the traditional esteem in which motherhood is held in Ireland, and applauds the native medical expertise of the Gaelicized practitioners, the 'O'Shiels, the O'Hickeys and the O'Lees' (14.37). Mr and Mrs Purefoy are granted a national status as the Ireland's most distinguished copulators and progenitors, although the fact that Mr Purefoy is a Methodist makes him an ironic representative of the fecund Catholic nation. The couple have produced nine live children, and Theodore is fulsomely praised as the colonizing migrant to the New World who saw his 'America' his lifetask, and charged 'to cover like the transpontine bison' (14.1430-31).

Eugenics, however, is not simply a matter of background discussion in 'Oxen'. The extraordinary biological aesthetics that visualizes artists shaping the process of racial natural selection is strongly implicated in the homologies between art and childbirth which are fundamental to the

---

[29] Mulligan's idea may have originated with George Bernard Shaw, who advocated 'a State Department of Evolution to pay women for their child-rearing services, and if necessary to regulate a "joint-stock human stud farm" ' (Weeks, *Sex, Politics and Society*, 134).

[30] It is perhaps worth pointing out that whilst Yeats's involvement with mainstream eugenics — his correspondence with the Eugenics Society, for example, and his championing of Raymond B. Cattells' *The Fight for Our National Intelligence* (1938) — was late, eugenics itself developed in the 1860s. Sir Francis Dalton, a cousin of Darwin's and leading figure in the English eugenics movement, published his *Hereditary Genius* in 1869. For a brief account of the history of eugenics in this period, see Weeks, *Sex, Politics and Society*, 128-38.

structure and design of 'Oxen'. From the outset physical and artistic gestation are related through the invocation to Apollo, god of poetry and bringer of fertility. In the Latinate opening, the Irishman is called upon to:

> become the exhortator and admonisher of his semblables and to tremble lest what had in the past been by the nation excellently commenced might be in the future not with similar excellence accomplished.
>
> (14.22-25)

This ironic incitement is specifically directed at the artist, constructed in this episode as 'the renewer and developer of ... inherited traditions'.[31] The whole idea of 'a woman of Eblana' (14.205) being delivered to the accompaniment of the genesis of literary style, seems to image precisely, too precisely, Yeats's view that art is a conduit for the lifeblood of the nation. The most fundamental irony, of course, is that, served-up along with the triumphant birth of the newest Purefoy, Joyce's parade of literary styles, is presented not as Irish at all, but as English cultural tradition. The likes of Swift and Burke may be represented, but they are represented as they would have been in the style handbooks of the period: as Irish participants in an English tradition. This tradition, as Robert Spoo has shown, was itself presented in developmental terms as a Whiggish or Darwinian 'progress'.[32] In the famous letter to Frank Budgen which appears to provide a detailed scheme for 'Oxen', Joyce emphasizes precisely the 'Englishness' of the literary traditions which he works on. He stresses the importance of an Anglo-Saxon rhythm and 'motive' which 'recurs from time to time' (*Letters 1*, 138-39). Budgen himself argues that 'a double thudding Anglo-Saxon motive continually recurs to give the feeling of trampling oxen'.[33]

It might be objected that this heavily produced 'procession' (*Letters 1*, 138) of styles and weight of symbolism is a form of parodic overkill,

---

[31] Peake, *Citizen and the Artist*, 254. However, Peake does not read this as an ironic tradition, and sees nothing problematic in Stephen inheriting English traditions.

[32] See Spoo, *Language of History*, 135-50.

[33] Budgen, *Making of 'Ulysses'*, 224.

a deployment of the proverbial sledge-hammer to crack what has been construed by English Yeatsians as nothing more objectionable than a quaint aristocratic eccentricity on Yeats's part. But then, Joyce's perception of the man who held unique significance as a representative of Irish culture is not English. From Joyce's perspective, Yeats's eugenic account of literary production is deeply offensive. It consigns the Catholic middle class that produced Joyce himself to the rubbish heap of racial history. Conversely, it hugely privileges the Ascendancy, 'the greatest breed in Europe',[34] who were devoted to the defence of landlordism at any price, including nationalism. Eugenics, for Yeats, was the one piece of modern 'scientific' rationalism that could underpin his long lament at the passing of noble blood and Joyce, if 'Oxen' is anything to go by, took unqualified delight in wrecking that support. Above all, however, eugenics produced a fallacious cultural historiography which Joyce could not tolerate. If Sir Francis Galton's invention of eugenics was Darwinism applied to society, Yeats's Literary Revival was eugenics applied to culture. The influential purist account of Irish literary culture that resulted was a deceit, understood by Joyce as Protestant ideology. With its joyous paralleling of an Irish birth with an English literary history, 'Oxen' shatters this organic, eugenicist articulation of culture. In fact, one of the most essential weapons Joyce deploys against the Yeatsian aesthetic is the surpassing pretentiousness that, ironically, so many critics have attacked for being over-the-top.

'womans higher functions': Molly and the homeland
The last episode of *Ulysses* has always been discussed in terms of gender issues, but the representation of Molly Bloom has rarely, if ever,[35] been understood in terms of nationalist culture. Just as 'The

---

[34] Attributed to Yeats by Joseph Cohen. See Stanfield, *Yeats and Politics*, 165.

[35] Darcy O'Brien has discussed some of the cultural influences on 'Penelope' in 'Some Determinants of Molly Bloom', in T. F Staley, ed., *Approaches to Ulysses*, (Pittsburgh: University of Pittsburgh Press, 1970), 137-56. But O'Brien sees nothing of the humour involved in Joyce constructing Molly out of Gea Tellus and Sheela-n-gig. Emer Nolan also discusses this episode in the context of nationalism, but concludes that 'Penelope' 'fails to depart from the stereotype' as far as representations of women are concerned. See Nolan, *Joyce and*

Dead' is a coda to *Dubliners*, 'Penelope' is most typically read as a coda to *Ulysses*. The Molly-discourse becomes a privileging of the female voice.³⁶ In this sense, 'Penelope' is divided from the rest of *Ulysses*. The boys are sleeping, and a new articulation takes the stage. An earthy, materialist, feminine kind of perception is released to close the book. Oddly, and despite some serious objections to a perceived stereotyping, most readers have found this a positive genderizing. There is a feminist consensus on Molly and it is essentially in favour.

I want to argue rather differently here. For all its innovation, 'Penelope' actually belongs much more substantially to a linear movement which is at work from the Telemachia through 'Scylla and Charybdis', 'Cyclops' and 'Circe' to the ricorso that this last chapter concludes. The movement I refer to starts with the word 'usurper' and ends with the embedding of a woman — a realistic figure drawn in great detail, but whose gender is also associated with a portentous symbolism, most of it taken from nationalist culture. In this respect, Joyce's Molly moves in on the territory staked out by, say, Yeats's Countess Cathleen. She is Joyce's wicked version of mother/mistress-Ireland. The Molly discussed here then is not situated at the margins of *Ulysses* as a coda, but rather at the centre of the novel as an ironic reconstruction of the feminized nation in the modern world. In this reading 'Penelope' becomes the 'clou' (*Letters 1*, 170) of the book, because it is the final stage in a dynamic which opens with an image of the dispossessed son and ends with a final act of cultural repossession.

Molly Bloom is a devastating riposte both to Yeats's detached, mysterious lady of the Great House and to the devout homemaker of the Catholic heartland. Before examining the detail of this engagement, it is worth emphasizing again that these alternative images of nation, which were hardly unique to Ireland, were formulated by competing social groups around distinct political agendas. Woman pictured as a denatured, domestic, helpmate to man was one of the cultural cornerstones of the Catholic nation as conceptualized by the Church and the Gaelic League. It was fully institutionalized in De Valera's

---

Nationalism, 163-81.

³⁶ Although it could be argued that, as a coda, the discourse is marginalized. Molly-speak is at the edge of culture, consigned to a private place, close to sleep and well-distanced from the huge and mostly masculine bulk of *Ulysses*.

Gaeltacht. On the other hand, the respectable had no great currency in Protestant revivalist culture.[37] The Revival at any rate generally allotted a wilder, more mysterious and even sensual role to women. A poem like Yeats's 'A Prayer for my Daughter' becomes quite exceptional in this respect. Here, an insecure father is a suppliant for a future where his daughter possesses beauty, but not 'overmuch ... to make a stranger's eye distraught'. She is to be educated in 'courtesy' and taught not to have 'opinions', (Yeats, *CPO*, 211-12) thus confirming Yeats's view that the Western philosophical tradition understood intellect and reason to be transcendent of the feminine.[38] This 'angel in the house' poem could have been assimilated into the repressive anti-feminism of De Valera's Pauline state without too much difficulty, but it is not characteristically Anglo-Irish. In pre-Treaty Ireland, images of nation produced less domesticated stereotypes of the feminine: Ireland as earth-goddess, or, as more commonly in Yeats, Ireland as the remote 'heroic mother moon' of 'Lines Written in Dejection'. This moon-image was more consistent with Yeats's conception of Ireland's tragic role and with his 'cult of the exceptional woman'.[39] In the latter, female power is connected to distance, reserve, even disdain — the aristocratic qualities so vital in Yeats's imagination. The result was an image of a feminized Ireland which was mysterious, static and archaic.

The cultural stereotypes of Catholic and Protestant Gaelicism were in some ways distinct. They became more so as the Irish nation became increasingly identified with the Catholic state, and as Yeats became an increasingly marginalized Senator. The Gaeltacht, in a piece of pure *realpolitick*, also identified Anglo-Ireland's intelligentsia as a fifth column gnawing away at the core of Irish morality. But for all this politicization of difference, there was a significant cultural crossover between Protestant and Catholic nationalists in the pre-Treaty period. In Joyce's view, it derived, not from a shared cultural heritage, but from a common reactionary position. The compelling adhesive was that both were purist, idealizing and patriarchal cultures which denatured women.

---

[37] See Mosse, where he discusses how, 'woman as a national symbol was the guardian of the continuity and immutability of the nation, the embodiment of its respectability' (*Sex and Nationalism*, 18).

[38] See Cullingford, *Gender and History*, 133.

[39] Ibid., 81.

'Penelope' both incorporates elements of these traditions and emerges as a text which is radically transgressive. There is a slight but interesting example of incorporation in the episode's absorption of the motif which was so central in Yeats's early representations of the feminized nation: the rose. In his notesheets for the episode, Joyce collected words with 'rose' in them: 'Rosia' the name of a district in Gibraltar; rosary and rosepoint; the student's name, Penrose. The word features throughout the finished 'Penelope' and the use of it grows more frequent, so that, between lines 1554 and 1609, for instance, 'rose' occurs some five times.[40] The most obvious, and controversial, appropriation, however, is of essentialist images of woman as nature. Indeed the whole structure and design of 'Penelope' apparently turns on an essentialist construction of woman. Joyce coined the word 'gynomorphic' to describe the chapter.[41] The dynamic is of an 'earthball slowly ... spinning' and Molly is mother-earth in the correspondences of the Linati schema. According to Joyce, the word 'yes', becomes a 'female word'. Moreover, the female was represented in the four words, 'because', 'bottom', 'woman' and 'yes'. These words apparently have no intellectual or emotional or spiritual significance for Joyce. They diagrammatize women because they somehow stand-in for 'the female breasts, arse, womb and cunt' (*Letters I*, 171). The 'numerology' of the episode, much of it concerned with the number 8, number of infinity and figure of a woman at rest, is a further demonstration of this episode's apparent overindulgence in what might be termed arche-stereotyping.

This is objectification with a vengeance. The joke here, as so often in *Ulysses*, is the consequence of a reproduction, exploitation and wild exaggeration of tendencies which are already constituents of a solemnly aristocratic culture. For all that, it is easy to see why 'Penelope' has sometimes alienated its modern readers. The line between the joke that liberates and the one that confirms the prejudice is perhaps particularly fine in this episode. This may be why so much of Joyce's articulation of the design of 'Penelope' is muted in the actual delivery. In fact, without the famous letter and the schema, it would be difficult to retrieve much

---

[40] Andrew Gibson makes this point in an unpublished essay entitled ' "Revising God's Order": "Penelope" '.

[41] Walton A. Litz, 'Joyce's Notes for the Last Episodes of *Ulysses*', *Modern Fiction Studies,* IV (1968), 16.

of Joyce's symbolizing intent.

The 'archetypal' configurations of Molly are also greatly softened by the sheer extent of her specificity. For a portrait of the 'essence' of woman, Molly is exceptionally individualised. She also belongs to a particular milieu. So much is revealed in her tastes. She sings the popular songs of the period and reads the popular literature, like Mrs Henry Wood's *The Shadow of Ashlydat* (1863), which sold 150,000 copies in 1899, and Mrs Mary Elizabeth Braddon's *Henry Dunbar* (1864). She reads popular magazines like *Lloyds Weekly News* and *The Gentlewoman*, turning to them for ideas in fashion and assimilating their idiom: the face lotion she uses, for instance, 'made my skin like new' (18.459). She has a dressy taste in clothes, which helps to place her as a cultural and social figure. She thinks of 'high buttoned boots'; 'violet garters'; 'orange petticoats'; 'kidfitting corsets', 'silkette stockings' and 'cream muslin dresses' (see 18.440-90). There are also suggestions of the unfashionable, like 'old brogues itself' (18.469). Molly's monologue is also full of references to contemporary figures, places and events. She calls Arthur Griffith and Val Dillon, the City Arms Hotel and the DBC to mind. She recalls the performance of Mr and Mrs William Hunter Kendal in *The Wife of Scarli* at the Gaiety Theatre and of Beerbohm Tree in *Trilby*. This immediacy is not a simple qualification of the symbolic earth-mother Molly. The spontaneous, materialist and middle-class Molly completely undermines the idea of Molly as female essence. The constant, immutable conception, which some readers have taken so seriously, is at odds with the immediacy of modish and stylish ephemera. In this sense, the 'realistic' Molly is in negation of the idealizing and conservative cultural practices which 'Penelope' itself seems to indulge on such a grand scale.

Joyce more than participates in the iconography of nationalist culture, but his earth-mother is hardly the eternal holy image of the land venerated by Yeats. Nor is she the pure, Gaelicized homemaker of Catholicism. Indeed, Molly is placed in precise opposition to these idealizations. She is urban and middle class. In many respects, she confirms the Revival's view of modern bourgeois life. She often expresses conventional views, and she is materialistic. Despite her transgression with Boylan — perhaps because of it — she is concerned to keep up appearances. She is angry that the Blooms do not have a maid and do not use visiting cards, for instance. But Molly is far from *just* conventional. Indeed part of her modern status is generated by her rejection of puritan views which *she* takes to be conventional and straightlaced. Molly despises Mrs Riordan, for instance, who is 'down on bathing suits and lownecks ... let us have a bit of fun first God help the world if all the women were of her sort' (18.9-10). On the other hand, Molly also criticizes the new brand of 'Irishers'. She thinks these young revivalists are snobbish, prissy and unsexy:

> Kathleen Kearney and her lot óf squealers Miss This Miss That Miss Theother lot of sparrowfarts skitting around talking about politics they know as much about as my backside anything in the world to make themselves someway interesting Irish homemade beauties soldiers daughter am I ay and whose are you bootmakers and publicans I beg your pardon coach I thought you were a wheelbarrow theyd die down dead off their feet if they ever got the chance of walking down the Alameda on an officers arm like me on the bandnight my eyes flash my bust that they havent passion God help their poor head I knew more about men and life when I was 15 then they'll all know at 50
>
> (18.878-87)

This may not be immediately recognizable as radical, but there is something challenging here, which derives not from the selflessness of the Yeatsian aristocrat, but precisely from vanity. In this sense, Molly's radicalism is something with which we all can identify, although it is culturally specific. It is contingent, not on the remote grandeur of a Lady Gregory, but on something much more human and ordinary.

There are further ways in which Molly derides convention. She knows that morality in Dublin is largely a matter of lip service, and she condemns the double standards that tie women to the home and allows men to behave as they like. She is not taken in by the mother-cult. She sees nothing romantic in childbirth and wishes men 'could have a touch of it themselves'. Although she is basically God-fearing, she is distrusts conventional morality. She is critical of the proprieties of the Church, and suggests that the guardians of the nation's chastity are not themselves so pure in thought. Most radical of all, she challenges creation itself. In particular, she questions the way in which women were made. Of menstruation she wonders 'whoever suggested that business for women what between clothes and cooking and children'. As for the design of sex organs, her views here, as so often, are contradictory, but she has this striking objection to female genitalia:

whats the idea making us like that with a big hole in the middle of us or like a Stallion driving it up into to you because thats all they want out of you
(18.151-152)

The most challenging characteristic of 'Penelope', however, is not its portrayal of Molly's modernity, but its detailed and insistent exposure of her sexuality. Of course, the two are related, but sexuality is of unique and particular importance in 'Penelope', and for good reason. The denial of female sexuality was part of the common ground uniting conservative nationalisms. Nationalism, as we have seen, helped to define 'respectable' sexuality and the family persona, 'the decent hardworking, God fearing man, his docile wife at his side and comely children romping sturdily around them'.[42] Sexual desire was considered to be antithetical to feminity. Sir William Acton, the Victorian surgeon often held to be representative in this respect, expected 'the best of mothers, wives and managers of households' to know 'little or nothing of sexual indulgence'.[43] Even amongst progressive liberals, like Elizabeth Blackwell, the pioneering doctor who challenged Acton's denial of female sexuality, chastity was held to be the 'highest law' and 'one natural to women'. Blackwell understood the maternal instinct to be the biological force driving women to tolerate what was regarded as the 'ungoverable lust of men'.[44]

'Penelope' completely overruns this consensus, and it is worth emphasizing the meticulous detail of its reply to the orthodoxy. The account of bodily functions — where we witness Molly urinating, menstruating, farting and suffering from an itchy 'hole'— is subversive enough. It would be difficult to sustain worship of a goddess exposed in this way, certainly in the high Yeatsian manner. The comprehensive coverage of sexuality in 'Penelope', however, completely ousts the virgin from the hearth. Rarely do five lines pass without some reference to sex. There are references to a range of fetishes, real and fantasized. Boylan seems to be a foot fetishist (see 18.250-60); Bloom nurses a

---

[42] Rosita Sweetman, *On Our Backs: Sexual Attitudes in a Changing Ireland* (London: Pan Books, 1979), 9.

[43] Sir William Action, a Victorian surgeon, quoted in Weeks, *Sex, Politics and Society*, 40.

[44] See Weeks, *Sex, Politics and Society*, 42.

rather more recherché desire to have Molly walk through horse manure (see 18.267). The fetish most associated with Bloom, however, is his underwear obsession. As distinguished from Boylan — who, Molly suspects, prefers women with 'no drawers at all' — Bloom is 'mad on the subject of drawers' (18.289). He asked Molly for a piece of her underwear when they were courting, and was given the drawers off Molly's doll. There is also a great deal of exhibitionism in the episode, with Molly lifting her 'orange petticoat' in public (18.308) and being asked by Bloom 'to pose for a picture naked' (18.560-61). At line 920, Molly thinks she was observed whilst washing, an experience she clearly enjoyed. She fantasizes about having sex in a train at line 365. At line 85 Molly expresses a desire for sex with a young man; at line 482 she tells us she'd like to try 'a black man's'. At 1143 she fancies 'feeling' a priest. Molly remembers being touched in the Gaiety Theatre at line 1040 and thinks about dirty books at line 969. There is considerable sexual activity around breasts, at lines 535, 578 and 800, and Molly fantasizes about being a whore at line 1418. Sadomadochism is alluded to at 493 and fantasized about at line 963. Masturbation is perhaps the sexual practice most frequently referred to in 'Penelope'. Molly masturbates Mulvey (see 18.810), and herself, fairly regularly, in fact '4 or 5 time a day sometimes' (18.1179). She masturbates Bloom with her feet at line 263 and would have tried a banana on herself at line 803, but was concerned that 'it might break'. She thinks about shaving off her pubic hair at 1135, and approves heartily of having sex during the day, on the floor because of the squeaky bed, at line 1130. Lesbianism is referred to at 1147 and oral sex, which Bloom does 'all wrong', at both lines 1250, and 1353 where Molly wants to kiss the statue of a boy 'all over also his lovely young cock'. Molly wonders about the sexual practices of her friends:

> Mrs Mastiansky told me her husband made her like the dogs do it and stick out her tongue as far as ever she could
>
> (18.417-18)

Some of the most vivid material is saved for Boylan and his 'tremendous big red brute of a thing' (18.144). He 'must have come 3 or 4 times' and Molly feels 'fucked yes and damn well fucked too up to my neck nearly not by him 5 or 6 times handrunning theres the mark of his spunk on the clean sheet' (18.1510-12). Although Molly asserting her sexual power over a debased Bloom can also be quite visually immediate:

> if he wants to kiss my bottom Ill drag open my drawers and bulge it right out in his face as large as life he can stick his tongue 7 miles up my hole as hes there my brown part then Ill tell him I want £1 or perhaps 30/-
> (18.1520-23)

Joyceans have claimed to be able to produce a sexually restrained Molly on the basis of Ulyssean biography. She has had penetrative sex, it seems, with only two men in her lifetime. But this is hardly the point. There really is little restraint in the 'Penelope' text and none of this sexual material concerns reproduction or the family. Molly's sexual drive is about desire, and such desire was a crime against the Irish nation of both Protestant and Catholic Gaelicism. In this culturally precise sense, this energized beauty who is fed up with being corseted, refusing outright to be a self-denying mother or a doting wife, is a deeply liberating figure. She answers the remote sirens of nationalist culture with the loud and radical assertion that sex is 'only nature'.

There is indisputably a modernizing position to this new image of nation. Anglo-Irish culture is outdated as well as outdone. The unattainable beauty of the Great House aristocrat is displaced as an image of Ireland by this close-up of Molly. But there is also an element of reclamation here, as there is so frequently in *Ulysses*. Certainly 'Penelope' writes against the traditions of Anglo-Irish cultural nationalism, but it also uses remnants from more raucous and rumbustious Gaelic traditions of an early period. In one old tradition, for instance, Ireland is presented as a goddess with whom the king must copulate before he can claim the throne. The myth of nationhood, here, is openly sexual and sovereignty is presented in terms of seduction:

> When unable to find the proper mate, the goddess becomes old, ugly and crazed, but she is miraculously restored to youth and beauty when she persuades some intrepid male to make love to her. The reward is kingship.[45]

This wild, copulating woman was already being written out from Irish culture in the seventeenth and early eighteenth centuries by post-bardic poets like O'Rathaille and Owen Roe Sullivan, and had vanished by the

---

[45] Cullingford, *Gender and History*, 58.

early nineteenth century. It is quite pointless to ask whether Joyce's representation of Molly is 'accurate'. There is no real Molly to measure her against. The point is that the 'Penelope' text frees the culture from the conservatism of revivalism and one wonders if this release owes something to an earlier formulation of Ireland as a more robust and sexual female figure. If this is the case then 'Penelope' effects a further repossession; not in flesh and blood, by any fictional male, but as culture and through the agency of the text itself.

Penelope' is a particular and dramatic illustration of a territorial instinct which animates Joyce's work from *Dubliners* onwards. The assault on Yeatsian mythopoetics, here in the last episode of *Ulysses*, is part of a much larger design which runs through all of these texts. Joyce's reply to the culture of revivalism is activated in the insistent realism of *Dubliners*, the ironic romantics of *A Portrait*, and the textual inventiveness of *Ulysses*. In their different ways, all these texts challenge the reality and the authenticity of the Irelands invented by revivalism generally and the Literary Revival in particular. Joyceans have seriously underestimated the importance of this challenge. They have also often depoliticized Joyce by constructing him as the chronic individualist who, in rejecting revivalism, heroically rejects an unproblematic concept called Ireland. This latter is partly a product of uncritical readings of the Revival's self-publicity. I have argued here, however, that Joyce understood revivalism, not as *the* Irish consciousness, but as an Anglicized and essentially conservative ideology. His encounter with the Revival is thus an expression of a political radicalism, but also and perhaps more centrally an expression of historical and social consciousness. The extraordinary volubility of *Ulysses* responds to the relative silence of Catholic Ireland in nineteenth and early twentieth-century literary culture, and, of course, to the sheer authority of the Protestant tradition. Without Joyce's massive intervention, the conservatism of revivalist Ireland would have gone much less seriously challenged as the authentic literary voice of the nation.

Yeats's place in the production of Joyce-texts is hard to overestimate. Yeats was not solely responsible for the creation of the Protestant culture of the Literary Revival, but he was its most eminent practitioner and elevated the drama of Ireland's cultural nationalism to the world stage. With Yeats, Joyce's contemporary target grew immeasurably. There is a clear sense, I think, in which Yeats is forever shadowing Joyce. The sheer grandeur of Yeats's last late mythologizing of landlordism must take some responsibility for the fabulous grandeur, equally, of both *Ulysses* and *Finnegans Wake*.

The conflict between Joyce and the Anglo-Irish has been presented here as a post-colonial issue. Of course, the distance between Joyce and Yeats could be seen in terms of a much more conventional literary teleology. In fact, the argument in this study seems not too far removed from the fairly standard view that understands Joyce's modernism as a 'naturally' progressive reaction against stale, nineteenth-century conventions which were being magnificently sustained by the last great romantic. But a purely literary history has not been able to account for, or even recognize, the insistence with which the Joycean aesthetic opposes revivalism. Nor has it been able to read the sheer comic energy and violence of Joyce's engagement with Yeats. It is quite inadequate to understand Joyce's fiction as some kind of 'development' from revivalism. The Joyce text splits away from revivalism; it is *devoted* to an undermining of revivalism's status as cultural nationalism, and to a displacement of the Yeatsian Protestant tradition from the round tower of Irish literary culture.

The social and cultural gulf between Joyce and Yeats finds expression in two aesthetics so different as to be radically incompatible. There is undeniably a sense in which Joyce measures the authenticity of his work against what he sees as the fake Ireland of revivalism. Equally, there is the compelling sense in which Joyce, writing 'Irish literature in English' is himself a product of Anglicization. Joyce's fictions are definitively alternative to revivalism, but they do not construct a substitute culture of ethnicity. Indeed, a good part of the integrity of Joyce's work derives from its refusal to project an alternative essentialism.

The complexity of Joyce's brand of literary strategics continues with *Finnegans Wake*, Joyce's last address to 'Gentes and laitymen, fullstoppers and semicolonials, hybred and lubberds' (*FW*. 152), which has seemed to many readers to be both the most universal and yet somehow the most Irish of Joyce's books. Of course, the main tradition of *Wake* criticism responds to the mechanics of universality, but many critics have detected a lyricism in the book which has often been related to the issue of cultural identity. Moreover, more recent post-colonial readings are beginning to understand the astonishing fullness and inclusiveness of the *Wake* as the reversal of post-colonial cultural spaces. Seamus Deane states the case admirably:

> *Finnegans Wake* is Joyce's Irish answer to an Irish problem. It is written in a ghost language about phantasmal figures; history is haunted by them and embodies them over and over again in specific people, places and tongues. If Ireland could not be herself, then, by way of compensation, the world would become Ireland. This is the problem of identity solved. Irish history is world history *in parvo*.[46]

The extremely difficult problem of precisely how to read the 'local' in the famously universalizing tendencies of the *Wake* remains to be addressed. The older orthodoxy which insists that '*Finnegans Wake* is about anybody, anywhere, anytime'[47] is compelling, but also needs to be integrated with newer readings which are insisting on the Irish dimension of the Joyce's last work. Such concerns go far beyond the boundaries of the present study. There is no doubt, however, that much of the most interesting current work claims a post-colonial provenance, and there is good reason to think that reading the *Wake* in relation to revivalism will feature in such readings. So much is suggested in the title which centralizes this last great work in deep contradictions of race and culture by referring to a Gael who is, somehow, both dead and alive.

---

[46] Seamus Deane, 'Joyce the Irishman', in Derek Attridge, ed., *The Cambridge Companion to James Joyce* (Cambridge: Cambridge University Press, 1990), 50.

[47] William York Tyndall, *A Reader's Guide to 'Finnegans Wake'* (London: Thames & Hudson, 1969), 3.

Appendix

The Deliverer and 'Circe'

Lady Gregory's *The Deliverer* works on J. F. Taylor's Jewish/Irish, England/Egypt metaphor in a curious way. Lady Gregory has Egypt's slaves, transported from some far off land by their persecutors, knocking up cement for pyramid building and talking in some dialect that purports to be Irish brogue. Their would-be saviour is 'The King's Nursling', a Moses/Parnell figure. Were Lady Gregory in full control of the comic potential of this crazy temporal and spatial displacement, we might have an interesting joke here. But she is not. The result is a mess of triteness that is inadvertently hilarious, and which is evoked in *Ulysses 15* where Bloom the messiah, receives his strongest support from women. Here is Lady Gregory's version:

ARD'S WIFE.	God love you! A thousand blessings on my two knees to you.
DAN'S WIFE:	That the world may wonder at the luck you'll have!
MALACHI'S WIFE:	That my blessing may comfort you, and make you that you'll never be broken up!
DAN'S WIFE:	May God increase you!
ARD'S WIFE:	The Lord have mercy on everyone belonging to you!
DAN'S WIFE:	And on everyone ever went from you!
MALACHI'S WIFE:	And on yourself at the latter end.
ARD'S WIFE:	The laugh that is in his eye should be sunshine to ripen the barley, and bleach the flax in the field![1]

Joyce has a similar kind of choral adoration, except that in his version the daft stage brogue is dropped and Joyce is rather more sensitive to the sexual connotations of hero-worship:

---

[1] Augusta Gregory, *Collected Plays* ed. Ann Saddlemeyer, (Gerrards Cross: Colin Symthe, 1970), I, 267.

A PAVIOUR AND FLAGGER
That's the famous Bloom now, the world's greatest reformer. Hats off! *(All uncover their heads. Women whisper eagerly)*

A MILLIONAIRESS
(richly) Isn't he simply wonderful!

A NOBLEWOMAN
(nobly) All that man has seen!

A FEMINIST
(masculinely) And done!
(15.1458-66)

In both texts the downfall of the hero martyr is initiated by the disapprobation of the priests and in both there is a choral reversal of the former glorification. This is *The Deliverer*:

MALACHI'S WIFE:	He has put on poor clothes like us for a mockery.
DAN'S WIFE:	Take care, he might be spying on us.
ARD'S WIFE:	To come on us as a spy and an informer, that is a foul thing to do.[2]

And this is 'Circe':

FATHER FARLEY
He is an episcopalian, an agnostic, an anythingarian seeking to overthrow our holy faith.

MRS RIORDAN
(tears up her will) I'm disappointed in you! You bad man!

MOTHER GROGAN
(removes her boot to throw it at Bloom) You beast! You abominable person!
(15.1711-18)

It might look as if Joyce shares Lady Gregory's view (a view commonly held amongst the Anglo-Irish intelligentsia) that in the end the Irish always betray their heroes, and usually at the behest of the priests. But quite apart from the fact that it was one thing for a Catholic

---

[2] Ibid., 272.

writer to hold this view, and something quite different for a Anglo-Irish aristocrat to hold it, Lady Gregory's text is meant to be taken seriously. It has the status of a contemporary political reading. Joyce's text, on the other hand, is a comic ordering of a well-established iconoclasm in which, incidentally, the crude image of Irish Catholic peasants betraying aristocratic heroes is decisively challenged. The 'noblewoman' and the 'millionairess' fawning at the feet of Bloom is along way from the usual mythopoetics of revivalist messianism.

Bibliography

Works by James Joyce
Dubliners, an annotated edition with introduction, notes and afterwords by John Wyse Jackson and Bernard McGinley (London: Sinclair-Stevenson, 1993).
Exiles, with the author's notes and an introduction by Padraic Colum (London: Jonathan Cape, 1952).
Finnegans Wake, third edition (London: Faber & Faber, 1964).
A Portrait of the Artist as a Young Man, the definitive text corrected from the Dublin holograph by Chester G. Anderson and edited by Richard Ellmann (London: Jonathan Cape, 1968).
Stephen Hero, edited by Theodore Spencer et al (London: Jonathan Cape, 1956).
Ulysses, the corrected text, edited by Hans Walter Gabler et al (London: Bodley Head, 1986).
The Critical Writings of James Joyce edited by Ellsworth Mason and Richard Ellmann (London: Faber and Faber, 1959).
Letters of James Joyce, Vols II and III, edited by Richard Ellmann (London: Faber and Faber, 1966).
Letters of James Joyce, edited by Stuart Gilbert (London: Faber and Faber, 1957).
Poems and Shorter Writings, including Epiphanies, Giacomo Joyce and 'A Portrait of the Artist', edited by Richard Ellmann, A. Walton Litz and John Whittier Ferguson (London: Faber and Faber 1991).

Works by W. B. Yeats
Autobiographies (London: Macmillan, 1959).
The Collected Plays (London: Macmillan, 1952).
The Collected Poems (London: Macmillan, 1950).
Essays and Introductions (London: Macmillan, 1961).
Explorations (London: Macmillan, 1961).
The Irish National Theatre (Roma: Accademia D'Italia, 1935).
Memoirs: Autobiography—First Draft Journal, transcribed and edited by Denis Donoghue (London: Macmillan, 1972).

Mythologies (London: Macmillan, 1989).
Uncollected Prose, edited by John P. Frayne and Colton Johnson (New York: Colombian University Press, 1970).
Yeats, W. B. with Edwin John Ellis, *The Works of William Blake, Poetic, Symbolic and Critical* (London: Bernard Quaritch, 1893).

Works by other authors

Anderson, Benedict, *Imagined Communities: Reflections on the Origin and Spread of Nationalism* (London: Verso, 1983).
Arnold, Matthew, *Culture and Anarchy* (Cambridge: Cambridge University Press, 1961 edn).
Arnold, Matthew, *On the Study of Celtic Literature and Other Essays* (London: Dent, 1910).
Attridge, Derek, *The Cambridge Companion to James Joyce* (Cambridge: Cambridge University Press, 1990).
Bakhtin, M. M., *The Dialogic Imagination*, edited by Michael Holquist (Austin: University of Texas Press, 1981).
Baldry, H. C., *Greek Literature for the Modern Reader* (Cambridge: Cambridge University Press, 1951).
Barrington Sir J., *Personal Sketches and Recollections of His Own Times* (London: Cameron and Ferguson, 1876).
Barry, M. J. ed., *The Songs of Ireland* (Dublin: James Duffy, 1869).
Bauerle, Ruth, *The James Joyce Songbook* (New York and London: Garland Publishing, 1982).
Behan, Dominic, *Ireland Sings* (London: Tro Essex Music, 1973).
Boyle, The Rev. R., ' "Two Gallants" and "Ivy Day" ', The *James Joyce Quarterly*, I/2 (Spring), 1963.
Boyd, Ernest, *The Irish Literary Renaissance*, revised edn (London: Grant Richards, 1922).
Brantl, George, *Catholicism* (London: Prentice-Hall, 1961).
Brown, Richard, *James Joyce and Sexuality* (Cambridge: Cambridge University Press, 1985).
Brown, Malcolm, *The Politics of Irish Literature: From Thomas Davis to W. B. Yeats* (London: Allen and Unwin, 1972).
Bryan, Donald, *The Great Earl of Kildare* (Dublin and Cork: The Talbot Press, 1933).
Budgen, Frank, *James Joyce and the Making of Ulysses*, new edition (London; Oxford University Press, 1972).
Butcher, S. H. and Andrew Lang, *The Odyssey of Homer — Done Into*

English Prose (London: Macmillan, 1893).
Cairns, David and Shaun Richards, *Writing Ireland: Colonialism, Nationalism and Culture* (Manchester: Manchester University Press, 1988).
Calder, Grace J., *George Petrie and the Ancient Music of Ireland* (Dublin: the Dolmen Press, 1968).
Castle, Terry, 'Lab'ring Bards: Birth Topoi and English Poetics, 1660-1820', *Journal of English and Germanic Philology*, 78, (1979).
Chambers, E. K., *Arnold: Poetry and Prose* (Oxford: Oxford University Press, 1939).
Chappell, William, *The Ballad Literature and Popular Music of Olden Time* with a new introduction by F.W. Sternfield, Vol. 2 (New York: Dover Publications, 1965).
Cheng, Vincent J. and Timothy Martin, eds *Joyce in Context* (Cambridge: Cambridge University Press, 1992).
Cheng, Vincent J., *Joyce, Race and Empire* (Cambridge: Cambridge University Press, 1995).
Cohn, Norman, *The Pursuit of the Millennium* (London: Secker and Warburg, 1957).
Conmee, The Very Reverend John S., *Old Times in The Barony* (Dublin: The Catholic Truth Society, 1907).
Conor, W. A., *History of the Irish People* (London: John Heywood, 1886).
Cullingford, Elizabeth, *Gender and History in Yeats's Love Poetry* (Melbourne and New York: Cambridge University Press, 1993).
Davis, Thomas, *The Spirit of the Nation* (Dublin: no publisher, 1845).
Davis, Thomas, *Essays Literary and Historical* (Dundalk: W. Tempest, 1914).
Deane, Seamus, *Celtic Revivals: Essays in Modern Irish Literature* (London: Faber and Faber, 1985).
Deane, Seamus, 'Poetry and Song 1800-1890', the introduction to *The Field Day Anthology of Irish Writing*, Vol. 2 (Derry: Field Day, 1991).
Dubois, L. Paul, *The Gaelic Movement in Contemporary Ireland* (Dublin: Maunsel, 1908).
Duffy, Sir Charles Gavan et al, *The Revival of Irish Literature* (Dublin: T. Fisher Unwin, 1894).
Eglinton, John et al, *Literary Ideals in Ireland* (Dublin: Maunsel, 1899).
Eglinton, John, *Irish Literary Portraits* (London: Macmillan, 1935).

Eglinton, John, *Anglo-Irish Essays* (Dublin: the Talbot Press, 1917).
Ellis, Havelock, *Studies in the Psychology of Sex*, Vol. 1 (Philadelphia: F. A. Davis, 1920).
Ellis, Steven G., *Tudor Ireland: Crown, Community and the Conflict of Culture 1470-1603* (Harlow: Longman, 1985).
Ellmann, Richard, *James Joyce,* revised edn. (New York: Oxford University Press, 1982).
Ellmann, Richard, *The Consciousness of Joyce* (London: Faber and Faber, 1977).
Fairhall, James, *James Joyce and the Question of History* (Cambridge: Cambridge University Press, 1993).
Fallis, R., *The Irish Renaissance* (Syracuse: Syracuse University Press, 1977).
Ferguson, Samuel, *The Lays of the Red Branch* (Dublin: Maunsel, 1987).
French, Marilyn, *The Book as World: James Joyce's 'Ulysses'*, (London: Abacus, 1982).
Fichter, Andrew 'The Dynastic Epic', in R. H. Draper, ed., *The Epic: Developments in Criticism* (London: Macmillan, 1990).
Flannery, James W., *W. B. Yeats and the Idea of a Theatre: the Early Abbey Theatre in Theory and Practice* (New Haven: Yale University Press, 1989).
Flood, Terence, *Silken Thomas* (Kilkenny: The People's Printing and Publishing Works, 1906).
Foster, R. F., *Modern Ireland 1600-1972* (Harmondsworth: Penguin, 1988).
Gibson, Andrew, ' "History, All That" ; Revival Historiography and Literary Strategy in the "Cyclops" Episode of *Ulysses*', *Essays and Studies*, 1991.
Gibson, Andrew, ed., *Reading Joyce's 'Circe'* (Amsterdam and Atlanta, GA: Rodopi, 1994).
Gibson, Andrew, ed., *Joyce's 'Ithaca'* (Amsterdam and Atlanta, GA: Rodopi, 1996).
Gilbert, Stuart, *James Joyce's 'Ulysses'* (London: Faber and Faber, 1952).
Gillen, Gerrard and Harry White, eds, *Irish Musical Studies 3: Music in Irish Cultural Studies* (Dublin: Irish Academy Press, 1995).
Goldberg, S. L., *The Classical Temper: A Study of James Joyce's 'Ulysses'* (London: Chatto and Windus, 1961).

Gorman, Herbert, *James Joyce* (London: John Lane, The Bodley Head, 1941).
Gramsci, Antonio, *Opere,* Vol. 4, *Il Risorgimento* (Turin: Turin Press, 1949).
Greene, David H. and Edward M. Stephens, *J. M. Synge* (New York: Collier Books, 1961).
Gregory, Lady Augusta, ed., *Ideals in Ireland* (London: Longman, 1907).
Gregory, Lady Augusta, *Collected Plays*, edited by Ann Saddlemeyer (Gerrards Cross: Colin Smythe, 1970).
Hart, Clive and David Hayman, eds, *James Joyce's 'Ulysses': Critical Essays* (Berkeley and Los Angeles, California University Press, 1974).
Henke, Suzette, *James Joyce and the Politics of Desire* (London: Routledge, 1990).
Hobsbawm, E. J., *Nations and Nationalism since 1780* (Cambridge: Cambridge University Press, 1990).
Hutchinson, J., *The Dynamics of Cultural Nationalism: The Gaelic Revival and the Creation of the Irish Free State* (London: Allen and Unwin, 1987).
Jeffares, A. Norman, *W. B. Yeats, Man and Poet* (London: Routledge and Kegan Paul, 1962).
Kenner, Hugh, *Dublin's Joyce* (London: Chatto and Windus, 1955).
Kenner, Hugh, *Joyce's Voices* (London: Faber and Faber, 1978).
Kettle, Arnold, *An Introduction to the English Novel*, 2 Vols (London: Hutchinson University Library, 1951).
Kettle, T. M., *Irish Oratory and Orators* (London: T. Fisher Unwin, nd.).
Kiberd, Declan, *Inventing Ireland* (London: Jonathan Cape, 1995).
Larkin, Emmet, 'Economic Growth, Capital Investment and the Roman Catholic Church in Nineteenth-Century Ireland', *The American Historical Review*, LXII/3 (April 1967).
Leerson, Joep, Mere Irish and Fíor-Ghael: *Studies in the Idea of Irish Nationality, its Development and Literary Expression Prior to the Nineteenth Century* (Cork: Cork University Press in association with Field Day, 1996).
Litz, Walton A., 'Joyce Notes for the Last Episodes of 'Ulysses', *Modern Fiction Studies* IV (1968).
Lyons, F. S. L., *Culture and Anarchy in Ireland, 1890-1939* (Oxford;

Oxford University Press, 1982).
Kingsley, Charles, *His Letters and Memories of His Life: Edited by his Wife* (London: H. S. King, 1877).
Joyce, Stanislaus, *The Dublin Diary*, ed. George Harris Healey (London: Faber and Faber, 1962).
McCabe, Colin, *James Joyce and the Revolution of the Word* (London: Macmillan, 1978).
McCabe, Colin (ed.), *James Joyce: New Perspectives* (Brighton: Harvester Press, 1982).
McCormack W. J. and Alistair Stead, eds., *James Joyce and Modern Literature* (London: Routledge and Kegan Paul, 1982).
McCormack, W. J., *From Burke to Beckett: Ascendancy, Tradition and Betrayal in Literary History*, revised and enlarged edn (Cork: Cork University Press, 1994).
McDonagh, Oliver, *States of Mind: A Study of Anglo-Irish Conflict, 1780-1980* (London: Allen and Unwin, 1983).
McDowell, R.B., *The Irish Administration 1801-1914* (London: Routledge and Kegan Paul, 1964).
Manganiello, Dominic, *Joyce's Politics* (London: Routledge and Kegan Paul, 1980).
Marcus, Phillip L.,'Notes of Irish Elements in "Scylla and Charybdis" ', *The James Joyce Quarterly*, X/3 (1973).
Martin, Augustine, ed., *James Joyce: the Artist and the Labyrinth* (London: Ryan Publishing, 1990).
Martyn, Edward, *The Heather Field and Maeve* (London: Duckworth, 1909).
Miller, David W., *Church, State and Nation in Ireland 1898-1921* (Dublin: Gill and Macmillan, 1973).
Moore, Thomas, *Irish Melodies* (London: Longman, 1869).
Moore, George, *The Untilled Field* (Gerrards Cross: Colin Smythe, 1976).
Moose, George L., *Nationalism and Sexuality: Middle-Class Morality and Sexual Norms in Modern Europe* (London and Wisconsin: Wisconsin University Press, 1985).
Moran, D. P., *The Philosophy of Irish Ireland* (Dublin; Maunsel, 1905).
Murray, Gilbert, The Rise of the Greek Epic, 4th edn (Oxford: Oxford University Press, 1934).
Nolan, Emer, *James Joyce and Nationalism* (London: Routledge, 1995).

Bibliography 243

O'Connell, M. (ed.), *The Correspondence of Daniel O'Connell*, 4 Vols (Shannon: Irish University Press, 1974).

O'Grady, Standish, *History of Ireland: The Heroic Period*, 2 Vols (London: Longman, 1878).

O'Grady, Standish, *History: Critical and Philosophical* (London: Sampson, Low, 1881).

O'Grady, Standish, *The Crisis in Ireland* (Dublin: E. Ponsonby, 1882).

O'Grady, H. A., *Standish O'Grady: The Man and the Writer* (Dublin:Talbot Press, 1927).

Oram, Hugh, *A History of Newspapers in Ireland 1649-1983* (Dublin: Mo Books, 1983).

Peake, Charles, *James Joyce: The Citizen and the Artist* (London: Edward Arnold, 1977).

Pearse, Padraic, *Collected Works: Political Writings and Speeches* (Dublin: Maunsel and Roberts, 1924).

Plunkett, Horace, *Ireland in the New Century* (London: John Murray, 1904).

Quint David, *Epic and Empire: Politics and Generic Form from Virgil to Milton* (New Jersey: Princeton University Press, 1993).

Riquelme, John Paul, *Teller and Tale in Joyce's Fiction: Oscillating Perspectives* (Baltimore: John Hopkins University Press, 1983).

Roche, Anthony, ' "The Strange Light of Some New World": Stephen's Vision in *A Portrait* ', *The James Joyce Quarterly*, XXV/3 (Spring 1988).

Saddlemeyer, Ann, 'Synge's Landscape', *Irish University Review*, XXII/1 (1992).

Salomone, A. W., 'The Risorgimento Between Ideology and History: The Political Myth of *Rivoluzione Mancata*' *American History Review*, XXVI, (1962).

Sanderson, Michael, ed., *The Universities in the Nineteenth Century* (London: Routledge and Kegan Paul, 1975).

Spoo, Robert, *James Joyce and the Language of History* (Oxford: Oxford University Press, 1994).

Stanfield, Paul Scott, *Yeats and Politics in the 1930s* (Basingstoke: Macmillan, 1988).

Staley, T. F., ed., *Approaches to Ulysses* (Pittsburgh: University of Pittsburgh Press, 1970).

Stone, Harry, ' "Araby" and the Writings of James Joyce', *The Antioch Review*, 3, (Fall), 1965.

Sultan, Stanley, *The Argument of 'Ulysses'* (Ohio: Ohio State University Press, 1964).
Super, R. H., *Democratic Education* (Ann Arbor: University of Michigan Press, 1962).
Sweetman, Rosita, *On Our Backs: Sexual Attitudes in a Changing Ireland* (London: Pan Books, 1979).
Synge, J. M., *Collected Works*: *Plays, Poetry and Prose,* edited by A. Price (London: Oxford University Press, 1967).
Synge, J. M., *Plays, Poems and Prose,* edited by Ernest Rhys (London: Dent, 1941).
Tagopoulos, Constance V., 'Joyce and Homer' in Cheng, Vincent J. and Timothy Martin, eds, *Joyce in Context* (Cambridge: Cambridge University Press, 1992).
Thalmann, William G., *The Odyssey: an Epic of Return* (New York: Twayne Publishers, 1992).
Thornton, Weldon, *Allusions in 'Ulysses'* (North Carolina: The North Carolina University Press, 1961).
Toomey, Deirdre, ed., *Yeats Annual No. 9* (Basingstoke; Macmillan, 1992).
Tyndall, William York, *A Reader's Guide to 'Finnegans Wake'*, (London: Thames and Hudson, 1969).
Walsh, E. J., *Ireland Sixty Years Ago* (Dublin; 1847) reprinted as *Rakes and Ruffians: The Underworld of the Georgian Dublin* (New Jersey: Totowa Press, 1977).
Weeks, Jeffrey, *Sex, Politics and Society: The Regulation of Sexuality Since 1800*, 2nd edn (London and New York: Longman, 1989).
White, Anna McBride, and Norman A. Jeffares, eds, *Always Your Friend: Letters Between Maud Gonne and W. B. Yeats, 1893 - 1938* (London: Hutchinson, 1992).
Wylde, James, ed., *Circles of the Sciences* (London: the London Printing and Publishing Co., n.d.).
Zimmermann, George-Denis, *Irish Political Street Ballads and Rebel Songs 1780-1900* (Geneva: Imprimerie la Sirine, 1966).

INDEX

Act of Union, (1800) 19, 26, 136
Acton, Sir William, 228
anarchism, 7, 13
The Annals of the Four Masters, 19
Aquinas, 8, 24, 76, 79
Aristotle, 8, 46, 73, 74, 77, 79, 101, 108, 117-18
Arnold, Matthew, 54-55, 100, 105-06, 109-10, 114, 116-18
Ascendancy, Anglo-Irish, 8, 12, 18-19, 20, 22, 25-27, 30, 34, 51-53, 55, 56, 58-61, 65-66, 74-76, 78-79, 81, 86, 89, 91, 93-94, 97, 108, 111-12, 115, 118-19, 121, 133, 136-38, 145, 148, 151, 157, 160, 168, 171, 178, 183, 190, 194, 196, 201, 219, 222, 224, 230-31, 235
Athanasian Creed, 79

Bagehot, William, 130
Bahktin, Mikhail, 133
Balfe, Michael William, 137
Barrington, Sir Jonah
  Personal Sketches, 92-94
Barry, M. J.
  Songs of Ireland, 136
Berard, Victor, 105
Berkeley, George, 26, 50, 52
Berlioz, Hector, 137
The Bible, 103
Blackwell, Elizabeth, 228
Blake, William, 175-6
Bloom, Leopold, 8, 62, 64, 66, 69, 71, 97, 99, 101-2, 115, 116-17, 118-27, 138, 139, 141, 147, 150, 152-55, 161-62, 164, 167, 171, 173-74, 176, 178, 181-82, 185, 187-88, 192-95, 197-201, 202, 212, 218-19, 222-23, 228-29, 234-36

Bloom, Molly, 97, 117, 125, 128, 141, 184, 192, 195, 200, 222-31
The Book of Kells, 9, 189
Boru, Brian, 181-82, 196, 201
Boyd, Ernest, 7, 8, 23
'The Boys of Wexford', 63, 133
British (English)
  JJ's attitude to, 7, 9, 18-21, 26-27, 35-37, 55, 57-59, 64, 70-72, 75, 78, 83-86, 89-90, 92, 95-96, 98, 100, 104, 106, 109-10, 115-16, 121, 123, 134, 136-39, 145, 150-51, 153-55, 160, 166, 169, 175, 178, 183, 189, 194, 201, 204, 214, 216, 219-21, 232
Bryan, Donagh
  The Great Earl of Kildare, 90-91
Budgen, Frank, 140, 219, 221
Bunting, Edward, 134
Burke, Edmund, 26, 52, 221
Butcher, S. H., 108
Butler, Samuel, 105

Catholic Church, 11-13, 20, 22, 23-25, 39-40, 46, 59-60, 68, 69, 70-71, 73, 76, 79-80, 87, 90, 94, 96, 151, 164-66, 175-76, 201, 209-10, 213-14, 223, 227
Catholic Emancipation, 19, 64
Cattell, R.B.
  *The Fight for National Intellig*ence, 207, 220
colonialism, imperialism, 13-14, 36, 48, 52-53, 58-59, 62, 70, 82, 84, 86, 90, 92-93, 95-96, 98, 100, 122-23, 136, 153, 154, 157, 174, 177, 184, 201, 205, 232, 233
Conmee, John S. J.
  Old Times in The Barony, 93

Connolly, James, 128-29,131
Copleston, Edward, 106
Corcoran, T., 10-11
'The Croppy Boy', 133, 136-37
Cuchulain, 19, 57, 120, 151, 170, 171

Darwinism, 130, 186, 204, 220-21
Dawson, Charles, 63-64, 70-71
De Valera, Eamon, 11-12, 208, 224
Deane, Seamus, 14, 135, 233-34
Dedalus, Stephen, 25, 29-30, 38, 39-47, 48, 49-86, 88, 92, 96-98, 158, 160, 162, 164, 167-68, 173-77, 181, 182, 188, 192-94, 197-201, 206, 210, 216, 219-20, 222
Delacroix, Eugene, 203
Dineen, The Rev. Patrick S., 75
Duffy, Charles Gavan, 28, 138

Edgeworth, R. L., 106
Eglinton, John, 15-17, 52, 73, 76, 82, 162, 168
Eliot, T. S., 73, 102
The Waste Land, 102
Ellis, Havelock, 205, 217-19
Ellmann, Richard, 102-3, 114
Emmet, Robert, 88, 89, 92, 133, 138, 152
Encumbered Estates Act, 20
epic, 12, 18, 66, 78, 79, 91, 100-02, 104-07, 109, 112, 114, 116, 121-22, 128, 134, 144, 148, 150, 172, 178, 180, 183, 185, 201-02
eugenics, 112, 124, 130, 204, 207-08, 219-222

fascism, 155
feminism, 224
Ferguson, Samuel, 10, 12, 19, 20, 25, 29, 52, 75, 93, 119, 134, 151
Fitzgerald, Lord Edward, 62, 87, 89-90, 91
Flaubert, Gustav, 8, 33
Flood, Terence

Silken Thomas, 90
The Freeman's Journal, 64, 66,168-69
Friel, Brian, 9
Froude, J.A., 52

Gaelic Athletic Association, 9, 131, 182
Gaelic League, 7, 9, 11, 14, 24, 32, 39, 131, 150, 161, 183, 223
Galen, 107
Galton, Sir Francis, 219, 222
Gilbert, Stuart, 69, 100-01, 139,
Goldsmith, Oliver, 26, 53, 55
Gonne, Maud, 209, 216
Gorman, Herbert, 100
Gramsci, Antonio, 131, 154
Grattan, Henry, 21, 52, 64, 87, 92, 119
Gray, Sir John, 66
Gregory, Lady Augusta, 13, 52, 74, 77, 120-22, 129, 144, 151, 171-72, 175, 216, 227, 234-36
The Deliverer, 171-72, 234-36
The White Cockade, 77, 172, 175
Griffiths, Arthur, 99

Harmsworth, Alfred, 62, 68, 70
Hasenclauer, Walter, 8
Hathaway, Anne, 84
Heaney, Seamus, 9
Higgins, Francis, 62, 88, 87
Hippocrates, 108
Hobsbawm, Eric, 130-31, 155, 184
Homer, 99-118, 199, 202
Odyssey, 25, 100, 104-06
Hume, David, 111
Hyde, Douglas, 10, 14, 52, 75, 128, 141, 151, 168, 174, 189
Literary History of Ireland, 75
The Lovesongs of Connaught, 75

Irish Literary Revival, 7-12, 15, 18, 22-25, 30, 35-36, 39, 41, 46-47, 51, 60, 75, 80, 100, 104, 109, 113-15, 119-20, 126,

132, 144-45, 149, 156, 170, 173, 178, 183, 197, 200, 205, 210, 214, 216, 222-23, 226, 231
Irish Literary Theatre, 27, 112, 157-80
Irish Penny Journal, 19
Irwin, T. Caulfield, 76

Jameson, Frederic, 143
Jews, anti-Semitism, 7, 130, 151
Johnson, Lionel, 28, 159-60
Joyce, James
  Critical Writings, 9, 14, 16, 23-26, 28-30, 57
  Dubliners, 30-39, 87, 223, 231
    'Araby', 37, 38
    'The Boarding House', 31, 37
    'Clay', 31
    'The Dead', 32-33, 38, 223
    'An Encounter', 37
    'Eveline', 31, 37, 214
    'Grace', 31, 137
    'Ivy Day', 31, 38
    'A Little Cloud', 33, 35, 36
    'A Mother', 31
    'A Painful Case', 31, 37, 134,
    'Two Gallants', 38
  A Portrait of the Artist as a Young Man, 16, 21, 25, 29, 38, 39-47, 97, 231
  Stephen Hero, 39-42, 47
  Ulysses, 7-9, 12-17, 27, 47, 49, 53, 57, 60, 64-65, 68, 73-74, 75, 85-86, 96-97, 100-01, 104, 109, 114-17, 120, 126, 133, 142-43, 155-56, 159,169, 173, 177, 180, 183, 191, 195, 201, 207, 215, 222-23, 225, 229-30, 232-34
    'Aeolus', 25, 48, 59, 60-73, 87, 88, 96, 100, 117
    'Calypso', 100, 116, 125
    'Circe', 61, 85, 100, 109, 127, 155-6, 158-79, 223, 234-36
    'Cyclops', 60, 98, 100, 127, 130, 133, 141, 142-56, 223
    'Eumaeus', 27, 180-81, 183, 184, 185-88, 190, 192, 195, 197, 200
    'Hades', 125
    'Ithaca', 98, 127, 180-202
    'Lestrygonians', 118-19
    'Lotuseaters', 100
    'Nausicaa', 123, 126, 133, 209-14
    'Nestor', 48, 49, 51, 100
    'Oxen of the Sun', 61, 214-22
    'Penelope', 116, 184, 222-31
    'Proteus', 48, 57, 61, 100, 117
    'Scylla and Charybdis', 25, 48, 59, 60, 65, 73-86, 95, 117, 168, 223
    'Sirens', 60, 83, 98, 100, 117, 126-27, 133-43, 148, 149
    'Telemachus', 48-59, 84-85, 96, 100, 109
    'Wandering Rocks', 48, 86, 87-99, 101, 110, 118
  Finnegans Wake, 30, 196, 232-23
Joyce, P.W., 135, 137
Jubainville, Marie Henri d'Arbois de, 75

Keating, Geoffrey
  History of Ireland, 75, 143
Kenner, Hugh, 99, 143
Kettle, T. M., 20, 64, 189
Kiberd, Declan, 14, 128-32
Kingsley, Charles, 52

Lang, A., 108
Lanigan, The Rev. Dr. John, 76
Larminie, William, 15, 73
Lawrence, D. H., 73
Linati, Carlo, 100, 180, 193, 211, 225
Locke, John, 59
Loyola, Ignatius, 79

Mahaffy, J. P., 16
Mallarmé, Stephen, 81, 113
Mananaun Maclir, 168

Mangan, James Clarence, 28-30
Marryat, Frederick, 59
Martyn, Edward
  Maeve, 113-14, 158
  The Heather Field, 113-14, 158
Mathers, MacGregor, 113, 167
McCabe, Colin, 13, 124
McCabe, Edward, Archbishop of Dublin, 139
'The Memory of the Dead', 133
millenarianism, 168, 171
Milligan, A, 113
Mitchel, John, 28
Moll, Albert, 205
Moore, George, 8, 16, 32, 39, 52, 78, 113
  The Untilled Field, 32
Moore, Thomas, 38, 56-59, 85, 135-137
  'Let Erin Remember the Days of Old', 56-59
  Melodies, 57-58, 135-37
Moran, D. P., 11, 21, 99, 178, 183, 190
Morris, William, 183
Moses, 62, 154
Mother Ireland, 215-16
Murphy, William, Martin, 69
Murray, Daniel, Archbishop of Dublin, 76
Murray, Gilbert, 99, 105-109, 114

The Nation, 66-68, 137
nationalism, cultural, 7, 11, 13, 18, 21, 30, 36-38, 45-46, 48, 60-61, 63, 65-67, 70, 72-73, 86, 95, 99, 111, 118, 121, 127, 131-35, 137, 141, 144, 150, 151-53, 156, 157, 170, 176, 178, 181, 184, 188-90, 194-96, 200, 202-03, 205-06, 214, 222, 228, 230-32
Nelson, Horatio, 59, 65, 67, 71, 73, 88
Newman, John, Henry, 106
Nietzsche, Friedrich, 217

O'Connell, Daniel, 18, 24, 61, 63, 66, 72, 88

O'Connor, T. P., 62
O'Curry, Eugene, 12, 19, 20, 134
O'Donovan, John, 12, 19, 134
O'Grady, Standish, 8, 12, 19, 20, 25, 27, 29, 52, 76, 81, 100, 111, 112, 120, 129, 146-47, 151, 188, 197
O'Leary, John, 197
O'Neill, Eoin, 24

Parnell, Charles Stewart, 11, 13, 60, 62, 66-68, 69, 71, 72, 88, 89, 119, 125, 150, 181, 188, 234
parody, 47, 85, 144-46, 166, 169, 172, 175
pastiche, 27, 144
Pearse, Patrick Henry, 171
Petrie, George, 12, 19, 20, 134, 135
  The Ancient Music of Ireland, 135
Plato, 73, 74, 81, 82, 101, 108, 117
Plunkett, Horace
  Ireland in the New Century, 168
Pope, Alexander, 105
Poynings Law, 91

Risorgimento, 111, 132
Rolleston, T. W., 53
Romain, Jules, 8
Rosetti, Dante Gabriel, 207
Royal Dublin Society, 18, 76, 186
Russell, George (AE), 16, 52, 74, 76-77, 80-82, 85, 118, 162, 168, 188, 193, 197
Ryan, W. P., 183

Salisbury, 3rd Marquess of, 64
Salvatorelli, Luigi, 131
Scotus, John Duns, 24
Shakespeare, William
  Cymberline, 95
  Hamlet, 53, 77, 82-83
  Henry V, 78, 90, 138
  Macbeth, 83
  The Tempest, 52, 83
Shaw, George Bernard, 55
Shelley, Percy Bysshe, 18, 197

Sheridan, Richard Brinsley, 55
Shklovsky, Victor, 96
Sigerson, George, 10, 75, 78
  Bards of the Gael and Gall, 75
  The Revival of Literature, 75
Sinn Fein, 142
Spenser, Edmund, 18, 197
Stackpole, Francis, 28
Sullivan, Owen Roe, 41, 230
Swift, Jonathan, 26, 29, 53, 221
Swinburne, Algernon Charles, 59, 81
Synge, J. M., 10, 13, 21, 39, 45-46, 52, 74-75, 124, 129, 140, 170, 173-74, 183, 197-200, 220
  In the Shadow of the Glen, 75
  Playboy of the Western World, 183
Taylor, J. F., 62, 64, 68
theosophy, 171
Thomas Davis
  The Spirit of the Nation, 136-37, 139, 142
Tone, Wolfe, 87, 137

Victory, Louis H., 75
Virgil
  The Aeneid, 104
  The Illiad, 104
von Flotow, Friedrich
  Martha, 137
Wagner, Richard, 162
Wallace, W. Vincent, 139
Walsh, Thomas, Archbishop of Cashel, 40, 56

'We Are the Boys of Wexford', 64
Wilde, Oscar, 51, 52, 55, 59, 113
women and nation, 11, 27, 52, 73, 75, 107, 115, 116, 126, 127, 141, 178, 191, 203-33
Wyse, Thomas, 5, 18

Yeats, W. B., 8, 10-16, 22-23, 25-35, 41-47, 51-52, 59, 69, 75, 81, 99, 110-15, 118, 120-22, 132, 141, 145-46, 148, 156-76, 179, 182, 183, 186-87, 189, 192-201, 209-13, 216-26, 231-31
  'Rosa Alchemica', 42, 43
  'The Adoration of the Magi', 41, 42, 45
  'The Tables of the Law', 41, 42, 45
  Cathleen ni Houlihan, 75, 152
  Collected Poetry, 6, 52, 207, 211, 213, 224
  The Countess Cathleen, 42, 113, 168
  Essays and Introductions, 6, 45, 160, 162, 163, 187, 197
  Explorations, 31, 33, 34, 217
  The Green Helmet, 157, 159
  The Hawk's Well, 159
  The King's Threshold, 218
  The Land of Heart's Desire, 158, 165, 175
  Mythologies, 33, 42, 43, 44, 45
  The Unicorn From the Stars, 168, 175
  A Vision, 169, 208

Zola, Emile, 8